The Doctor Will Not See You Now

The Doctor Will Not See You Now

Jane Poulson

NOVALIS

NOVALIS

© 2002 Novalis, Saint Paul University, Ottawa, Canada

Cover design: Blair Turner
Layout: Caroline Gagnon
Back cover flap painting: Frederick Sebastian
Interior photographs courtesy of Barbara Poulson, Elizabeth MacCallum, Margaret
de Chazal, Anne Poulson (Riley), Tom Fitches, Ann Dillon and Joan York

Business Office:
Novalis
49 Front Street East, 2nd Floor
Toronto, Ontario, Canada
M5E 1B3

Phone: 1-800-387-7164 or (416) 363-3303
Fax: 1-800-204-4140 or (416) 363-9409
E-mail: cservice@novalis.ca

National Library of Canada Cataloguing in Publication Data

Poulson, Jane, 1952–2001
        The doctor will not see you now

ISBN 2-89507-243-4

        1. Poulson, Jane, 1952–2001. 2. Physicians–Canada–Biography.
3. Blind–Canada–Biography. 4. Diabetes–Patients–Canada– Biography.
5. Cancer–Patients–Canada–Biography.
I. Title.

R464.P68A3 2002   610'.92   C2002-900935-9

Printed in Canada.

We acknowledge the financial support of the Government of Canada through the
Book Publishing Industry Development Program (BPIDP) for our publishing activities.

10 9 8 7 6 5 4 3 2 1   10 09 08 07 06 05 04 03 02

Contents

You cannot imagine how time… can be… so still.
It hangs. It weighs.
And yet there is so little of it.
It goes so slowly, and yet it is so scarce.

Margaret Edson, *Wit*
(New York: Faber and Faber, 1999)

Acknowledgments

As literary executors for Jane Poulson, we would like to thank the many people who assisted Jane in this project, which was such an important focus for her final three years in this life.

First and foremost, the idea of this project was originally put to Jane by the Most Reverend Edward Scott, archbishop and former primate of the Anglican Church of Canada. Two other spiritual mentors who helped Jane with ideas incorporated in her book were Father Paul Geraghty of Montreal and the Very Reverend Douglas Stoute of Toronto.

Stephen Scharper, a member of the Massey College community, set up the crucial meeting that led to Jane's manuscript finding a publisher. Without his intervention, this book might not have come to be.

Jane was always grateful for the editing help she received from many people; in particular, she was substantially helped by Jennifer Glossop, Barbara Moon and the editors at Novalis.

Practical assistance was crucial to Jane in many aspects of writing and preparing this book. Colleagues from her private, professional and academic lives assisted her mightily: we would like to make special mention of Oscar Guerra, Karima Kada-Bekhaled, Kim Vicente, Dorothy Lo, Colette Hegarty, Jenny Richardson, David Goldbloom, Nancy Epstein, Joanna Campion, Joan York and David Robertson.

To Jane's large family we extend special thanks, but especially to her mother, Mrs. Barbara Poulson; her brother, David Poulson; and her sister, Anne Riley. We are particularly grateful for the family's co-operation and for the use of photographs from their private collection.

Thanks also to all those who helped Jane in ways large and small who are not named here but who are all a part of the story of Jane Poulson.

Elizabeth MacCallum
John Fraser
Kevin Burns
Literary Executors for the Estate of Jane Poulson

Introduction

by John Fraser and Elizabeth MacCallum

We are Dr. Jane Poulson's literary executors, along with Kevin Burns, Commissioning Editor at Novalis. We were also her friends. This introduction is our effort to offer a small portrait of the Jane we knew during her last decade, both to supplement her own story and to show, as humbly and gratefully as we are able, the extraordinary effect she had on the people who came into her life.

(1) "Lucky" Jane (John)

This is a story of a disease – juvenile diabetes – and what it did to a young girl from North Toronto. It is a story of singular ambition in the face of seemingly insuperable odds, of an all-encompassing love that enveloped all her friends and relations and colleagues in a conspiracy of protective admiration, and of a transforming faith that simply defied rational analysis. This is the story of Jane Poulson, M.D., the first blind person in Canada to become a practising doctor, who proved in acts both great and small that she not only could practise her own medicine, but that she had prescriptions from her own terrible confrontation with disease which had the power to change the course of other people's lives.

As you read her story, you must remember this: at no point along her tale would she not have gladly traded for a more ordinary life every one of the extraordinary insights and metaphysical breakthroughs which blindness and other afflictions bequeathed her. A part of Jane Poulson – the most remarkable person her friends will ever know – longed to drift anonymously back into the faceless throng of the sighted.

"Oh, Jane," a well-intentioned person at her church once said to her during the tragedy of Rwandan genocide, "you're so lucky you can't see these dreadful photographs of slaughter."

Such luck!

Jane would have worked in the thick of the slaughter for years if anyone could have restored her eyesight. For most of her life, Jane dealt with personal catastrophe. As disease worked its way through her body, she suffered not just the well-known affliction of diabetes – daily needles, regular daily urine tests, blood sugar tests, diet restrictions, feeling crummy, insulin "reactions" – but because she was learned in medicine, she also calmly (well, mostly calmly) observed the attacks on her vascular system which robbed her of her eyesight and then started attacking her heart. And each and every time, she fought back. She would establish a working order for herself – clinical work here, a stint in the emergency section of a major urban hospital there, then a teaching program or helping create a comprehensive palliative care unit, and offering medical advice to her friends and family when she could no longer practise with the public, in addition to writing widely-admired articles in leading medical journals thrown in for good measure.

Out of all this endurance and accomplishment emerged the Jane Poulson who has written this book. The writing of it was suggested to her by her dear friend Ted Scott, the oldest and wisest of her priest friends. Well, he wasn't just a priest. He was the Anglican Primate of Canada once and the head of the World Council of Churches. A widely regarded international religious leader who, in the presence of Jane, was grateful – as we all were – just to be her friend and to try and get some measure of her secret of living.

We were all after that, really. All Jane Poulson's family and friends and colleagues who came into her orbit. We may actually have come thinking we wanted to help her, but in the end the giving was mostly from the other direction: we would be warmed by her spirit, sustained by her unquestioning friendship, spurred on by her faith, healed by her learning, and utterly amazed by her endurance and struggle. If you were in Jane's orbit, it was no easier to sustain faith in an intervening deity than it was to sustain non-faith in the face of her radiant assurance.

She was a crucially important person in our lives. For my wife, Elizabeth, as you will read shortly, she was a rescue saint; for me, she was a spectacular goad to a better life, both physically and spiritually. My God, as you will also read, she used the catastrophe of her cancer as a sly means to get me to stop smoking!

The writing of this book was done in the last two years of Jane's life. Although she knew she was dying, she fought death every inch of the way, right up to her last breath. She did manage in her dying moments, however, to tell her mother that although she wasn't pleased at the prospect of leaving this world, she was struggling to accept it with grace, and she did have a sense of fulfillment. Kevin Burns, her editor at Novalis, was taking corrections and making editing changes with Jane just a few days before she died, and although he came late into her story, her luminous hold on life grabbed hold of him too. We were all gibbering idiots when she finally agreed to die, with all her family around her as they had been throughout her life.

"It's not easy to be related to me," Jane once told her mother. That was true. In some ways, it was far easier to be Jane's friend than to be her mother or sister or cousin. I think, though, her family mostly understood this business. They had the front-line assignments and they never faltered, especially her mother, the redoubtable Bobbie Poulson. The interplay between family, friends, profession and faith form the matrix of Jane's book. The mix could sometimes be volatile – everyone was human, after all – but the dynamic was unique because Jane Poulson was unique.

(2)   Work (Elizabeth)

In telling the story of her gutsy career as a blind doctor, Jane does not fully divulge or probably did not understand – nor would she have believed if she were ever told – the effect she had not just on patients, but also on colleagues.

Even before she went blind, she must have been an endearing and forceful character because medical superiors gladly came to her aid. When disaster hit, Dr. Robert Gardiner, her own endocrinologist and a colleague of the ophthalmologist who was treating Jane when she lost her sight, took considerable professional risks by encouraging her to begin her internship and to perform her first tryouts in his own clinic. Typically of Jane, her first encounter with a patient began with a disaster which she made into one of her funniest "blind doctor stories" and which she recounts in these memoirs.

Her classmate Diane Leith recalls, "We all took turns reading to her for the finals. She could remember everything. She was so brilliant." When asked about Jane's earlier unexceptional academic career, Leith replied, "Maybe this was her calling. Once she was in meds, she lived it and she loved it. Everyone felt sick about Jane going blind. She was in the older married group in our year. She attracted people. She never had any enemies. Ever, ever, ever."

Colleagues and family also recorded textbooks and articles so Jane could study for her finals, three months after losing her sight. Unsolicited editorial comments on the text from friends drove her crazy and became notorious among her crowd. Meanwhile, her mother gained renown for diligently recording the entire Harrison textbook of internal medicine, which most students probably never read cover to cover.

When she graduated, her classmates gave her a standing ovation and a tandem bicycle.

Dr. Phil Gold, the Montreal General Chief of Medicine who kept her medical career alive, says, "I didn't think we were really doing anything so strange. Jane never threw around her blindness. She didn't use it as a crutch."

That is crucial to understanding Jane's ability to lead an unusually rich life despite her disability.

"When Jane was just Senior Resident on the wards," Dr. Gold recalls, "she was already mentoring students. On rounds, they would turn to her for help.

"Jane saw the world much more clearly than we did. Blindness was not just a disability to overcome. It gave her access and understanding. Jane told us, 'When I need you, I'll ask you for help.' And she did.

"Jane was not a difficult person to love. Everyone took Jane on as their own. She was everybody's 'Jane.' We all wanted her for ourselves."

That was true till her final days, when nurses had to discourage Jane from exhausting herself by seeing too many close friends who could not stand to be away from her.

Gold admits to being surprised that Jane wanted to continue medicine after losing her sight, but plays down his own role in her career. Dr. Tim Meagher of McGill Medical School emphasizes what a crucial ally Gold was. He managed to get rules changed. It was he who created a nurse-assistant position and led the struggle to make the Royal College of Physicians and Surgeons of Canada more flexible, a feat that Meagher still insists was "a *huge* deal."

Getting Jane through residency repeatedly forced her supervisors to question, if not challenge, the rules. "People knew she would practise in a sheltered position," Meagher explains, "and the rules were interpreted in that regard. A lot of accommodations were required to get her through, but there was never a question of lowering professional levels."

Clearly, Jane was special.

Meagher, her first supervising medical resident, says, "One of the nice things was how Jane's classmates rallied round. There's no doubt her presence lent a different feeling to the residency program at that time. It's *very* tough for everyone, both physically and psychologically. Seeing Jane created extraordinary perspective for everybody else. Yes, it was remarkable for her to do it without sight, but it was also remarkable for her classmates with sight. They never left her unattended."

Once Jane became a staff doctor, two charitable foundations paid for her nurse-assistant. Her first nurse, Margaret de Chazal, who fortunately shared Jane's sense of gallows humour in the face of adversity, called Jane's work "hugely challenging." De Chazal remains in awe. "Jane fine-tuned her ear to become an exceptional listener. She knew she could listen better than anyone else could and picked up audible clues no one else noticed. Her touch was incredible. I remember her discovering a tumour that no one else could find. For things like colour, she would ask me.

"She immediately told patients she was blind. Afterwards she would ask me what their reaction was, whether they were looking at me for answers. When Jane answered their questions, not *me*, then they looked at her. Jane never went in 'blind.' I always read the chart and we went over the history first."

After a full career at the Montreal General, Jane decided to move to the Royal Victoria Hospital in Montreal to specialize in palliative care. Margaret de Chazal says Jane put a great deal of thought into this change of direction. "She felt she would have a good rapport, and she listened well." Palliative care was also less demanding physically – an important consideration as Jane was now having to deal with her own aging frame.

Soon, people were coming to study palliative care with Jane. Dr. Colette Hegarty, an anesthetist, recalls getting to know Jane. "I had really only just met her, but I intuited her sense of humour. One afternoon, the program was sort of 'soft,' you know, and I didn't think it would be Jane's kind of thing. I arrived late after lunch and saw Jane sitting on the floor, playing the bongo drums. Everyone else was sitting there too. So, even though I hardly knew her, I went up to her and said, 'So, Dr. Poulson, I see you play the bongo drums well.'

" 'Get me out of here,' Jane hissed back, 'if you want to learn any palliative care in the next six months.' "

Jane could make a mess into a lark, and accomplices have enthusiastically responded to the "Get me out of here!" order, usually escaping just in time to explode into gales of laughter.

At one point in her life, the get-me-out-of-here line was not so funny. When she returned to Toronto from Montreal, her work led her into a tightly knit old boys' doctor clique. She was overwhelmed with frustration at not being able to do what she had been hired to do. She would rail at her impotence, at the waste of time, and at the relentless cold shoulder that she met.

About five years later, Jane ran into a nurse who had worked in an intensive care unit at that hospital during that time. They greeted each other with obvious affection. Jane brought up a specific case and how difficult it had been. She still retained all the technical details. Another nurse who knew the gruelling history of those years told me, "Dr. Poulson might have said she'd done nothing all week, but probably she'd have given 45 I.C.U. consults, which *she* considered nothing. The good nurses all knew her. She'd come down and work through the most complicated cases. She was the one who really knew pain control. She really knew palliative care. Since she left, they've never had consults like that. She was brilliant, brilliant, brilliant."

That wasn't the only time Jane underestimated her influence or was unaware of her effect on others.

Dr. Jon Hunter, of the Department of Psychiatry at Mount Sinai Hospital, wrote after Jane died, "I know that Jane often felt she had 'missed the boat' at times with her communications to people with serious illness. I believe I can attest, however, to the fact that she hit the nail on the head most of the time, as I would often be hearing from patients about their relationship with other physicians. It would be typical that the patient would identify Jane as a trusted and forthright physician whose contact they appreciated both for the reduction in suffering it brought them in the medical sense, but also for the comfort of being attended to by a caring person."

A few years into her battle with cancer, she began writing what Dr. Neil Macdonald refers to as seminal articles on patient care and cancer. She wrote to Macdonald, "I am no longer a private person" once she had written professionally about how it felt to be a patient. After giving a lecture on patient care using her now double-sided experience, the first talk she'd given in over a year of her illness, she was subdued.

"There wasn't much audience reaction," Jane reported. After considerable silence she went on: "I was surprised how many women who have breast cancer came to speak to me afterwards." After more discussion she said, "The guy who invited me to talk came to me later and asked if everybody always cried during my lectures."

If you're blind, others' tears are secret.

When she gave "grand rounds" at McGill, not a year before she died and when she was not at all well, she spoke for 50 minutes, from memory as usual. In 24 years Dr. Macdonald had never seen the lecture theatre so full. At the end, people applauded. "They never applaud," he said.

The intellectual effort Jane put into her work became stunningly obvious to my husband, John, and me when she asked us to help her proofread galleys of a chapter on pain management for an important new text on treating women with cancer. She had written it over a year before, when she herself was undergoing brutal chemotherapy. It was a text full of charts using highly technical terms, each of which one of us had to read aloud, column by column.

"Shit! Did I write that?" Pause. "Okay. Four pages earlier, on the left side, there should be another chart. What's the title?" [Mispronounced, garbled reply.] "Third line should begin with [incomprehensible technical term]... Okay. Fifth column over what does it say? ... F*#*! Okay, back to the other chart. Change 4.6 to..." And so it went.

The book appeared, with Jane's chapter advocating radically aggressive dosages – for which she was legally responsible in case of any adverse effects.

Even more demanding in many ways, her final articles required trial by fire – chemotherapy, surgery, radiation. Jane did not like to dwell on her illnesses, particularly in public, but by using her joint experience as doctor and patient she could explain how it really feels to be treated by doctors who *don't* know, and how it feels to try to live a normal life when nothing left is normal. Her articles shook up many in the medical profession. Finally, by making so-called fatigue in cancer patients an important and distinct issue in her article in the *Journal of Clinical Oncology*, which was published three months after she died (and reprinted in this memoir), Jane used her own grisly battle – scrutinized by her incisive steel-trap logic – to draw attention to a significant hole in medical research.

Three days before she died, when she was gasping for each breath, Jane dictated several letters of thanks to mentors and administrators. One was to Dr. Neil Macdonald. He later wrote to her mother:

I treasure my association with Jane and my memories of her. A mentor for her? Much more was she a teacher and inspiration for me. She exhibited that most noble of all human attributes – the courage to convert personal adversity into a benefit for others.

As an example, Jane's article on fatigue conveys more clearly than anything I have read the nature of this devastating problem for our trainees and ourselves. After reading Jane's work I finally "got it" – gaining a heightened understanding of fatigue, its impact on my patients and some practical ideas on how to manage it. The articles and Jane's related presentations and manuscript have had an enormous influence on palliative care practice and research.

I will hold dear until my last days the letter she left for me.

(3) Massey College (John)

The moment I was elected administrator of Massey College in the University of Toronto, complete with the eccentric title of "Master," Jane figured out how to capitalize on what I had thought was my new opportunity, but turned out to be hers. "O Master," she would say on the phone, with just that slight amount of whimsy and sarcasm that was meant to register both affection and a certain edge, "I was thinking, what you need at that college of yours is a good chapel mistress, and I'm volunteering."

She was right. I had revived services in Massey College's tiny crypt chapel; Jane loved its atmosphere. What some of the sighted thought claustrophobic, she decided was "intense." Organizing the services became her special operation. She knew all the priests, or so it seemed, and she organized the music and the readings and phoned up all the outside members of the College community who she felt would enjoy getting up at 6:30 a.m. for a 7:30 a.m. Sung Eucharist. The college's chapel choir always co-operated and the services were inevitably imbued with Jane's spirit. Occasionally she would do the intercessions, but for the most part she preferred to be the grand organizer, phoning students – or Junior Fellows, as they are called at Massey – and the Senior Fellows to get them to read the intercessions. The chapel is hallowed by her labours and her strong affection; no one who went to a service organized by Jane, or who presided, would disagree.

And what a mentor she was for the Junior Fellows – and not just those who were medical students. They took to her instantly and experienced the same mixed-up sentiments we all felt. They thought they had come into Jane's company to help her, and always came to the extraordinary realization that Jane was the one doing most of the giving. Students flocked to her side, to her home, to the chairs beside her in the dining hall. She somehow managed to turn her blindness into an asset in personal relations. Not only would she face you directly, using the sound of your voice for directions, but she concentrated totally so that, if you weren't careful, you soon found yourself babbling to her as if she was a priest-confessor, which I guess she was in a rather wonderful way.

Certainly she knew how to make use of all the Massey facilities. Whenever she felt she had a triumph – beating back cancer, getting a new job, greeting the return of spring, et cetera – she would dial up the College catering office and book the Common Room or the small dining room or the Upper Library and throw a party. Usually with a band, always with an open bar and the very best food. These parties, I am convinced, were an extension of her duties as the Chapel Mistress. She not only ennobled all the people who came into her life, she wined and dined them so well that they actually came to believe her when she said her friends meant everything to her. How could it have been otherwise, as she showered on us all her talent for loving and healing? Massey College, where she reigned as one of the most amazing Senior Fellows ever elected to that office, was transformed by her time there. It is a lesser place without her.

(4)   Friends (Elizabeth)

Colette Hegarty, Jane's friend, colleague and, in the end, palliative care physician, was sifting through Jane's professional papers and correspondence after her death. Even though they had often worked closely together, Colette was astounded at the extent of Jane's wide-ranging network. Jane had repeatedly gone out of her way to search out and get to know different people in her field, to find out what others were doing, to explore what they could do together. "The effort Jane made was simply staggering," Hegarty says. "Even when she was sick, she still was at it."

When she finally stopped treatment, thus acknowledging that she was ceding the ultimate battle, Jane fretted about letting people down. To her last gasp Jane Poulson looked after her friends.

From what Jane's oldest friends describe as an extremely shy child – an adolescent so prudish she asked for chicken "chests" at the butcher to avoid saying aloud that problematic body part (how ironic, in retrospect) – Jane became an astonishing catalyst of human activity. It was Jane who was the social centre of the lives of her "dear friends" or even "dear, dear friends," as she would say again and again.

At her funeral, people who did not know her well but who had been profoundly touched by her after only a few conversations remarked on the variety of people – of all ages, races, rank and economic status – slowly processing up the church aisle for communion.

To onlookers, Jane's friends seemed so kind to drive her places or include her in their plans. Those outsiders just didn't know Jane, or they too would have been lining up to partake in her life. Friends *wanted* to be with her, to do anything for her, because she was fun to be with, and always caring and thoughtful. To be asked to take Jane to a medical appointment, let alone a concert, was a coveted honour.

She hired medical students to help her with research; soon they would start calling to invite her to go for a walk. One dropped off a bouquet of lily of the valley, a flower with a lovely scent for her to smell, on Mother's Day. There was a note explaining that even though Jane had not had children, she was the most important influence in this medical student's life, as she was for so many medical students whom Jane never met but who learned from her and looked up to her as their model. Two foreign graduate students helped Jane write this book, providing computer organization skills and basic editing. They wouldn't let her pay them, so she got even by paying for their wedding reception instead.

When Jane's own friends were sick, she'd get them to the best doctor available. Fast. On one occasion, one such physician was relieved to hear that Jane was out of town. "At least she won't be on the phone to me this afternoon to see how you are," she commented with wry affection.

Friends who lived far away often came to stay for the weekend. She would make certain they met other friends while they were there as well. When her Toronto friends had *their* friends to town, or if they had friends who were in bad health, these friends of friends were taken, almost as if on a pilgrimage, to meet Jane. They already would have heard all about her, but they *had* to meet her, to be enfolded in her friendship too. And if someone who was ill was part of the group, Jane would always manage to work around to their illness and discuss it, making them feel comfortable enough to ask intimate questions and listen to her wise, caring advice, which was usually liberally strewn with outrageous commentary on life's course.

Jane may have loved her friends and accepted their help when necessary, but she still coveted her independence. As she became riddled with disease and secondary health problems, she reluctantly realized that she needed more than a cleaning woman once a week. Fortunately, Jenny Richardson came into Jane's life and ended up being her saving grace.

Jenny worked part-time for Jane's brother's family as a mother's helper, and started working more and more for Jane. At first she cooked and cleaned and helped Jane deal with her mail and sort her beloved but accursed CDs and tapes, which were always in a muddle. When it was time to take Berry, Jane's crabby miniature dachshund, out for a walk, Jenny would put on her running shoes and head off down the street with this ridiculous-looking dog beetling along after her, leaving bystanders doubled over with laughter. Jane and Jenny would walk together over to the stores or the hairdresser, or take the bus or a taxi to appointments and treatments.

Jenny commuted a long way from the suburbs to Jane's apartment by public transit each day. More than once I came to be with Jane when she suddenly became too ill to be alone, while Jenny went home in rush hour to get what she needed and then returned to stay with Jane overnight. Gradually, Jenny became not just cook and assistant, but a beloved companion and confidant.

Others – family or friends – would stay overnight, too; as Jane became sicker, more and more friends were over more often, with Jenny there too. Jenny's sensitivity to the slightest nuance was a marvel to behold. She could melt away when she was not needed or when privacy was required, and reappear with tea at the perfect moment. When Jane was in the hospital, Jenny would be there, making sure Jane had what she needed, helping her up when she could get out of bed, listening to Jane's innermost thoughts, and then disappearing again when others arrived, unless she sensed we needed her too. We relied on Jenny – to find out how Jane was doing, to know what was happening, to hear what the treatment plans were, and to weep together. Jenny became one of the gang, as Jane called us. And now, inspired by Jane, this warm, intelligent woman is back at school part-time, preparing to apply to train as a hospital technician or a nurse, as Jane urged her to do.

In her memoirs, Jane neglects to mention her endless and endlessly imaginative generosity. A classic example came at one of the darkest moments of her life, when she threatened John that she would not have chemotherapy to combat her first rapacious breast cancer. She railed about decades as a juvenile diabetic punctuated by four daily injections of insulin and endless stabs with a nib-like needle in the ends of her fingers to test blood sugar, and decades of blindness. Why should she put herself through chemical torture on top of all that? she challenged.

"But Jane," John said, "you can't give up! Your friends *need* you."

Jane paused and said, "Well, maybe if someone else suffers or *gives up* something too."

She looked at John, using her highly refined technique of making you feel as if she were looking you right in the eye.

"Maybe if you give up smoking for six months then I'll have chemo for six months."

Knowing the weakness of smokers, Jane added an economic incentive whereby friends could place wagers. If John indulged in a cigarette, money would go into a fund to pay for anti-nausea drugs for breast cancer patients, pills that cost up to $27 a pop. If John lasted the course, money would go into a Massey College fund.

Jane being Jane, she threw a Butt Out Party for John the night before her first "red poison" chemotherapy treatment. A huge sign emblazoned her apartment door: NO SMOKING! She had invited her "dear friend" Ted Scott, who presided at the simple Eucharist we celebrated before the drinking and desperate but sincere fun began. John breathed his last sweet puffs, and Jane made sure the filthy ashtray was preserved.

The next morning, on the way to the Princess Margaret Hospital, in a car full of friends, Jane ordered a regal drive-past of Massey College. Those in the car honked and waved flags out the window, making what felt to Jane like a death march, or at best a ride to Passchendaele, into the start of a victorious battle – for her friends' sake.

Months later, after chemotherapy, mastectomy and biopsies, Jane was given a verdict of three to six months to live. A friend immediately organized another party. Jane had friends visiting from Montreal; we didn't know how we would all get through it, a party under a death sentence. When we collected them, out waltzed Jane, dazzling in a Venetian-style half mask with outrageous red feathers sprouting above her classic chemo fuzz of hair. Jane knew what we needed.

If such parties seem inappropriate, then you never knew Jane. She would sit in her living room armchair, armed with her touch-tone phone, banging out numbers at a ferocious rate to make a party happen immediately. And it would. Whoever was around dropped everything to come over. The wine flowed, the scotch was poured – in the most dire straits, Jane banned tea entirely: "Only scotch!" would be the order – and everybody exulted in having a good time with Jane.

On and on, through the years of cancer and open-heart surgery, Jane threw formal dinner dances as well as impromptu parties. She and her friend Joanna would spend hours working out the place settings, up to a hundred people, all arranged table by table, in Jane's computer-like mind. She could leave Emily Post in the shade. You don't need Martha Stewart when you're blind.

With Jane, life became relative. One impromptu dinner just before her second mastectomy became a good news celebration. The latest tests showed that it was *only* breast cancer, a new primary, *not* a metastasized cancer that had spread. Another victory for Jane!

These soirees became survival parties – another year had passed and she could still dance – but they were also dress-up versions of Jane's constant efforts to get her friends together, to make everyone have a good time, to look after her friends.

Jane's last big party, in February 2001, was her most grand celebration, marking the fact that she had made it well and truly into the new millennium. For her, it was a victorious evening. She brought a hundred "dear friends" into the Dining Hall at Massey, uniting nearly all the Montreal gang – who had coaxed, cajoled and walked with her as she battled her way into the Royal College of Physicians and Surgeons and a full-fledged medical career – with her ridiculously extended family and her "dear friends" from Toronto: from Brownies, high school, Queen's University, medicine, Massey College and church.

When she bought a new outfit for the party and was climbing into the car with her purchases she muttered, "I'll be so pissed off if I've spent all this money and get f*#!ing pulmonary mets."

"What?" asked her friend.

"Metastatic lung disease," she snarled.

"Might as well spend your money while you can," her friend rationalized.

The night of the party, for the first time in her life, Jane mounted the Grace Pulpit in Ondaatje Hall, with John holding her arm, quietly explaining the layout of the small steps and the curve in the stair, the location of the railing and bell pull. She rang the bell, which is just like an old-fashioned recess bell, that hung next to her on the wall. That was the only way to silence the deafening din of conversation. Jane, after all, was an expert seating arranger.

"I've always wanted to do that!" she said, throwing her head back in her full-throated, infectious laughter.

Then Jane began her welcome, particularly for her Montreal friends, who were strangers to many of the Torontonians. She told the hilarious story of how, after she went blind, she was badgered back into clinical practice by Dr. Robert Gardiner. Only Jane could make that funny. As she put it, he was so aggressive that she would have had to change churches to avoid him, her fellow parishioner and would-be mentor, or do an internship, "And I wasn't going to change churches!" She introduced everyone group by group, in a way, recounting her life story.

Tom Fitches, Jane's "church" friend and favourite organist, videotaped her speech. Watching it now, I find it impossible to believe that such a vibrant bundle of enthusiasm and zest for life, though she was even then full of disease, would be gone six months later.

She danced her heart out with her brother, David, her favourite and only truly worthy dance partner. As a teenager, she had insisted on teaching her little brother how to dance at home in their rec room so she could have fun dancing, since no dumb boys were asking her out on dates. On that festive night in February 2001, she found herself out of breath after dancing and resolved to work out more often on her treadmill, despite her gout-inflamed knees.

Lots of people were sure that Jane knew she was dying and that it was a goodbye party. Jane was astounded. She insisted that it was song of triumph. Even if she knew she would not be around for as long as some of us, she had long outlived her oncologist's bleak prognosis of 1996. She had also seen good friends die before she did, and was surprised and jolted in a way to lose them when *she* was supposed to have "pegged out" first, as she would have said.

But with only half a year left she had a lot of life to live, a lot of friends to see, and a lot of writing to do for professional talks and for her memoirs, for within weeks she would have a publisher.

(5) Church (John)

Although Jane worshipped for some years at Christ Church Cathedral in Montreal, her spiritual home – the church of her youth and the place she returned to in her final decade – was St. Clement's, Eglinton Anglican Church in North Toronto. It is no architectural gem and does not try to pretend to be other than what it is – a solid, middle-class parish church serving solid, middle-class Christians of various degrees of faith and faithlessness.

In Jane's final years, St. Clement's was particularly important to her for two very salient reasons: her family and closest friends gathered there most Sundays and it was a great way to keep in touch; and the building's interior and exterior were implanted visually in her brain from youthful experience. She knew the place; the physical knowing – the "seeing" – was a source of great comfort to her. Any changes in the church's internal structure – a new doorway, say, or an elevator for people who couldn't manage stairs where a washroom had once been – were first regarded with annoyance and then scrutinized to the last inch so that she could place the changes within her visual record.

As Elizabeth describes shortly, Jane and I were pewmates, our friendship beginning in our joint Sunday School teaching experience. Although the time would come when hardly a day would go by without my seeing Jane or speaking to her, even in those first days of tentative friendship, our meetings were weekly. As I sat beside her as she prayed or chuckled during sermons, our relationship soon became very close. It is very hard to go there now, to sit in that same pew, without her. Every time a hymn or a prayer makes mention that Jesus restored the sight of the blind, I can feel her heat. She had a confident and mystical faith, but I do not believe it incorporated the kind of God who could make such intimate adjustments to biological fate. God intervened in human affairs to give us Jesus, she firmly believed, but how all that came about remained a mystery which did not tax her credulity. I think she merely accepted that it was unanswerable and concentrated on taking advantage of whatever aspects of life were given to her.

"The Days That Will Still Be Mine" is the title of one of her magnificent essays (reproduced elsewhere in this book); the resignation and fight equally implied in that title give you as good an impression as any of the Jane we knew and loved. The resignation acknowledged that she knew her allotted span of years was shorter than most; the fight cried out that she was determined not to waste one minute of them. The

only thing that really sent her into a rage (well, sometimes the permutations of her physical fate got the pillows flying around her apartment)
was stupidity. I remember sitting with her in our pew during a sermon
by a visiting medical missionary, who told the miraculous story of being
saved by God from a terrible accident which would have blinded him.
Jane squeezed my wrist till I thought her nails would draw blood. "Well,
isn't he the lucky one," she hissed at me, rather more loudly than she
usually commented on inept preaching. She spent the rest of the sermon glaring at him, but he was blind to her reaction.

The deepest sources of Jane's faith were secret and died with
her. That's as it should be, but the bereft feeling she left behind in her
parish church cannot truly be quantified. I daresay there are those whose
own faith was sustained simply by her courage and the feeling that if
Jane still believed, who were they to question? It's not a sophisticated
answer to the dilemma and challenges of faith, but it worked well enough
on many otherwise bleak mornings. Jane Poulson was so clearly aiming
herself towards light and translucent clarity that anyone who got on her
bandwagon felt immediately exhilarated simply by his or her proximity
to Jane.

(6)   Our Friend Jane (Elizabeth)

John and I are two of the luckiest people in the world. For the
better part of a decade, Jane Poulson was our dearly beloved friend, and
for me, the last six years of the friendship were intense. The summer she
died, a friend from Jane's sighted days asked how long we had known
each other. He was surprised at how few years it had been. "We didn't
waste time," Jane replied. "It got close fast."

John tends to pick up people and announce how absolutely *wonderful* they are and that I will *just love them!* This is often not the case. And
even if it is eventually, it takes time.

John picked up Jane soon after she returned to Toronto from
Montreal. She naively thought teaching Sunday School at her old church
would be a good idea. As Jane reported, "The first week the little darlings were scared of me. The second week they realized they could do
things behind my back. The third week they realized they could do
anything right in my face!"

She felt frustrated and defeated, but John was furious because
his own usually somewhat raucous class was even worse than normal
one Sunday. The din of acting out the story of King Solomon – John did

happen to be on a chair on top of a table with a gangly five-foot-four-inch girl with disabilities on his knee, helping *her* play the king – was so loud that the Superintendent came in to scold him for disturbing "a blind lady teaching next door."

When they actually met, the blind lady said, "You've got to get me out of this mess," and so John fell in love with her. It turned out that Jane went to the same service as John and our three choir member daughters, so they picked her up and drove her home every Sunday. She would wait for them outside her apartment, standing erect, always looking smart, listening for the car and always looking so alone.

"Hel-lo, Horrors!" she would cheerily greet the girls in the back seat as they sat in various heaps of somnolence.

Jane tried to make friends with me, inviting me to concerts, calling up to chat, but I kept my distance to a certain extent. It was not a great time in my life and I wasn't responsive to much of anything. It was only when I ran away to France with an old friend to recuperate from my teenagers and my chronic pain that things really changed: Jane discovered she had breast cancer and John was one of the first to know.

Immediately, my walls were down. Watching someone battle a particularly aggressive cancer and stagger in and out of hospital with potentially lethal infections when their white cell count repeatedly hit bottom is a good way to get to know them intimately, fast. We happen to live within walking distance of the major university hospital district and her apartment was five minutes up the hill by car, so it was easy to drop by.

The rest of Jane's life was a long-term medical battle which included two primary breast cancers, open-heart surgery, gout in her knees, frozen shoulders, both arms bloated by mastectomies, and one arm that lost all feeling except for electric shock sensations and pins and needles. She told me, "I was sitting in my chair and suddenly someone put their hand on my knee. I didn't know anyone was in the apartment! It was my own left hand but I didn't know."

Not only did this further rob Jane's independence, it meant she couldn't play her piano. She had started music lessons again, using tapes provided by her teacher. When her arm went dead she thought about changing to singing lessons, but got sick again before she could start. Eventually, after nearly every doctor in town basically said her arm had nothing to do with them, a neurologist realized she could treat it with hemoglobin transfusions. With luck, after a number of transfusions, her arm would recover permanently. Of course, with Jane, it didn't and she had to have transfusions about every five weeks, which made her feel sick, but gave her back her arm. And how she hated transfusions of any type. They began long enough ago that she could grumble, "And they haven't even discovered Hepatitis C yet." At least she died before she had to deal with that affliction.

One day she called John: "Listen to this." After quite a bit of rustling and crashing noises on the phone, John heard slow, tentative notes on her piano. Jane's left hand hesitantly picked out the beginning of a Bach Two-Part Invention that she had been able to play before. He cried.

Having Jane as a friend meant lots of talking on the phone. If there was ever a moment of calm, a moment of happiness, a hilarious disaster, particularly salacious gossip, personal crisis, frustration, rage or boredom, we called Jane. She depended on the phone to keep up with the world, but she also controlled it, simply turning it off when she was too tired, sick or depressed to talk. And she called, too. Her classic message was, "Hu-low. What's the scoop?" Even when she was in dire straits, even near the end, if she had any energy, that old familiar message would be waiting.

And what an experience it was talking to Jane! She had two kinds of laughs: an outright hoot followed by bell-like chimes, and her scandalized, stifled chuckle that was particularly satisfying to me because it meant I had outraged her. We always said, "You can take the girl out of North Toronto, but you can't take North Toronto out of the girl." This was the "chicken chest" side of Jane, which made it all the more worthwhile to shock her, and make her laugh when she knew she shouldn't.

Jane's friends had many different roles. One of my self-appointed roles was to challenge her sense of propriety, either with dreadful tales or by making fun of her predicament. One day when she was contemplating her funeral – which was all decided more than four years before she died – John suggested that her little dog could follow the coffin down the aisle of the church. That was bad enough. Jane retorted that she was going to be cremated. So I immediately proposed that Berry, the beast, should be cremated with her.

She gasped, clutching Berry to her breast.

"Well, it was good enough for Hindu wives," I pointed out. "Should be good enough for Berry."

In case it appears that I am particularly callous and not a friend you would want, Jane could dish it out quite handily herself. Another member of our gang, an extraordinary hospital chaplain, was diagnosed with liver cancer. Suddenly, he couldn't drink scotch anymore. Jane could, and so she was teasing him about it. "Just you wait, Poulson," he threatened. "I'll be there ahead of you, waiting for you at the gates, with a single malt in my hand."

It's not often that dying *first* becomes key to one-upmanship; it took even my breath away.

Jane was no goody two-shoes, and while she did admit to being a cock-eyed optimist, she still got depressed. One evening a friend arrived to drive her to her book club. Jane burst into tears, swore several blue streaks and cursed the God who made her. Then she pulled herself together and said, "Let's go." With friends, she solved the horrible how-are-you-feeling question by answering, "Couldn't be better!" Definitely a bad day. There were many periods when we constructed phone calls so she didn't have to make any comment on her state unless she wished to do so. Little old ladies telling her how wonderful she looked "even though we've been praying for you for weeks at church" drove her crazy.

"It's just because I'm so f#*!ing full of chemicals," she would snort as we walked away. "It makes me glow!"

When she felt up to it, Jane did everything in spades. She loved to dance – any kind of dance, not just ballroom dancing, when she was carefully held by her partner. At my 50th birthday party, she was out on the floor doing Celtic dancing, an Irish version of square-dancing, delighted to be tripping her way through a set of eight dancers, which was quite demanding for some of us with vision.

She missed seeing the stars, and she missed driving her car. We couldn't help with the night sky, but one day out in the country, John found a quiet dirt road and put Jane at the wheel of our old gearshift Volvo. Our organist friend Tom Fitches was in the back seat, as Jane exulted in the feeling of adjusting clutch and gears. To make the experience complete, John talked her through a three-point turn at the end of the road.

Poor Fitches. "A three-point turn?" he gasped. "Watch out! There's a DITCH!"

Everything was under control – just – as Jane, in glory, drove back to the other end of the road. When Jane was riding high, she shared her happiness with everyone and did whatever she could.

While the history of her last five years looks exceedingly bleak in synopsis, you have to remember that during this time she travelled to France, England, the Bahamas, Barbados, Georgian Bay, Muskoka and

New York City; threw more parties than most of us do in a lifetime; bought a new grand piano to practise her Bach; sat on various active committees at church; energetically participated at Massey College as a Senior Fellow; played a significant role in the medical community; and wrote this book.

A few years ago, six of us (all women) went to Barbados with our former priest, a Barbadian. We stayed at his brother's empty holiday house while our host stayed with his father. It was all very proper – except for the conversation. Jane made it so much better for everyone else. We all had been with her through her years of hell, but there was a brief time when things were looking up. Her arm was recovering from its mysterious malaise. Two of us were swimming in the pool with Jane. When we got out and watched, we suddenly realized that she was swimming the front crawl, with *two* arms. Both her lifeguards were in tears. Another victory. Another defeat of the odds.

Several times during that hilarious sunny week, when there was a pause Jane would be exultant. "I haven't felt this good for years. For *years!*" We didn't think we had either.

Part of the reason for her sense of well-being was that Jane and I had recently finished a nine-week course called Mindfulness Stress Reduction. The name grates on a cynic like myself, but it changed my life, and certainly improved Jane's. Doing that course together, with our lives enmeshed in each other's, symbolizes much of our relationship.

Because of a lifelong back deformity and arthritis, I have chronic pain. When Jane and I became friends I was in something of a downward spiral due to increasingly active, undiagnosed arthritis and the effects of age on my fused back. Jane being a doctor, and so empathetic, I began asking her for advice. Gradually, once my arthritis was diagnosed and anti-inflammatory pills improved my condition somewhat, Jane became my chief medical adviser.

John, too, called her "my personal physician."

Such a personal physician.

Jane directed my pain management. She would suggest medication to confuse pain pathways and hence reduce the pain I felt. Then I would see my receptive G.P., who would check in his book and say, "She's right" and write out the prescription. Later on, she directed me to a pain clinic where I was put on morphine and other painkillers. But though my symptoms improved, I was still a wreck, in terrible pain, an inadequate parent, and hardly able to remember my own name.

Her psychiatrist, a specialist who treated people with medical problems such as cancer, suggested that Jane enroll in the new Mindfulness program at the Toronto Hospital. Jane started it but had to stop because she was too ill from chemotherapy. Together, we registered for the next session. We took it as a team. The two of us would stagger in at 9 a.m., me bleary-eyed and clumsy, and Jane carrying her thermos of coffee for me. She relied on me to find us a spot in the large room with an amorphous grouping of chairs.

Together we had what might be termed a negative attitude. As we were instructed to assume a positive attitude toward our bodies we muttered: "You've got to be kidding! This wreck?" Together we learned yoga. The instructor got us all standing up, double arms' width apart, which involved a certain amount of me disrespectfully pushing Jane around. Then he told us to close our eyes because this helps focus on your inner being, on how your body feels. "Yeah," Jane whispered fiercely at me. "Close them *real* tight."

I was astonished at how insecure she was about Mindfulness. She was afraid I would find it too flaky. She kept asking me if I thought it was nuts. After all, here was a hard-nosed rationalist scientist listening to proverbs told by Buddhist monks. But when only halfway through the course I could begin cutting down on painkillers, and when by the end of the course I was completely off supplementary breakthrough painkillers and had halved my morphine, I certainly wasn't ready to make fun of any Buddhist monks. We also found ourselves pursuing other less official paths of dealing with drug side effects, and accepting that not always pushing ourselves beyond sensible limits in order to justify our existences was a possible, acceptable course of action.

For all her talents and achievements, her many friends and admirers, Jane basically could only defend her place on earth because she was a doctor. When cancer and heart disease felled her, the fact that she was on disability leave shook her frail confidence. After all, she wasn't *doing* anything – except, of course, waging a major war against ill health. In fact, through almost all of those years she did have professional activities on the go: writing papers, orchestrating studies, delivering lectures and advising friends. A classic example of the latter was when, after being in bed most of the day, she dug out her stethoscope to visit my 92-year-old father, who was having congestive heart failure and couldn't bear to face the Emergency Department one more time. On the way home, she kept talking about how sorry she felt for my parents being in such distress.

It took Mindfulness, time and a good psychiatrist for Jane to accept that a weekly massage was not self-indulgence, it was a way of improving her quality of life. If she was too tired to get out of bed, then she should stay in bed – guilt free. Well, almost guilt free.

One of Jane's oldest friends says that despite all the agony of her final year of life, Jane seemed most content then. Perhaps finally she accepted that she was loved and respected. It would have been difficult even for Jane to ignore as praises and awards came her way, along with her friends who travelled continents expressly to see her – Jane, who couldn't do much more than sit in her big chair in her apartment.

When the cancer returned for the last time, Jane said that this time, she was ready to die. If she was told she would die next week, she wouldn't change the way she was living. But when it came down to it, just days before she actually did die, when she had to decide to abandon all treatment and accept palliative care as the only way to be more comfortable, she was shocked.

During one conversation in the Princess Margaret Hospital, she denied she had agreed to palliative care. "The disease decided," she finally admitted. She paused, "I always thought it would be clear, that you would know when you were *really* sick. I was just swimming in Muskoka last week, and now I'm supposed to need palliative care."

She knew by then that her lungs, pleura and liver were full of cancer. There was bone cancer in her spine and pelvis, and cancer in her brain. At this point Jane was agreeing to take Tylenol when necessary.

Jane's palliative care doctor wasn't surprised at the fight Jane put up. She had many patients in hospital who were much sicker than Jane, she said, "but there was Dr. Poulson, off with a rubber tube sticking out between her ribs to drain malignant fluid from her chest cavity, up in cottage country, whizzing about in boats, and going in swimming." The drain, a flexible tube covered haphazardly with tape and plastic for swimming, did not keep Jane out of the water.

Five weeks earlier she had been on the verge of death with pneumonia, and having her chest drained regularly: so sick that I was ready to cancel a holiday out of the country. Then she announced proudly that she had learned how to drain her own chest cavity so she was going to Muskoka for the long weekend!

The first time she donned her new life jacket (her arms were too weak to hold her up), she asked cheerily, "Why should a girl from North Toronto wear a yellow and black life jacket? ... Because I'm a WASP!" Another defeat made into a party trick.

After so many close calls, after foiling death so many times, Jane and most of her friends couldn't believe in August of 2001 that this was really it. Intellectually, I suppose, it was obvious, but it had often been obvious before. Even in the palliative care unit of the Grace Hospital she was hoping to stabilize enough to bring her computer in to write another chapter for this book, a treatise on parties, and maybe even go home.

You could tell it was Jane's room. There was a corkscrew lying around, opened bottles of wine, and mini bottles of scotch to share with her friends; the nurses in the Salvation Army hospital graciously supplied the ice. It was late August, and as usual, Jane was clocking the return of all her friends and family to mark the end of summer. Then she would know that everyone was safe and sound, and ready to share their lives with her again.

She was a terrible patient. The nurses and doctors had to negotiate every drop of painkiller as she made outrageous pronouncements about the difference between codeine and morphine. "She certainly never would have said that to any patient," her doctor snorted. "She would have encouraged them to take the medication to relieve the pain." She certainly never said it to me. Just the opposite.

Her friends were returning from holiday. Her eldest niece, just back from summer camp, came to visit her and Jane recognized her. Jane was declining rapidly, but her doctor predicted she would wait another five days till the rest of her close friends returned.

Perhaps with her niece home, she knew the holidays were over. Jane died 15 hours later.

Now there is a big black hole in our lives. That will remain because no one lived life like Jane. No one so gloriously shared her existence, heart and soul with anyone open to her generous spirit as did Jane Poulson, right to the end.

John Fraser
Elizabeth MacCallum
January 31, 2002

Prologue

Say something, Jesus

Holy Week 1966 passed in much the same manner as it always had. Palm Sunday was among my favourite liturgies of the year. It had excitement and anticipation without the commercial overlay of the Advent and Christmas services. I enjoyed the service right up to the point when we enacted Christ's passion; I always felt a little anxious when we got to the trial. Each year I wanted to change the part when Jesus stands silent before his accusers. "Say something, Jesus," I would think. "You didn't do those things." I was 13 and I wondered if it would make any difference this many years later if the person playing Jesus in our church denied the charges. I knew it wouldn't, but it might make me feel better. Another difficult part for me was when we, the crowds, preferred to spare Barabbas over Jesus. I remember leaving church that Sunday feeling sad and confused. I comforted myself by thinking that Jesus and all the bad guys were just following God's instructions. If Jesus had denied the charges and defended himself, or if we, the crowd, had released him rather than Barabbas, then the whole Christian story could never have happened.

The Good Friday liturgy was without a doubt the most difficult. We were happy that it was Good Friday because that meant we had a day off school, but I dreaded the three-hour service of prayers and contemplation, which seemed like ten hours rather than three. My great (and secret) fear was that someone would see me cry during the singing of the hymn "There Is a Green Hill Far Away." It is a beautiful tune but the words are so sad, I always cried. I squirmed at the thought of someone hammering a living person to a cross. The words "crucify," "suffer" and "pain" overwhelmed me. I truly did not know what they were talking about when they spoke of Him being crucified to save us all: "We do not know, we cannot tell, what pains He had to bear, but we believe it was for us he hung and suffered there."

That was so long ago; how could he be saving *me*? I was not alive back in Jesus' time, so what did my sins have to do with it? I wasn't all that sure that I was so sinful anyway. I was always relieved when the service was over.

Easter Sunday was always good. I remember it more for all the chocolates than for the liturgy, but I did love the smell of all the Easter lilies as I walked through the front door of the church. We always had a new outfit to wear on Easter – usually a dress, sometimes a new hat. Often we had new white gloves or a new purse.

Easter would not have been Easter without Laura Secord. The greatest signs of Easter for us as children were the Laura Secord eggs. They were heavy and they were all candy. Underneath the generous layer of chocolate was a cream filling. As you sliced through the egg the melt-in-your-mouth filling was white and eventually a yellow centre appeared, like in a real egg. These eggs always went on sale for half-price following Easter, so we would save our allowance and buy another egg at the sale. Another Easter delight was the small mesh bags of brightly coloured foil-wrapped eggs. I still recall the luminous metallic sheens of green, blue, gold and silver.

Family rules required that we leave the large eggs at home in the fridge, but the small eggs we could conceal in our pockets or new Easter purses. They were fiddly to open but it was worth the effort. They were solid chocolate; I liked eating them by pressing them lengthwise along the roof of my mouth with my tongue. As they melted the chocolate would trickle out between my tongue and my teeth. For us, Ascension did not mark the end of the Easter season. No, Easter was a much shorter season that drew to a symbolic close as soon as we had finished off all our chocolate eggs, which usually took about 10 days. That year I slowly savoured what was to be my last egg, blissfully unaware that this would be the last time I would ever eat something sweet, delicious and inviting unencumbered by a sense of dreadful guilt.

Part I: 1966 to 1980

Chapter 1: Early Days

April 26, 1966

April 26, 1966, dawned raw and chilly. The sky was mainly overcast. Occasional patches of blue sky were quickly blown away by a sharp breeze. The trees had small buds upon their branches but there was no trace of green emerging to break the monotony of the grey and white scene outside.

Despite the dreary day, I awoke with a sense of anticipation. Today was the opening of April Lyrics, the spring concert at Lawrence Park Collegiate. Piano was my favourite instrument. I had been studying and practising for five years when my teacher died suddenly and those lessons stopped. The transition to high school gave me the chance to explore other instruments. I was assigned to the woodwind class and given a clarinet. I loved it! I took it home with me each weekend to practise and was very pleased with my progress. I was in the Junior Band and tonight was to be our first-ever public performance. I could not wait for the show to begin.

I dressed and went downstairs for our usual breakfast. Because it was damp and cold outside, our mother had made us hot oatmeal porridge. I loved the mixture of brown sugar and milk on top of the porridge. My spoon cut ripples of sweetness in the soggy oatmeal as the cold milk ran through the steaming oats. Next came toast with peanut butter and honey, followed by a tall glass of orange juice. I was so thirsty I also had a glass of milk. I gathered my things together and went off to band practice. I stopped on my way out the door to grab a glass of cold water as nothing seemed to slake my thirst.

I liked to get to school a little before the practice began. For some reason, I always needed to use the washroom by the time I got to school, despite the fact that I had done so only 15 minutes earlier. I usually did the same thing after band, by which time I was thirsty yet again. This thirst/urination pattern was something new for me, and it seemed to be getting worse. I felt irritated with my body about this, but was pleased with it for losing so much weight. It was "in" to be exceptionally thin those days. My friends were all starving themselves in an attempt to emulate Twiggy, the aptly named leading fashion model of the day, while I was losing weight without having to deprive myself at all. I knew that several of the girls in my class were jealous of my new slim figure. My gym teacher asked me about my weight. I knew she was worried about anorexia nervosa so I told her that I was eating well – even more than I usually ate. She seemed reassured. I thought I would be perfectly content if I could only beat this thirst problem.

One girl in our class had leukemia. Our whispered conversations confirmed that she was going to die. Her presence made me slightly anxious. Her locker was across the hall from mine. She had been so jealous of my losing weight that she had commented only the day before that I looked really sick. I had told my family what she had said. How outrageous, I thought, that someone who was dying would tell me that I looked sick. My parents had asked if anyone else had said anything, so I told them about the gym teacher's questions.

Our morning band practice went well and my excitement mounted. I thought the day would never end.

When I returned home for lunch, I noticed that Mom seemed less cheerful than usual. She told me that she had called Dr. Turner, our family doctor, that morning and that he wanted to see me right after school. She would pick me up at 3:15. She said that she and Dad had been concerned about my stories of people at school telling me that I did not look well. I could not believe that my parents would get upset about something that a girl dying of leukemia had said to me. I felt mildly irritated as I returned to school for the afternoon, but the imminent concert soon took over my thoughts.

Mom picked me up at the end of the school day and we proceeded to the doctor's office. His nurse weighed me and then asked for a urine sample. I hated doing this. We always had to do this at our annual check-up and I resented having to do it twice in the same year. I was going to bargain with him to let this sample replace the annual collection, which was due two months later, in June. I could not explain why I felt so uncomfortable walking out of a bathroom with a little container of my urine, but I hated the thought of urine getting on my hand. I felt dirty and washed my hands several times after providing the sample. I knew that there was still urine on the outside of the cup, and that I could never get my fingers completely clean.

The nurse took my offering and showed us into the doctor's office. Mom sat there looking tense. Dr. Turner asked me a few questions. It was so embarrassing – he asked me how many times I went to the bathroom each day. I could not believe that I had to talk about this out loud. I could feel myself blushing uncontrollably. Next he listened to me breathe and touched my stomach. I got dressed and he asked me to wait outside for my mother. The waiting room was crowded with crying babies waiting their turn to see the doctor. In a sudden moment of silence I overheard him say to my mother that unfortunately she was not crying wolf. As the noise in the waiting room increased again I wondered what he meant by that.

I did not have long to wait, for they called me in a few moments later. It was like a scene from a bad movie, with the doctor shifting in his chair and my mother sitting there looking anxious as he told me that I had a disease called diabetes. This meant too much sugar in the blood, which got into the urine and made me go to the bathroom frequently. "What mark did you get on your last report card?" asked the doctor. I told him it was an A.

"I thought as much," he said. "Only the smartest and prettiest patients get diabetes." With that, Mom and I left his office. I walked down to the car in a shocked and stunned silence. The only person I knew who had diabetes was my grandmother. She was old and had had this strange sugar disease for 10 years. Whenever she had dinner at our house she would always have fresh fruit instead of the dessert that the rest of us were enjoying. I had always thought that this must be boring for her. I consoled myself by thinking that at least she had been able to eat dessert for most of her life. Mom had told us that Nanny had to give herself a needle each day. We had never seen her do this, or even seen the needle itself, so it was all somewhat mysterious. Older people seemed to get many different kinds of sickness and I wondered why the doctor had called my illness the same thing as hers. I was only 13! Surely diabetes was something that only happened to old people.

It was bitterly cold as we stood in the parking lot. The breeze had turned into quite a strong wind. The blue patches of sky had all been blown away. I gathered my coat around me. I had bought it before

I had started to lose weight and now it hung on me awkwardly. The wind seemed to blow easily up the sleeves and under the hem.

"Is this like Nanny?" I asked my mother.

"Yes," she said.

"Do many teenagers get this?" I asked.

"I don't know," she answered.

We drove home in silence. All I could think of was that I wanted to be alone in my room.

When we pulled into the driveway, I got out of the car and went directly upstairs, went into my room and closed the door. I ripped off my coat and stared at myself in the mirror. I glared at my body reflected in the mirror and asked, "How could you do this to me? I hate you, I hate you!" I sat down to do my homework, but I could not concentrate. I looked at the veins and lines across my hand and again told it and the rest of my body that I hated it. I paced around my room, agitated but unable to cry or scream.

I heard my sister, Anne, come home from school. A few minutes later my mother and Anne came upstairs and opened my door. They were both crying. I could not remember ever seeing my mother cry before and I was frightened. Anne had Brownies that evening and wondered if she should still go. What a stupid question, I thought. Of course she should go. She was turning 12 in two days and we had planned a party at our house. "Should we cancel the party?" she asked in a panic.

"Of course not," I said. "Why are you asking me that?"

Their crying made me very nervous. I closed the door and told them to leave me alone. I had to get my homework done as I had my band concert that evening. I looked at my work half-heartedly. Questions swirled furiously in my brain. What did all this mean? Why were my mother and Anne crying? I had had diseases before – chicken pox, measles and mumps. You felt unwell for a week and then you gradually got better on your own. I didn't feel sick now, only thirsty. I wished that I had never mentioned the stupid comments from school. Then I started counting. My grandmother had had diabetes for 10 years. Would I have it for 10 years too?

I heard my dad come home – he was earlier than usual. There was a long delay before he came upstairs to change out of his business suit. Then I heard him go downstairs again. I eventually closed my homework book and went down to see what was happening. I found a very subdued atmosphere. Anne and my seven-year-old brother, David, were watching TV with the sound quite low. Mom and Dad were in the kitchen, trying to prepare for a meeting of Mom's church group, which was being held at our house that evening. Everyone was very quiet and sombre. Dad kissed me. Then he said that he and Mom thought I should not go to the band concert that evening.

"Are you crazy?" I blurted out. "There is no way I am going to miss opening night." I had made the junior band and nothing could prevent me from playing. "What is everyone so upset about?"

Awkward silence.

Because of Mom's meeting, we did not have dinner in the dining room. Mom gave me fresh fruit for dessert. I thought that this was rather stingy as the house was full of brownies, date squares and my favourite: peanut butter cookies. I was anxious to go to school to tune up so I did not take the time to protest. I would have a brownie and a glass of milk when I got home.

The various music ensembles played endlessly. At last it was our turn to go on stage. My knees buckled slightly and I had butterflies in my stomach as I looked out into the full auditorium. My heart was beating quickly. I saw the door at the back open; to my surprise, in walked my mother. What was she doing here? She was supposed to be having her meeting right now. She and Dad had tickets for the Friday night show, because I thought that we would be at our best by then. I was not certain that all would go well tonight during our very first performance – there were too many strange things happening today. The conductor raised his baton and I nervously squeaked out the first notes of our first piece, a march.

When I got home, our house was indeed full of the women of the church auxiliary. There was my mother sitting with the rest of them. When she heard me come in she came to the kitchen to greet me. I was looking around for the most scrumptious brownie. She told me that we had played well.

"Why did you come tonight?" I asked her.

"I wanted to hear you play just in case you cannot play on the other nights," she said.

She's insane, I thought. I was high from the experience even though I knew we had made a few mistakes. She told me not to have a brownie and instead gave me a plain cookie. She opened the refrigerator and took out a bottle of sugar-free ginger ale. She had been on a reducing diet, and this was the only pop made with artificial sweetener. It tasted so terrible that none of us would drink it. She poured some into a big glass for me and added a few ice cubes.

"Here," she said, "why don't you have this instead of milk?" Pop had always been a special treat in our household and it was strange for Mom to offer this instead of milk.

"I am not drinking that stuff!" I exclaimed. She looked upset and told me that I should try it. Reluctantly, I took it. I did not want to make a scene with all her friends here. It was nice and cold, and not that bad. I suddenly felt very tired and went upstairs to bed. Why was everyone acting so weird? I wondered. I looked at myself in the mirror and told my body that it had wrecked my concert debut.

The Babcock–Poulson Clan

I grew up with an extremely strong sense of family. My family was not rich but we had a nice lifestyle and wanted for very little. My father, Andrew, had moved from Montreal to Toronto for business. He met my mother, Barbara Babcock, at Lake Couchiching. After two years of courtship they married in Toronto in February 1950. They had three children. I was their first, born in 1952. My sister, Anne, was born in 1954 and my brother, David, in 1959.

The Babcock family was unusual in some respects. My mother and her two sisters, Mary and Janet, were extraordinarily close friends with each other and with their mother, Elspeth. They grew up in a house on Sheldrake Boulevard in Toronto. My grandfather, Harold, built this house as well as a house next door for his parents. After they died, he kept the house for future family use. When my Aunt Mary was married, she and her new husband, Bob Dale, moved in there. Two years later, when Mom and Dad married, Nan and Granddad built a new home for themselves and my parents moved into the house where my mother had grown up. A large fence surrounded the combined gardens and so my cousins and I grew up in what was a kind of shared compound. For many years we were each other's only friends. Even as an adult I feel closer to most of my cousins than many people feel to their siblings. Although we all eventually outgrew these homes and bought bigger ones, the three Babcock sisters and their families still lived within a 10-minute walk of each other.

Incredibly strong bonds formed throughout years of shared experiences. Every year for 24 years, we gathered to celebrate each major festival. These celebrations led to traditions that we still cherish.

On the evening of the fourth Sunday of Advent, our church had a festival of lights, a carol service with a candlelight procession. I remember the smoky wax smell of the candles and their flickering reflections in the stained glass windows. Following the service, everyone went back to Auntie Janet's house for a party. Uncle Bob dressed up as Santa Claus and began a lifetime of denying it. The cousins have all grown up and the Babcock family now numbers 49. Still, each year we attend the Advent carol service and go back to my aunt's. The fourth generation of Babcocks is now investigating the identity of Santa.

We always celebrated Christmas night as a group. Each year the party took place at the home of one of the Babcock sisters. The before-dinner activities followed a rigid format: two games were essential and the children of the host household were responsible for them. First, each person had a piece of paper pinned to his or her back. Written upon the paper was the name of someone famous. Each of us had to guess who we were by asking questions that could only be answered with "yes" or "no." Not until we had identified every last person could we move into the face game. In this game, magazine pictures of notable people were cut out and glued onto cardboard cards. Each card was numbered. Everybody had a chance to view the cards and write down who they thought they recognized. (It is extraordinary how difficult it can be to put a name to a face.)

Following dinner, there were two more competitions. One was the hat game, which is like musical chairs except it is played with a grand collection of old hats. We all stood in a circle. When the music started, we grabbed the hat from the person on our right. Because there was always one less hat than the number of participants, vicious melees ensued as each person attempted to be in possession of a hat when the music stopped. The person without a hat was out of the game. Then one hat was removed and another round commenced. For a family that appeared to be so loving and committed to each other, the aggression displayed during the hat game was phenomenal. Lives were often at stake as the tension rose. As each of the eight cousins began to marry, one of our private criteria for suitability was how we thought the proposed new family member would get along in the hat game.

At the same time as the playoffs were happening in the hat game, the annual ping-pong championship was taking place in the basement. Everyone had to play, including the grandmothers, even the one with diabetes. The organizing committee would give each person a handicap so that not playing ping-pong during the year apparently did not affect your chances of winning. Everyone was involved in the final round. Cheering could not have been louder for a Toronto Argonauts football game. As the cousins married one by one, the circle became larger. We all stood in stunned silence when, the year after my eldest cousin's marriage, his brother-in-law won the tournament. This was the first time in the history of the Babcock dynasty that anyone outside the family had won. As more cousins married and the tribe continued to grow, it became too difficult to carry on these traditions. Christmas parties became much smaller and decidedly more sedate.

Each year there were what seemed like golden, endless summers in Muskoka, where my grandfather had built a beautiful cottage on Lake of Bays. It was a fabulous piece of land with something for everyone. There was a sand beach and a swimming dock, a boathouse and garage. There was a swing hanging from a big old pine tree and a shuffleboard court. We all used the cottage, sometimes in groups and sometimes as individual families. My grandparents had a smaller cottage on the property, a refuge for when the playing got too aggressive. In order to keep us outside, one of my uncles measured the distance around the main house and determined that 22 laps made one mile. We were all desperate to get out there and see who could get the most miles clocked.

We had two boats that can only be described as hysterical, although as children we thought they were marvellous. Both boats were pitifully underpowered. For years, the little blue boat, which had a 15-horsepower motor, was our only craft. We all learned how to waterski behind that boat. As we grew older we acquired "the big pink boat," an awkward barge with a 40-horsepower motor.

To this day, my happiest dreams take place in this setting, with the cottage serving both as the stage as well as one of the main characters. My cousins now all have cottages of their own, also in Muskoka. On rainy days they make trips to see the old family cottage. One summer, no fewer than three of them made separate treks there within a four-week period. The current owner remarked that it must have been a special haven for them. They had never heard of so many people wanting to come back 30 years later to see a cottage and to show it to their children.

Sensing the Presence of God

In between these seemingly endless summers, the rituals of Christmas, and the metal foil and chocolate of Easter, I also remember my childhood as a struggle to figure out who God was, this God whose birth meant parties and games and whose death and resurrection meant an endless supply of chocolate that would last a little over a week if we were lucky. I was vaguely aware that this God was present throughout the significant and trivial details of my youthful life as well as in these seasonal celebrations.

I had some assistance in this theological inquiry. In Sunday school we learned that God was the father of Jesus. We were also told that God was very good and had made mountains, lakes and flowers. In fact, God had made the whole world and the stars and the sun and moon. We were supposed to love God very much because of all the good things He had done for us. I found this image of such a powerful and good person difficult to reconcile with the person who gave His son to be crucified. If He was strong enough to make the whole world, surely He could have done something to stop His son from suffering such brutal torture and humiliating execution: death on a cross in a public place.

My visual images of God and Jesus changed over time, even before I could no longer see the depictions and interpretations by artists throughout the centuries. As children, we had many pictures of Jesus from Sunday school. He was a white man with a beard and a very kind face. He wore odd clothes but apparently that was what they wore in Galilee at the time. Initially, I imagined a strong family resemblance between God and His son, Jesus, just as there had always been a strong likeness between the generations in my own family. I also knew that God lived in St. Clement's, the big Anglican church near where I lived. We always had to be quiet and behave well there, since this was God's house. When we said grace before meals at home I always wondered how he was going to hear us when the church was a mile away.

My theological speculations on the nature of God became somewhat more complicated when I was seven years old and we moved next door to the Ryan family. Cathy Ryan was the only daughter in this large Roman Catholic family and she quickly became my new "best friend." She did not go to John Ross Robertson School, even though she lived right next door. She went to Blessed Sacrament School. We got to talking about this on several occasions. She assured me that God was not, in fact, an Anglican. My God was not the real thing, since only Roman Catholics had the real God. She thoughtfully warned me that I would not go to heaven when I died. Her not-very-secret agenda was to entice me to become a Roman Catholic so that I too could go to heaven. She spoke with a certainty that made me nervous. Nevertheless, with all the effort I could muster, I continued to cling to what I had been taught, that St. Clement's was indeed God's house – despite Cathy's constant assurances that God lived at Blessed Sacrament Church. To preserve our friendship, and in a spirit of ecumenical largesse, we reached an agreement that it would be possible for God to live part-time at St. Clement's and part-time at Blessed Sacrament, since the two churches were so close together. We found it easier to agree on one certainty that united us: God could not possibly live in any of the other churches in the neighbourhood. We could not even imagine why all of those other churches had been built in the first place. Such a waste.

But certainty creates its own form of doubt. I tried hard to see God when He was at St. Clement's; Cathy did the same over at Blessed Sacrament. But I was not too sure that I would recognize God. As hard as I looked, I never saw anything like the pictures we were shown in Sunday school. Then I learned that God lived in heaven. Was this a third location? No one could tell us exactly where heaven was, although it was widely assumed that this was in the sky somewhere.

The movie *The Wizard of Oz* helped me in my investigations into the nature of the divine. I imagined that God might look something like the Wizard. The film was suitably nebulous about the Land of Oz. I decided that it was the same sort of thing with God and heaven. I was also old enough to start struggling with the difficult but essential concept of uncertainty. I continued to receive comfort from the knowledge that God lived, at least some of the time, at St. Clement's.

Another feature of God that caused me some concern related to the concept of time. At school we learned that the world was very old. At Sunday school we learned that God made the earth. How could this same God who had made all the mountains millions of years ago be still busy at this very moment making all the new babies that were being born? This was a troublesome challenge to my childhood concept of God. It was difficult enough to imagine that my own grandparents had grandparents of their own, and that they too had had grandparents and on and on into the fog of our unwritten ancient family history.

Family history – so mythologized and, for the most part, unwritten. Like many families, we were so busy living and experiencing the events and encounters of our lives that few of us ever took the time to write out the details for each other. As I write this, a personal and family story, I am using fragments of a journal I have kept, off and on, for many years, together with the many filters of my memory.

Great Expectations

My father was the epitome of capitalism at its best. I grew up knowing that achievements were not lauded so much as expected in the

Poulson household. The Second World War interrupted his university education. When the war was over he was offered a job with the company where he had worked during the summer as mailroom clerk. He took the job, intending to save some money and then return to school. He received a series of promotions and never looked back. The fact that he had no university degree bothered my father all his life. Despite not having a degree, my father worked very hard and when he retired he was the president and chief executive officer of his company. He had been chair of many industry groups and was widely recognized for his contribution to the field.

It was clear that none of us would be allowed to take shortcuts or abbreviate our academic careers. My mother and her sisters had all attended St. Clement's School – a private school for girls. Naturally, it was decided that I should attend St. Clement's as well. In the mid-1950s there was no kindergarten; five-year-old girls could go directly into Grade 1. If there were social or psychological problems or anything to suggest unpreparedness for academic pursuits, the child was asked to return the next year. I cannot now remember how this message was articulated to me, but on my first day in Grade 1 I knew clearly that I had to make this work. This was not difficult for me. There were only three girls in our class – Jane, Joan and Julie. We were the darlings of the school. The junior school was operated from a small house next door to the senior school, and had a separate schoolyard. Within this was a special protected yard for Grades 1 and 2. We had our own sandbox. One of the Grade 7 girls was assigned as the prefect to take care of the Grade 1 children.

The school headmistress at the time was Dr. Effie Gordon Waugh. She had a stern and mannish appearance, and I was terrified of her. I had never heard of a woman being called Gordon. Furthermore, I could not conceive of a woman being a doctor. It was my grave misfortune to share a birthday with Miss Waugh. Each year the school had a party for the headmistress on her birthday in the auditorium of the senior school. All the girls were lined up in even rows. I had to walk up in front of everyone and sit upon Miss Waugh's knee. My recollection at the time was that this was the one day in the year that I wished I had never been born.

After our family moved from Sheldrake Boulevard into a larger home on Chatsworth Drive, my sister and I attended John Ross Robertson public school. It was quite a shock to move from being one of three girls in an incredibly sheltered environment to being one of 500 or 600 children where every girl had to fend for herself. Yet I loved school and proved to be a bright and capable student.

I learned that this was not going to be enough for my father. One day in Grade 6 I brought home what I thought to be a good report card. I had two A pluses, two A's and two B pluses. I was looking forward to the requisite meeting following the presentation of report cards at home, so I was flabbergasted when my father told me seriously that he was concerned about my report. He said that I must buckle down and take my work more seriously. Outraged, I challenged him on his comment. Beside each mark was a column where the teacher indicated whether she thought we were doing our best, were improving or could do better. Beside three of my top marks, the check indicated that I could be doing better. This was the source of my father's concern. I reasoned that if you got good marks without much effort, why try harder? After all, you could not get higher than A plus. This enraged Dad, who stated that he would be more content with a card showing all C's if the checks indicated that I was doing my best.

My mom and dad were typical of their generation I think, but Dad was slightly ahead of his time in some respects. He expected good academic performances from Anne and me. Furthermore, he always told us that we must never be financially dependent upon someone else; we must be able to fend ably for ourselves should the need arise. One of my earliest goals as a child was to be a nurse. "Why be a nurse?" he would ask. "Why not become a doctor?" There were no female medical role models in the 1960s and I thought it quite an odd suggestion. The only other lady "doctor" I knew was Dr. Waugh, the school headmistress, and she was not even involved in medicine. Despite my father's advice to work hard in school and have a career, it was my parents' shared expectation that Anne and I would each eventually marry and raise families just as Mom had done. She had never worked outside the home despite having a degree in physiotherapy. Women did not work at that time unless they were single or had to supplement the family income. My brother, David, however, was expected to get a good job and support a family as the sole breadwinner, like Dad.

Dad's pressure paid off for us all in the end. Both my sister and brother followed my father into the business world, completing Commerce degrees at Queen's University and Master's degrees in Business Administration. The journey I took through the sciences before becoming a medical doctor is the story of this book. As with any story, certain formative events and influences shaped how I responded years

later to that knock on the door, the sudden silence, the ring of the telephone, the cruel overheard remark, or the diagnosis given so casually
in an examination room that is not even soundproof. I keep returning to
the idea of family that I learned from my parents, and which they, no
doubt, learned from theirs.

Mom and Dad were both deeply involved in the life of our
church, where Dad taught Bible class to young adults. On Sunday evenings we often went to our grandparents' house for dinner, or they came
to us. The evening meal was always a special occasion. We all had to be
present. We all sat around the dining table and talked about activities
during the day. We had to eat everything which was put in front of us
and help in setting and clearing the table. We were then allowed to go
outside to play for a short period of time, then we would watch *Lassie*
and *The Ed Sullivan Show*.

Each summer we went on a family trip, to places like British
Columbia or to Prince Edward Island. Mom and Dad were both musical
and we sang songs by the hour wherever we travelled around the country.

From my father I inherited drive and determination. I developed very high standards for myself – so high that I could never reach
them. From my mother I inherited passion and a wonderful capacity to
engage life, an infectious sense of humour and the ability to see the
funny side of every situation. This ability to laugh even when in severe
pain has been invaluable to me. But the day after my initial diagnosis of
diabetes was not to be one of those days when laughter was possible.

April 27, 1966

The day after my diagnosis was bright and clear. The blue sky
and the sunlight seemed to coax a little green colour from the mostly
brown grass. It was warm and the air was rich with the scent of thawing
soil. I got dressed and went downstairs with a slight feeling of apprehension. I was still upset from all the strange events of the day before.

There was a small bowl of plain corn flakes awaiting me. "No
sugar, just milk," my mother directed me. At noon, when I came home
for lunch as usual, I was surprised to see my father's car in the driveway.
What was he doing home? When I went inside, hoping that everything
was all right, my parents greeted me with sad looks.

"The doctor telephoned this morning," said my mother. "Dad
and I have to take you down to the hospital."

"What for? I have band practice," I said. It was no use – I had no
choice. I had to go at 1:00 and I would have to stay in the hospital.

"No way," I argued. "What about April Lyrics?"

"You will have to miss the rest of the performances," said my mother firmly.

Dad told me that he and I would go to the school and explain the situation to the vice-principal. What was really going on? I thought. I had missed school before. You bring in a note when you get back. What's the big deal?

The seniors were still at lunch when Dad and I walked into the school. I felt like a freak walking through the crowds of Grade 11 and 12 students with my father. We went into the vice-principal's office. I was afraid of him so I sat with my eyes cast down. I heard my father speaking but it did not sound like his voice. I looked over and saw to my utter amazement that he was crying. I was stunned: I had never seen my father cry. I did not even know that men *could* cry. I felt a small amount of panic developing in the pit of my stomach as the vice-principal assured us that we did not have to worry. "Take as much time as you need," he said encouragingly.

I did not feel reassured.

We all drove downtown to the Hospital for Sick Children. While we waited in the admitting department, Mom told me that I would have diabetes for the rest of my life. The rest of my life was an inconceivable concept for me. The future consisted mainly of getting into Grade 12 and thus being eligible to try out for the senior band. Suddenly a question occurred to me.

"Can you be allergic to insulin?" I asked. (I had recently heard a story about someone who had died after a shot of penicillin.)

"I don't think so," said my mother, not very reassuringly.

"Why do I have to come into the hospital to get this medicine? Why can't we get the pills at a drugstore?"

"Insulin does not come in pills. You will have to take a needle every day, just like Nanny."

I did not like the answers to my questions so I stopped asking them.

We eventually went upstairs into my hospital room. I was quite anxious. I had never been in a hospital before. There were many children younger than I playing in the corridor; I seemed to be the oldest patient there. When I presented myself to the nursing desk, everything began to move at an increasingly faster pace. A nurse weighed me and made a comment about how skinny I was. Then she asked me for a urine sample.

"I gave one to the doctor yesterday," I said, implying that I did not intend to give her any more.

"Oh, but we need some right now," she said.

I could not believe that I would have to do this two days in a row. To make matters worse, she told me to flush all the urine away and then call her in 15 minutes when we would get fresh urine. This seemed like a contradiction in terms. Urine had poison in it. How could she talk about fresh urine? I went into the bathroom as instructed. When I came out she was waiting for me.

"Have you emptied your bladder fully?" she inquired.

"None of your business!" was the answer that sprang to mind. I did not like this nurse. She was nosy and rude. She asked me every 10 minutes if I could produce more urine. I eventually produced a small sample in order to get her off my case. I heard her telling another nurse that my urine was "very high." What did that mean? I wondered. Then someone came in to take a blood sample. "They already took blood downstairs," I told the technician, showing her the bandage as proof. She went and got the nurse. The nurse told me that I needed another blood test. My blood was so high that the doctor could not believe it. What were they talking about? No one came in to ask if I felt okay. I wished they would – I was frightened and wanted to cry, but 13 was too old to cry. I wished I could be with my friends in the band. Even though it had been scary performing the night before, this was a lot scarier.

The next several days passed in a blur. I continued to lose weight, which caused the nurses some concern. I did not think that they should be surprised; they were not giving me very much to eat. One day, a doctor came in to take some blood. My arms were bruised from all this bloodletting. "What? Another blood test?" I complained to the nurse. She told me that the doctor could not believe that the blood was still so high and wanted to draw the blood himself and take it to the lab.

Worse than all the blood tests were the urine tests. They asked me for urine samples many times each day. Nurses were always asking me if I had just emptied my bladder. I could not believe that so many people were interested in my bladder and my urine. I longed to run away from the place. Mom came every day to see how I was. She always seemed very upset. Every time she got ready to leave I wanted to ask her if I could come home with her, but I never did, as I suspected that this would upset her too much. Anyway, I knew that the answer would be a resounding "No."

After four or five days I stopped losing weight. Whatever it was in my blood and urine that interested them seemed to be lower. They told me that now I had to start learning to "control" this disease by myself. I still did not feel sick and did not know why they were calling this a disease. I felt as I always had. What was there to control? If they had this mystery substance out of my blood now, why could I not go home and get back to my life?

"You Will Die if You Do Not Follow the Rules"

Before I was allowed to return home, I entered what we would now call a steep learning curve. After nearly a week of saying very little, doctors, nurses and various medical professionals began telling me about this disease and my role in it. My first shock was that the disease would never go away. Although my mother had told me this, it only sank in when I heard it from the doctors. The worst was yet to come, however. It seemed as if this team of doctors, nurses, dieticians and physiotherapists were competing with each other to see who could make my life more miserable. The dietician must have won that contest. To this day, she remains the meanest person I have ever met, because she gave me the worst news. Every time I met with her she would tell me all about the things I could no longer eat. She was very strict. (I recall her favourite expression: "No, not ever again." This was her answer every time I asked her when I would get to eat something that I really wanted, like candy, chocolate or soft drinks.) I had to learn the exact amount of food that I could eat at each meal. After I began to get the hang of it, I asked her, "What do I do on the weekend when I sleep in? Do I consume the food plan for breakfast and lunch at the same time?"

"Your sleeping-in days are over," she said. "You have to get up every morning at the same time and take your insulin right away and then eat breakfast. This is something you will have to do every day for the rest of your life. You will die if you do not follow the rules."

The rest of my life? That seemed a long time to me.

They told me that I could never smoke cigarettes. For some reason they also told me that with careful management I could probably have a baby. This seemed to be the only positive thing they had to say. They could keep their baby. I wanted to sleep in and eat French fries.

I had to learn how to check my urine for sugar. This was quite a tedious undertaking which required voiding twice at 15-minute intervals for each test. I had to do this four times a day. I was given a notebook to record the results of each test and told to take this book to each doctor's visit. When I was finally ready to go home, I had a large box full of equipment for weighing food, checking urine and taking insulin injections. The syringes were glass and I had to have special pans for sterilizing the needles.

Two things prevented me from falling into utter despair during my hospital stay. First, even before this, I had been thinking about working in a hospital. During this brief time in the hospital I entertained myself with thoughts of whether I wanted to be a nurse, physiotherapist or other paramedical technician. Since none of my doctors were female I did not consider this as an option. Even then, I was attracted to being the person who made the decisions rather than the one who followed orders.

Second, I discovered the extent of my scientific curiosity. I caught on quite quickly to the essential relationship between food, insulin and exercise. My disgust at constant urine testing was mitigated by my interest in observing the effect of interventions aimed at lowering urine sugars. I also learned another, bitter lesson about diabetes in those early days. Sometimes there was absolutely no rhyme or reason for the results. I weighed my food and followed all the rules, but still the tests would come back unacceptably high.

Once I got home, I was initially intrigued by the challenge of getting the urine tests right. I had my little food sample book telling me how much of each food I should eat. At first I saw it as a bit of a game. I would take a portion and then weigh it to see how close I could get. I noticed that my estimated portion was always larger than what I could have. The novelty wore off after about two weeks. I had had enough of this strict regimen. I said that I was not going to do it anymore. Then I recalled the words of the wicked dietician: "If you do not follow the rules every day of your life, you will die." A deep melancholy overcame me and I felt an overwhelming despair. I cried frequently but knew that this upset my parents. I began to retreat to my room and express my anger, fear and outrage by crying alone and punching my pillows. I hated my body.

My days were all the same. They started with an alarm ringing to tell me to get up and start the day's voiding routine. Then I weighed myself. To my dismay my ultraslim figure was a thing of the past; I could no longer compete with Twiggy. Then there was insulin preparation and injection and urine testing. All that before moving on to breakfast. This meant going downstairs to the kitchen and getting out my weigh scale. I had to make choices. If I had a bowl of cereal I could only have one slice of toast. I measured out the exact amount of each food group and then ate. I began to resent my brother and sister who could leap out of bed at the last moment, dress, run downstairs, eat as much or as little as they liked and still get to school on time. They did not have to choose between two foods they wanted and could consume. They could have as much of everything as they wished.

This routine was repeated at lunchtime and again at 4 p.m., for it was important for the doctor to know the sugar content of my urine throughout the day. This was awkward if I stayed after school to play sports or went to a friend's home. At dinnertime I weighed out my food for dinner and checked urine sugar again before bed. I woke up the next day to the same routine. I felt that my days had been taken over by the diabetes and I no longer had a life.

"You Are Doing Just Fine"

Frequent visits to the doctor soon became part of my routine. Each visit to the doctor started with a weigh-in. As I recall, there was an extremely narrow range of acceptable weight. I always seemed to be heavier than the doctor wanted, but if I lost weight, he wondered if I was managing the diabetes properly. I resented my sister's slim body and the ease with which she could shed five pounds in a week by not eating for a few days. I had to eat three meals and two snacks every day, so losing weight was difficult. Increasing exercise often threw off the insulin dosage, which got me into trouble again. I tried to resign myself to the fact that, like so many people I have met throughout my life, I would always be the "wrong" weight no matter what that weight might be.

In addition to seeing the doctor regularly, once every six weeks I had to go to a laboratory to have my blood checked four times in the same day. I had to do a urine test at the same time so that the results could be compared.

In those early years, the doctor thought I was doing "just fine" as long as my weight and my blood and urine test results were within reasonable ranges. My obsessive streak required that the results be satisfactory.

No one ever asked me if it was difficult to get these results. My grandmother told me one day that it was not difficult having diabetes. You took your needle in the morning and the rest of the day was normal. We were not allowed to disagree with our grandparents or be rude, but I wanted to shriek as loud as I could that day, telling her and everyone else that I hated having diabetes. I had not been "fine" a single day since I got the diagnosis, and could never imagine being happy again.

My return to school had not been made any easier by my teachers' reactions. The day before I was supposed to return, my homeroom teacher announced to the class that a tragedy had occurred: I had been diagnosed with diabetes. That afternoon, some boys chased my little brother home from school, taunting him, saying, "Your sister is diabetic!" My brother was upset by this and wanted to know what was the matter with me.

I felt strange and awkward returning to school, as if I now came from another planet. My anxiety was not relieved when several teachers approached me and said that where I was concerned, all rules were void. If I felt an insulin "fit" coming on I could leave the class without permission. I had the feeling that my teachers were afraid of having me in their class.

Before I left Sick Children's Hospital, they tried to make me experience an episode of hypoglycemia, or low blood sugar. The appropriate term for this is "insulin reaction," not a "fit," as my teachers called it. It is an extremely strange feeling when the blood sugar falls below the level required for normal function of the brain and muscles. The body's reaction to this is to release adrenaline and other hormones in an attempt to raise the sugar level. The liver and muscles all store energy in the form of glycogen. This product can be broken down into glucose by adrenaline. Adrenaline, of course, does many other things as well. The effect of all of these internal chemical processes can produce an insulin reaction. Adrenaline is the hormone that is released in the "fight or flight" response. It prepares us to marshal all our resources in a situation of stress. This causes us to tremble, perspire or feel weak. Sometimes the sugar level can get low enough to disturb the function of the nervous system, causing the person to become tired, have headaches or become confused. Serious reactions may include seizures, paralysis or loss of consciousness. Each year many diabetics are thrown into jail for drunken behaviour in the street. Rather than being troublesome drunks, these diabetics are experiencing severe low blood sugar. Once thrown into a cell, they sink more deeply into a comatose state. The problem is compounded as alcohol itself can produce low blood sugars. If they have had some alcohol then they both look and smell the part of someone who is drunk.

The hospital had not been successful in lowering my blood sugar enough so I could experience hypoglycemia. I had, however, been well informed about seizures and weird behaviours that it can cause and I had many discussions with the nurses and doctors about what to expect.

My lifelong capacity to remain calm despite deep distress only made matters worse: I was terrified by the thought of hypogycemia but I didn't tell anyone. My teachers' references to insulin "fits" did not help. This was the first time I had heard the term "fit" used and all I could think of was people falling to the ground and flailing around with epilepsy.

Fear of hypoglycemia has been a big part of my life. Because adrenaline, the mediating hormone for hypoglycemia, is also the mediating hormone for nervousness, anxiety and fear, I always carried with me the spectre of imminent seizure or loss of consciousness whenever I became nervous. I have had to do many performances and presentations of different kinds during my studies and career. As the normal "nerves" acted up before the performance I always felt it was an impending insulin reaction. I would tell myself that this could not be possible as I had eaten only an hour earlier. This was probably correct, but one feature of diabetes is that it can be "brittle." This means that the blood sugar can rise or fall dramatically for no apparent reason. The only way I have been able to resolve this situation has been always to take a high carbohydrate snack before making a presentation. Mind you, this does nothing to help weight or blood sugar control.

So I lived in terror of my first insulin reaction. It did not occur for eight months. I woke up one morning feeling very tired and lazy. We were on a family ski trip and could not stay in bed in the morning. As we started breakfast in the dining room about half an hour later, we remembered that I had left the sugar-free fruit spread in our room. When I got back to the dining room I was not looking well. I drank orange juice with sugar, which made me appear somewhat livelier. Because of one's sense of panic, the tendency is always to overshoot the mark and take more carbohydrate than you need. This results in a dramatic rise in the sugar level. I felt tired, unwell and depressed for the rest of the day, but this was all masked by my participation in ski school and other activities on the slope. Whenever I found myself standing alone on the hill I thought, "I am only 14 and I have to do this for the rest of my life."

In those early days, there were no synthetic insulins. In fact, the preparation of insulin was fairly crude until the 1970s. Insulin was prepared by extracting the hormone from crushed pancreas of cows and pigs. This beef and pork insulin, as it was called, did lower blood sugar in humans, but unfortunately that was not all it did. The human body recognized that this was not a native human protein and created antibodies to the hormone. There were also other impurities in the insulin. For reasons that were never well understood, injections of this drug resulted in damage to the underlying subcutaneous and fatty tissues. Some people were more affected by this than others. I had this reaction in spades: within a matter of months my arms and legs looked like a war zone. Hollowed-out pits were surrounded by hard, indurate tissues. My arms and legs looked like a ribbed washboard. Wearing a swimsuit was an assault on my already fractured sense of self-confidence. "Oh! Oh! Oh!" some people shrieked. "What are all those bumps on your arms and legs?" "Do you lift weights?" others would ask. I preferred not to go swimming rather than reveal my arms and legs. Finally, synthetic insulins became available. These are either totally synthetic or use co-opting e-coli bacteria which have been genetically manipulated so that one of the proteins they produce is human insulin. With the advent of these newer formulations, my disfigured limbs became somewhat more presentable, but those lumps and bumps certainly played a significant role in the shame I had about my body.

In the 1960s there were few sugar substitutes. Saccharin, available mainly in liquid or tablet form for use in tea and coffee, was the most widely used replacement. Cooking with saccharin was out of the question, though; heating it changed its properties and the taste was horrid. The impact that my inability to consume sugar had on my life was enormous. When kids went out after school or on Friday or Saturday night, activities revolved around eating and drinking soft drinks. These drinks were strictly off limits for me. I could choose milk, coffee or tea, but this is not what my friends were drinking. There was no room for pizza or ice cream sundaes on my food list. Other than to decline joining the gang as they set off for the Dairy Queen or some other equally forbidden destination, I had no solution to this problem. I bitterly resented my situation and would go home to my room afterwards and cry to vent my rage. Unfortunately, the result would always be the same. I would always end up hating my body and blame it for all of my distress. I was so disgusted by my body and so full of self-loathing that I must have projected this to any boys I met. I now know that I was not alone and that many non-diabetic girls had similar experiences in their adolescent years.

My Uncle Bob Dale worked in the food industry in Canada, so he had access to many American products. Soon after I developed diabetes, cartons of artificially sweetened jams began arriving at our door. He was also able to buy artificially sweetened canned fruits and Jell-O. In order to keep everything straight, my mother cleared out one cupboard and put "Jane's food" in it. I feel very sorry for my mother as I look back at those horrible days. My brother and sister resented the fact that they had no special foods but had to eat what was put in front of them. For my part I wanted nothing more than regular old food, whenever I liked and in portions of my choosing. Half an apple after school did not compete with peanut butter cookies. Many mornings I would be in tears because I had to have special jam on my toast. David and Anne were in tears because all they could have was the same old peanut butter and honey. They wanted to choose between raspberry, peach or blueberry spread. We had always eaten fairly healthy foods in our household, so dinners remained pretty much the same, but dessert became a disaster. Mom tried to give all of us fresh fruit in a different format. This met with dreadful opposition from the others, who protested loudly at the disappearance of lemon meringue pie. I think we all breathed a collective sigh of relief when I left home in 1970 to attend Queen's University and our household once again had free access to soft drinks, junk food and chocolate.

This battle with food left me scarred for my entire life. Many teenage diabetics say "forget it" to the doctors and dieticians. They eat what they want and then face the consequences. Many teens are admitted to hospital with either severe low blood sugars and coma or severely elevated sugars resulting in diabetic ketoacidosis and coma, a life-threatening situation. Perhaps because in our family we had been taught always to do what we were told, or perhaps because it was my nature, I heeded all the warnings of the dieticians. As a result, I have lost the ability to enjoy food. If I am eating something forbidden I get an initial rush of pleasure, but this is soon replaced by guilt. I absolutely must eat chocolate, but while I enjoy it, I feel very guilty. Eventually I feel resentful that I cannot eat it without guilt. To this day, I look at a meal as a ration of carbohydrate and fat content rather than as a delicious plate of lasagna or confit.

Many teenage girls with diabetes develop eating disorders, such as anorexia or bulimia, in part because of the constant focus on food and body weight. I never developed what might be considered an official eating disorder, but I continue to struggle with many of the features of these disabling conditions. While eating I am thinking about the effect this food will have on my weight and blood sugar level. Even though I have remained within the normal range of body mass index throughout my life (my tendency is always to creep up towards the upper limits), my self-image is grossly distorted and I feel like a blimp. Rather than being an object of pleasure or satisfaction, food remains more an object of reward or punishment for me.

A recurring pattern, which I am unable to shake, has cost me a lot of emotion. When I am angry, anxious or depressed, I frequently resort to a cache of chocolate or other foods kept in reserve for visitors or severe insulin reactions. I eat the entire cache. This is not a particularly pleasant event after the first few bites. After my gorge is over, I feel overfed, angry and depressed. I turn upon myself and flagellate myself for once again falling into this trap, which has haunted me for more than 30 years. These patterns are not rational or intelligent, and I tell myself that a doctor of all people should know that this is a no-win situation. I know now that this sort of behaviour has nothing to do with one's capacity for rational thought. Such behaviour was certainly not fitting for someone about to begin academic life at Queen's University.

Queen's University and McGill

The loud snap of the clock radio turning itself on rudely interrupted a pleasant dream. "How could it be 7:15 a.m. already?" I thought. "Maybe I will stay snuggled in here for a few extra minutes," I bargained with myself. I resented getting up this early on a Saturday morning.

Weekends were meant for sleeping in. Goodness knows no one else in the women's dormitory at Queen's University got up at this hour. But I had to get up and start the morning urine-testing procedure. I had to go twice. The first time removed the urine that had been made during the night. Fifteen minutes later, the urine sugar content was more representative of the present blood sugar. How I hated doing this! At least no one else was up at this hour, so I did not have to bother with housecoat and slippers – I slipped across the hall to the bathroom in my pyjamas. Ban Righ Hall, the women's dining room, closed at 8:30 a.m. on weekends. If I did not get up and get going I might miss breakfast, and then what would I do? The vending machines in my residence sold only foods rich in fat and carbohydrates. None of them would have been sanctioned by my arch-enemy, that humourless dietician at Sick Children's Hospital who had wrecked my life four years before.

It was good for me to be getting up relatively early today. It was Homecoming Weekend. I had been living in residence at Queen's for four weeks, and I was in love with the idea and the experience of being a university student. I had been to my first football game during Frosh Week, when the first-year students had orientation. It was a ball! We were all draped in red, gold and blue, our new school's colours. We marched down the road shrieking out the school songs we had learned. The seniors made us sing louder and louder. I thought on that Homecoming morning how lucky I was to be doing this. I could not wait until the game that afternoon. I was not a big follower of football, but we had so much fun in the stands it did not matter if I understood what was going on.

My course work was very heavy, so it was best to try and get some work done before the festivities started. As I walked across campus to Ban Righ Hall for breakfast, I was quite content to be outside, virtually alone. It was a glorious fall morning – cool air but bright sunshine illuminating the autumn trees. Homecoming Weekend was full of special events. I did not have an invitation to any of the dances, but there were lots of parties all over campus. I had already decided that today was the day I was going to drink a beer. I suppressed the internal warning that alcohol is discouraged on a diabetic diet.

They made it sound particularly bad. I did not know what was worse for me: alcohol or chocolate. I resigned myself to the fact that I was not supposed to have either of them. As I was 19 and under the legal drinking age, I was reluctant to push the discussion of alcohol with the dietician. In my last year of high school, I drank ice water while the others imbibed stronger stuff. (I hoped that they might think it was vodka or gin, but most people knew I only drank water.) Because I felt I could not speak to them about the diabetes, I was unable to point out that it was dietary rather than moral restrictions that kept me drinking water.

I was already anticipating with some delight this evening's transgression. I had drunk so little beer up to that point in my life that I did not have a preferred brand. Most people did, so I too would state a definite preference at the appropriate time this evening. Our team lost the game that day, but this did little to discourage the crowds. My friend Sarah Welch and I had met some interesting characters at the game. One of the boys suggested that we come to their house for a party that evening. We were thrilled, and with some anxiety we presented ourselves at their University Avenue house at the appointed hour of 8:00. It was full of rowdy students drinking beer and smoking. Sarah pulled out her cigarettes. I must have been the only person not smoking. The Sick Children's team had warned me that smoking was very, very bad for me and that people with diabetes should never smoke.

Several people offered me cigarettes. "No, thanks," I said, smiling as much as I could. I hoped that they would think I had just finished one and was not refusing on moral or religious grounds. "Want a beer?"

one of the boys asked me. I looked at the bottle in his hand and replied, "Yeah, I'll have a 50." I felt a small thrill as I wrapped my hand around the forbidden bottle. After I had emptied that bottle, the same boy brought me another beer. I told him, "No, thank you." He looked at me strangely.

"What do you mean?" he asked. "You've only had one beer."

"Right," I said, and reached out for another bottle. Now I was feeling nervous. Sarah came over to speak to me and I poured half my new beer into her glass. I clung to this half glass quite carefully, but someone crashed into me and it spilled. "Here, I'll get you another one," someone else said helpfully. By this point in the party, everyone seemed to be sharing their beers and you took a good gulp as it was passed to you. I had completely lost track of how much beer I had consumed. This one party seemed to be making up for all the other parties I had watched in high school where I would sit drinking water, feeling like a nun, as my friends consumed forbidden beverages. For the first time ever, I felt like one of the gang.

Sarah and I escorted each other home at about 1:00 a.m. I think this was the latest I had stayed out for some time. Light-headed with the combined effect of the alcohol and the fun, I dropped into my bed without giving a single thought to testing urine. I awoke the following day with a strange sensation on my face. Warm, bright sunlight was streaming through my window. It shone upon a poster of a kitten hanging on the wall. The cat was holding on to a chin-up bar. The caption said, "Hang in there, Baby." This was strange. I could not remember waking with sun on my face on other mornings. I rolled over and enjoyed the feeling of the warm sunlight. Then a strange thought began to percolate through my grey matter. My room got the afternoon sun. I rolled over to look at my clock radio. It said 11:37 a.m. "What?" I thought. "What is going on around here?" My clock radio was in the off position. I pushed it on only to hear the announcer talking about the songs leading up to the noon-hour newscast.

I felt as if I had been struck by a thunderbolt. Surely I had not slept in and missed my morning urine test and breakfast? The dietician had told me that I would die if I was ever late with my insulin or my meal. Was I dead or alive? Was I bathing in all this bright, warm sunshine because I was in heaven? The familiar poster on the wall brought me back to reality. It seemed that rather than having died and ascended into heaven I was alive but decidedly hung over in my dorm in Kingston, Ontario. My mind was paralyzed. What should I do now? What were my choices? It did not take me long to figure out that my only option was to get up, shower and dress like all the other girls in the residence. I took my insulin nearly five hours late, walked out into the fresh, bright air with my friends and ate lunch. This was new territory and I was filled with a strange sense of wonder mixed with fear. I had never slept in or missed a meal or snack since April 1966. The dietician had managed to put the fear of God into me about this very thing.

So I was not dead. But maybe later in the day my body would begin to notice that the insulin was absorbing at a different time and that it had been cheated out of early morning fruit, protein and bread exchanges. I stayed relatively close to home all that day, half anticipating a disaster. Nothing of the sort happened. I had dinner with my friends and fell into my bed very much alive despite my major transgression of the night before. This was a decisive and liberating moment for me.

My years at Queen's (1970–1976) were, as Dickens said in another context, both the best of times and the worst of times. I arrived in Kingston a young and naive girl who had not been through most of the experiences of adolescence that prepare us for adulthood. I was in for a lot more learning than my intended studies in physics and biology would provide.

It did not help that I was not well-prepared academically. In the 1960s, the curriculum at my next school, Havergal College, did not adequately prepare young women for careers in science. For example, we did not finish our calculus textbook, and no one considered this to be a problem. I am sure that it never became a problem for most of my classmates, who flooded into English and history and eventually law or business. It was, however, a huge problem for me. I enrolled in the sciences because I was interested in health sciences. After the first few classes in calculus, physics and chemistry, I found myself scrambling to keep up. The professors kept saying, "This is like what you learned in Grade 13, only a little trickier."

By mid-September it was all new to me. I essentially did Grade 13 and first-year university all together. I spent a lot of extra time with the class tutors, learning the basics before learning how to do the more challenging problems. I had arrived with poor self-esteem, largely due to physical and biochemical problems; much of my academic capacity had been lost to this inner torment, which was threatening to consume me. I knew that I had not been properly prepared for first-year Honours sciences, but this rational knowledge became twisted and distorted and I believed that not only was I metabolically deranged, I was also stupid.

Second year was easier for me except that I was now carrying a secret label of "intellectually impaired." My friends did not help. The medical students do the same first two years as the Honours science students, so many of my friends were part of the medical class. They, of course, were all very bright and used to being at the top of the class. The rest of our class was competing for the remaining slots in the medical class. It was not the most conducive environment for someone struggling to overcome an inferiority complex. I bumbled along, presuming stupidity, unless good marks forced me to question my hypothesis. These started coming to me in third year, when we left behind all the abstract subjects like statistics and organic chemistry. We were now focusing on the health sciences, such as physiology and biochemistry. My love affair with the human body started then. I never tired of reading about the marvels of the living body. It was quite clear to me that the human body was not a coincidence. Although at the time I would not have been able, or even inclined, to describe it thus, the seeds of a lifelong reverence for God and nature were sown during that difficult academic year.

At this point it became crystal clear to me that I wanted to become a doctor. It felt like my vocation. Surrounded by students who wanted to go to medical school, I became almost completely absorbed and preoccupied with my decision. By this time, my poor parents were at their wits' end. I had frequently been in tears because I thought I was stupid, or because I had no idea what I was going to do with my life. They could not understand why I was now crying because I had had this call, this undeniable knowledge that with all my energies, all my creative and technical abilities, I would pursue a career in medicine.

While I had developed a better sense of control on the academic side of things, third year brought me pain from an unexpected source. My effervescent sister, Anne, became a freshman at Queen's. She was outgoing and popular. She had lots of boyfriends and once again showed me what was supposed to happen to young women. Wherever she went she seemed to attract attention. Every time she played squash, some young man or other always came by to watch the game. One night, some drunken engineering students created a fuss by painting a message of love on the pavement outside her residence window. I came over to admire it and while I was in her room, one of her roommates entered. "Are you thinking of choosing Queen's for university?" she asked kindly. Shattered, I told her that I had been studying here for three years and that her famous friend was my younger sister.

Although I dated during my years at Queen's, I spent a lot of my time feeling like an ugly duckling. When I discussed these events with my sister many years later, we were both painfully aware of the different filters each of us used when looking over the events in our lives. For me, my sister was the epitome of everything that seemed to underline what was wrong with me. She had no worries about her body. She could eat or drink as much or as little as she wished. She never had to be concerned about low blood sugars. She was beautiful, I was not. She had boyfriends, I did not. My wrath and resentment were mainly focused on my sister rather than on my friends or the other women at Queen's. Somehow, it was much harder for me to handle my sister's carefree life than the lives of the other carefree people around me.

The experience was quite different for Anne. She eventually told me that she felt that I had been blessed with an easy and likeable manner that made it easy for me to make friends. In contrast, she felt uncomfortable in new situations and felt she could only attend Queen's because I was there to support her. So, it turns out that we were both attending Queen's believing that the other had it so easy, and neither was aware of the other's suffering.

Besides my sister and her circle, I had a great group of friends at Queen's. They liked me despite the constant challenges of my diabetes. I got up the courage to tell my friend Janet Stephens my dreadful secret. "So what's the big deal? I figured as much. There is always a vial of insulin in your fridge," was her response. That was all there was to it. I screwed up all my courage to tell my boyfriend at the time, Ross Pennie, about the diabetes. Ross was a brilliant and devoted medical student, and a group of us were going to his home in Ottawa to ski for a weekend. I had dreadful fears about having an insulin reaction while in his home. "Do you want me to do anything special?" he asked, not missing a beat. Telling Ross had been one of my greatest concerns. I could not believe that it had gone so smoothly. We were very close friends throughout our time at Queen's and we continue to be in touch 30 years later.

Our circle of fellow students formed a grand gang of loyal friends. During my fourth year, I shared an apartment with other med students. Then for two years a group of us, including Ross, lived in an old hotel that had been converted into relatively low-cost housing. We each had our own room but had many meals and parties together.

In May 1976, my world took a major hit. My friends all finished medical school and, with very few exceptions, left Kingston for further training. Ross became an intern at the University of Western Ontario in

London. To assure the authorities that I was serious about studying medicine, I had applied after both third and fourth year despite my slow academic start. Following fourth year they said I was close but they wanted to see a more sustained academic output. Despite my feeling that I was profoundly intellectually challenged, I managed to win a scholarship to graduate school in pharmacology. After my first year of graduate studies, the university implemented a rule not to accept any Queen's graduate students until they had successfully defended their thesis. Mine was a two-year program, so I still had a way to go before I could apply again. I still had a thesis to write, but I was totally depressed and unmotivated. All my friends had moved away and some were married already. The new class was filling up and it seemed likely that I would have to postpone medical studies by another year. Once again I felt like a stupid ugly duckling whose future seemed murky at best.

In spite of my earlier conviction that medicine was to be my life, I was still not enrolled in medical school. It seemed foolish to drop out of graduate studies after two years of research and not write the thesis. This was indeed a miserable time.

As for Ross Pennie, it was never clear whether we were "going out" or not. In any case, his ambition was to work in Papua, New Guinea, following his internship at Western. There did not seem to be much room for me in those plans. Just as we had drifted around together during our Queen's years, we drifted apart when he went off to pursue his medical goals. For the next two months I was distraught. What was I going to do with my life? I was beginning to receive some interest from some of the pharmaceutical companies about possible postgraduate employment, but none of them sounded like the job I had always wanted to do and all of them required that I complete my thesis.

I received a badly needed shot of adrenaline in early July, when McGill offered me a place in the first-year medical class. I had to get my thesis written and had fewer than six weeks to do it!

Dr. Poulson?

I literally talked my way into med school at McGill. In the mid-1970s, there was a move afoot to broaden entrance requirements. Previously, only transcripts of academic performance had counted. The McGill application required that applicants include a personal letter telling why they should be admitted. I seized this opportunity. I addressed the issue of unacceptable early marks and explained the poor preparation I had received in Grade 13. Then I spoke of my realization in third year that

I had to pursue a career in clinical medicine. I cannot remember the details of what I wrote in that letter, but I believe I even went so far as to say that I was not enjoying life as a basic scientist, and that I doubted I would ever win a Nobel Prize. Whatever I wrote earned me an interview.

I took the train from Kingston to Montreal. It was a gorgeous day and I arrived three hours before my appointment. What else to do but go shopping at Place Ville Marie? After a productive spree, I arrived at my interview laden with parcels. There was no secretary with whom to leave my purchases so I marched into the office of the vice-dean of admissions with my arms full. We talked about Montreal as a place to live. Then he started asking me about Kingston. I said that I liked it because I could cycle everywhere.

"Where do you ride?" he asked.

I spoke of riding along the St. Lawrence River on my free evenings.

"Are the Dupont plants still operating?"

I said that they were but were no longer out in the "boonies" – they were now in a well-developed area.

"What else do you do in the evening?" he asked.

I spoke of visiting women in the prison for women there. I told him that they often wanted to play volleyball, and seemed to take pleasure in drilling the ball at our heads. I was getting slightly anxious. When would the interview begin?

To my amazement and despair, he soon ended our discussion following a recitation about trips to ski in upper New York with the Queen's ski club. His last question threw me for a real loop. "Why would a graduate student in pharmacology be enrolled in undergraduate economics?"

I cried all the way back on the train. I had prepared answers to questions about why I wanted to be a doctor. What special talent did I have to offer to the world? All we had spoken of was my riding my bike and playing volleyball with women prisoners. Even so, I was accepted and had to move from Kingston to Montreal, and from student to student doctor.

Jane Poulson, M.Sc.

I tried to appear nonchalant as I walked into the main amphitheatre of the Strathcona Building at McGill University in September

1976. This was the home of the anatomy department. I told myself that it was the seventh year in a row that I had enrolled in a university program. I was on time. There was no reason to be nervous. I counted over 150 people sitting in the theatre. I tried to scan my colleagues as unobtrusively as possible. They all seemed young. Why did this group feel like enemies rather than friends?

Shortly after I arrived, a very dapper man entered. He turned out to be the co-ordinator of the anatomy program. He told us there were handouts at the front that we should pick up on our way out, then said he was going to show us a video. I presumed that it would be a "Welcome to McGill Med School" tape and I settled in to enjoy it. It was in black and white. The opening scene was a skeleton hanging from a hook through its skull – not what I had been expecting, but perhaps a good way to greet a new medical class. A dull voice described what is meant by the anatomical position. The skeleton was turned sideways and we were informed that the arms were lateral to the midline and that the front was anterior and the back posterior. The skeleton kept turning and for some reason I sat there waiting for someone on the tape to say, "Congratulations, kiddo! You made it into medical school."

Eventually I noticed that everyone else around me was scribbling furiously. I had missed the opening 10 minutes of my first medical lecture. I rooted about in my purse and found a pen. Sheepishly I asked the person beside me if I could borrow some paper.

The first six weeks of medical school were not easy. For one thing, I had not had time to find a place of my own. I was living with Nora and Gordon Pim, who were good friends of my father and who were very hospitable and kind to me. What's more, I still had some work to do before I could put graduate school behind me. This required several weekend trips to Kingston. My thesis defence was in the first week of October. I tried to concentrate on medicine during the week and worked on my defence on the weekends. I was well prepared and successfully defended my thesis, but I did not feel settled in this new phase of my life. I was not well prepared for our first set of mid-terms.

We had seven exams that week: written exams in the morning, and "bell ringer" lab exams in the afternoons. The lab was set into 50 stations. Each station had a specific specimen, with pins of different colours inserted at various places on the specimen. A card at each station held questions: for example, "Blood supply to the structure with the red pin is from which vessel?" Or "Stimulation of the structure at the blue pin results in...?"

Each student took a place at a station. We were allowed two minutes at each one. At the end of two minutes, a bell, loud enough to raise the pickled, pinned cadavers, rang to signal a shift to the next station. Fifty hyped up and nearly hysterical med students tried to push classmates out of the next station. Two minutes is plenty of time to answer if you recognize what you are looking at, but if you are having difficulty orienting yourself to an eyeball extricated from its socket and turned upside down, it can take much of the 120 seconds figuring out which side is up. Then, back to the question. Did they want the name of that muscle, or its blood supply? Or perhaps they wanted to know about its innervation or maybe the consequences of its contraction? You had to jot quick notes to yourself to help yourself remember at a station where you might still have a few spare seconds. Sweat was flowing freely from practically the entire group by the end of this brutal exercise.

Another legendary hurdle at the McGill med school was the mid-term histology exam. Histology is the study of the structure and function of cells, both individually and severally, as they join together to form organs. The exam was always in two parts. Half the marks were assigned to one single question, to be answered longhand. The other half of the marks were assigned to multiple-choice questions. The single question was always the subject of great speculation and concern before the exam. In past years it had been to describe the course of the demise of liver tissue following exposure to the hepatitis virus. Once it had been to compare the development of hard and soft bone. I had been so busy defending my thesis that I had not heard any conjectures for this year. I felt at a disadvantage until I heard the collective gasp of 100 med students as they whipped through the exam paper: "Describe the structure and function of the Golgi Apparatus."

Who cares about that? I thought in my panic and outrage. The Golgi Apparatus is an ugly little collection of membranes floating around a cell. The only time it had come up was on that first morning when I did not have any paper with me. Even then, we did not speak about it. There was a line pointing at it, labelled "GA." I tried to dredge my mind for scraps of information about it from undergraduate days. My overwhelming recollection was that very little was known about it, and that no one seemed to care. So why did this esteemed doctor/professor care enough about it to make it the topic of this dreaded exam? What those of us who were new to the McGill Department of Anatomy did not know was that the life work of the teacher in question was the function of the Golgi in the adult testicular cell. He was one of the world's experts on the subject. Had I known this at the time, I might have confronted him as he sat calmly overseeing our distress. I would have pointed out to him that he was the only person in the world who cared about the structure or function of that ugly cell infrastructure. It was only Tuesday morning and I was sure that I had already flunked out of medicine.

The week finally drew to a close, and surprisingly, my worst fears were not realized. I did not fail any of the exams. My marks were all in the high 60s, with one or two in the 70s. The class average was 75 per cent. I was definitely way down there. Although this confirmed my sense that I was stupid, I was still a student doctor.

Wernicke Korsakoff Syndrome

Following the Christmas of my first year at McGill, my focus was entirely upon my medical studies and I settled into my work. I loved medical school. I could not read enough about the body and how it worked. Knowing that I was going to be a doctor gave me a rudder, which had so far been lacking in my life. I now had a reason for living. I was full of a delicious feeling of contentment, and an even stronger sense of determination to succeed as a doctor.

Following the Christmas of my second year in medical school, we began a year of pre-clinical work. We had learned the principles of history-taking and had practised the physical exam upon each other. Now, under close supervision, we would work with our first live patients. We had no role in their care, but we asked permission to "work them up" as if we were their physician. We spent an entire year, from mid-second until mid-third year, in this pre-clinical phase, rotating through the different hospitals in the city.

I started with internal medicine. Four of us were assigned to Ward 10 East at the Montreal General Hospital. Over the three months on this rotation, we had to do 12 complete patient reports. We started with the patient's history and then gave them a thorough examination. We had to work out all the possible diagnoses, say what tests were appropriate and suggest case management. Theory would meet practice, or at least that was the idea.

The student locker room was in the basement of the interns' residence. With trembling hands I put on my white jacket. (To identify us as students our jackets were short, ending about eight inches below the waist.) I put my new stethoscope and shiny reflex hammer in the hip pocket. I put on my name tag, popped my pen into the breast pocket and looked at myself in the mirror. No matter how hard I tried to look the part, it was a young, insecure face looking back at me. I leaned over to pull up my socks and everything from my pockets promptly tumbled onto the concrete floor. Good start, Jane, I thought.

I left the locker room, happy that no one had seen my inauspicious beginning. I could feel my heart pound and my stomach contort as I approached the main hospital corridor. There seemed to be about a hundred people milling about. All were wearing long white coats. After controlling my panicked breathing, I stepped boldly towards the elevators. I felt as if all eyes were upon me as I asked for the 10th floor. When I got off the elevator I was so weak I had to sit and rest on the benches between the east and west units.

Through the glass doors leading to the ward, I could see a doctor who seemed to be in charge. He looked pleasant. I took a deep breath and stepped onto the ward. What I had not seen through the doors was that this doctor had all the medical team with him. When he saw me, he asked if he could help me. With a very dry mouth I introduced myself, apologizing profusely for having been born. I told him I was one of the new med students. Could he assign me my first patient? He looked through the list and suggested one Mrs. G. Did I detect a smirk on the faces of the team? No, they were giving me a welcoming smile.

I noted the patient's room. I did several laps of the ward for reconnaissance purposes, trying to identify and size up my prey. She looked like a kind little old woman sitting quietly in her bed wearing a pretty pink bed jacket. I was afraid that the doctors would see me hanging around, so I entered the room as if I were about to disturb the reigning monarch.

"Are you Mrs. G?" I asked.

"Yes, dear, I am."

I explained who I was and what I wanted from her.

"Why, yes, dear, please sit down. I would be pleased to help you."

I collapsed into the chair and caught my breath. So far it had gone well. There were many famous medical school stories of students being thrown out by irate patients. I secretly thanked my tutor for starting me off with such a sweet and gentle little old lady.

I noted her demographic data and began the interview. She apparently had been admitted for chest pain. I felt encouraged, as I knew right away that this meant heart trouble, stomach reflux or a problem with her muscles or ribs. I set out to distinguish these possibilities with my clever questions.

"Do you get this pain when you are walking?"

"Yes, I do."

"Are you short of breath when this happens?"

"Yes, I am."

Right on, Jane! You are on your way to bagging your first case.

"Do your symptoms get better when you slow down or stop?" I asked, almost smugly. . I was sure that she had angina, and I knew that the pain would settle with rest

"Oh, no, dear, they are worse."

"The pain and shortness of breath get worse when you stop walking?"

"Yes, dear."

"Do you get this pain if you are just sitting?"

"Oh, yes, dear."

I was now quite puzzled. This did not sound like any pain I had studied. Perhaps she was a bit forgetful and I might yet get her story to fit my diagnosis. I verified her date of birth and address. I could not catch her out here. Suddenly I had a brain wave. Ask about family history. Some families have siblings with the same disease.

"Do you have brothers and sisters?"

"Yes," she said, "I have 17 sisters and brothers."

I felt sick. Could this be possible? Well, she was born in Quebec in the era when large families were the norm. I took down the long, convoluted medical history of her siblings. I was both frustrated and bored. Worse than that, nothing was fitting together. I checked her out on date of birth again. She was right on again. By this point I had spent over 90 minutes with her, and I had not done the physical exam yet. We had been instructed to complete the entire process in 60 minutes maximum. Exhausted, I said goodbye to Mrs. G and dragged myself towards the exit, where I ran into my tutor and the entire team.

"Any problems?" he asked brightly.

"Oh, no," I said weakly.

"See you tomorrow, then," he said warmly.

Ward rounds had already started when I arrived the next day. I was alarmed as I could see the team gathered near my patient's room. My fear increased as I saw that they were discussing my patient, Mrs G. Despite hours of poring over medical texts the evening before, I had not come across any disease that could explain her odd assortment of complaints. Surely they would not ask a second-year med student for analysis. I stared at the floor in the hopes that I might become invisible to the interrogator. I felt my face beginning to grow very red and flushed as the team discussed my patient.

"This is classical Wernicke Korsakoff syndrome," said the tutor. "What is the classic feature of this disease?"

"Confabulation," said a clever intern.

"Correct," replied our tutor. "These patients have consumed so much alcohol that they have completely destroyed the new memory centre in the brain. They retain old information such as birth date and address, but for everything else they make up an answer. You can have quite a long conversation with them and never learn anything useful," he chuckled.

Not All Roses

As this year of practical work continued, we were rotated through the different clinical areas. As junior interns, we would be the ones who would run, literally, to the radiology department for the forgotten films. We were the ones who would do all the tedious filling out of reports. Even so, it took us out of the classroom and into the world of medical routines, with occasional miracles and ever-present mysteries.

My first clinical rotation was Obstetrics where, to my alarm, I found that I was on call the first Saturday of the rotation. I had made other plans but quickly discovered that personal plans always take second place to the call schedule and I had better get used to it.

I timidly walked up to the information desk and asked where the locker room was. "Which locker room?" asked the kindly volunteer.

"The doctors' locker room," I replied.

She said that she was unaware of such a facility. I decided I would go up to the case room with my coat and packed lunch. As it turned out there were call rooms on the Obstetrics floor. I left my things there and put on my lab jacket. I went to the nursing station, where the nurses told me that I would have to change into surgical scrubs – the uniforms worn in the operating theatres. I saw them smile at each other. My pupils must have flashed. Surely they did not plan for me to go into an operating room – I was only in second year! After changing into my scrubs I looked at myself in a mirror. I looked like a young child dressed up for a Halloween party. I did my best to look self-assured and returned to the nursing station for assignment.

My first job was to admit a new maternity patient. The nurses felt that she had come in too early in her labour, but allowed her to stay as this was her first child and she was frightened. I was relieved to know that my first "real" patient was not going to deliver during my admission. It was lucky she did come early – the admission took me nearly an hour to do. (By the end of the rotation I would be doing the same thing in under 15 minutes.) As I was finishing, the nurse came to the door and said that I was wanted in Delivery 1.

On this, my first real clinical encounter, I would confront my first misgivings about how "we" do things. During our obstetrics instruction we had had a panel discussion with a practising obstetrician, a midwife and a new mother who had delivered her baby at home. The two women had attacked the way our profession has "medicalized" the birth process, starting from the demeaning position we force women to assume once they climb up onto the table. Doctors were turning women undergoing a normal experience into sick patients, they argued. Furthermore, they alleged that this was a course of action taken for the convenience of the doctors. How ridiculous, I thought. What do these women's lib types know about anything? I was totally convinced by the male obstetrician, who spoke about how quickly things could go wrong and how disasters could be easily avoided with the current system.

These arguments were rolling around my head as I entered Delivery 1 to see a distressed woman being strapped onto the table and her legs tied into the shiny metal stirrups. I felt my anxiety rising. She did not look at all comfortable and I was not entirely happy to be part of the team that was hooking her into its system. Very quickly I came back to the matter at hand and tried to remember how to do the surgical draping. I wondered about the utility of all this sterile process. Didn't most Chinese women give birth right there in the rice paddies? I was diverted from my musings by what was happening before my eyes.

I was floored by the experience of watching my first birth. The illustrations in my obstetrics textbook had made it all look so clean and straightforward. One picture showed the child *in utero*, ready for launching. The next picture showed the child in the birth canal and the final illustration showed the child emerging through the vagina. I cannot say that I had never wondered how a 10-pound human could pass through both a small cervix and a small vagina without any difficulty. Perhaps I had chosen to ignore the obvious discrepancy in dimensions. I had always chalked it up to God, who invented the process, thinking it must be another of those daily miracles. Until that day, I had never wondered why the process of childbirth was called labour.

When we were all prepared, with drapes in place and lighting right, we all began encouraging the young woman, who was the same age as me, to push. Our encouragement and her valiant effort went on for some time, and I was getting a little stiff from standing around. Then a strange thing happened. With each push a dark, furry-looking object appeared between her legs. I had never seen this in my book. I asked the other med student who was with me what in the world he thought it was. "Maybe it's the head," he whispered, as naive as I.

"That couldn't be the head of anything," I told him. As time passed, more and more of this strange object filled her expanding vagina. I cringed as I acknowledged that my partner had been correct. It *was* going to be a head! I was greatly embarrassed and hoped that my partner would not tell any of our classmates that I had asked what was emerging through the vagina. Of course, he had not known either.

Suddenly, events took an alarming turn. Our professor began telling us which type of episiotomy (a surgical cut made at the opening of the vagina to enlarge the birth canal and aid delivery) he preferred. Each doctor had his or her preferred type, he told us. Then he picked up surgical scissors and moved towards the patient. I nearly screamed and grabbed his hand. I had been prepared to help drape this poor woman in place on the hard operating room table, but I could not stand by and allow him to assault her with that instrument. Somehow, I held myself back but had to sit down on a stool after the deed was done. No one else in the room seemed the least bit troubled by what he was doing. Apparently it was a common procedure for the time.

I was shaken free of my introspection as things were moving quickly now. Within minutes, the baby's head and then shoulders emerged fully, like the illustrations in our textbooks. The child howled at his distress from the ordeal and both parents wept with joy. I was stunned. I had witnessed a miracle. This helpless child was a tiny but perfect human. Tiny little ears flat against his head. Perfect little hands with tiny fingernails. Unlike the emerging infants illustrated in our texts, this baby had a full head of thick, curly dark hair. It was a complete mystery to me how this child had been created, developed and then delivered intact from its mother's womb. If I had ever had any doubts about the existence of God the Creator, they were permanently and profoundly extinguished in this single moment in Delivery 1. For me, procreation is constant living proof of God. Whenever people ask me why I believe in God, all I can answer comes from this experience of witnessing the miracle of birth for the first time. Studying embryology and knowing all the things that might go wrong during development only served to increase my sense of awe.

Later, when it was finally time to complete all the paperwork, I was glad for the break. I felt dizzy from the turbulence of my emotional journey. I had experienced the entire range of human emotion. I had felt doubt and shame, fear, anger and joy. As a young doctor-in-training, I had suddenly become an advocate for birthing suites on the case room floor. I imagined myself as that woman in labour, locked into – both literally and metaphorically – what has to be one of the most exhilarating experiences of life. I felt the helplessness of her anxious husband as he looked on. I experienced a profound theological moment. Then, with some dismay, I realized that I had imagined myself to be each person in that drama *except* the doctor. I was going to have to work on developing my "compassionate detachment," a term I developed years later as a teacher of medical students. I encouraged them never to lose the capacity for compassion towards a fellow human, but to stay detached in order to help them. That labouring woman in Montreal did not want my squeamish emotions as she gave birth. She wanted me to deliver her son safely.

Thoughts of babies and children had been on my mind during the summer between first and second year medical school. I had entered into what would turn out to be a very unsatisfactory marriage.

Why do you hide your face?
Why do you forget our affliction and oppression?
For we sink down to the dust; our bodies cling to the ground.
Rise up, come to our help.
Redeem us for the sake out your steadfast love.

Psalm 44:24-26

Chapter 2: Cosmic Error

On August 13, 1977, I promised to love and care for, in sickness and in health, share my life with, for richer and for poorer, and create new life with a man I hardly knew. Rather than feeling sick with despair, I recall that I felt something approaching contentment. I thought that my husband was a good man and that as the years passed, we would learn to love each other. On that lovely sunny summer afternoon when we got married, I had no idea how differently I would feel eight days later when I returned from a week-long honeymoon. After being with him for only seven days, I felt as if I was trapped in a horrifying dream from which there was no escape. I wanted nothing more than to retreat to the familiarity of my family home. I imagine that he, too, wished to spend the night somewhere else, away from me. Although my optimistic lenses were scratched, a little crooked and considerably less rose coloured, I reassured myself that it would not be possible for a marriage to fail in one week when the partners were so well suited.

There may very well be worse personality traits than unbridled optimism. My persistently positive spin on the world even in the face of overwhelming odds is a valuable part of who I am. Presuming that every story would eventually have a happy ending gave me the energy to "keep on trucking" despite appalling circumstances. My detractors might go so far as to say that I can be stubborn. While this characteristic has often proven invaluable in my life, it has also caused me to misinterpret all the signs in certain situations and lead me to make some very unfortunate decisions. I made one such decision in 1977.

It is a tribute to my parents that they made marriage and family life look easy. I cannot ever remember them exchanging an angry word.

They always seemed to agree with each other and always presented a united front. The same could be said of my aunts and uncles. None of my friends came from "broken" families. I think that all the adults in our neighbourhood must have done their fighting in hermetically sealed houses. I never saw examples of marital discord. Divorce was still a sticky political matter in the 70s. Before getting divorced, couples had to be separated for seven years or prove one of the following: adultery, physical abuse or mental cruelty. I knew of people who were separated or divorced but at some fundamental level believed that to fail in marriage indicated a basic personality disorder.

Although we did not have extensive discussions on the topic in our family, my parents and I assumed that when I grew up I, too, would marry and have children. The only dark cloud over this assumption was the diabetes, which had struck at a very fragile moment in a young girl's life: on the brink of adolescence and an emerging sexuality. My body was a source of shame and embarrassment to me, and my sense of self-esteem suffered immensely. Paradoxically, even though I had serious self-doubts about the value of my body, I still expected to marry and raise children.

By the end of my undergraduate studies, a number of my former roommates were already married. When they invited me over for dinner, I felt jealous of their lifestyle. Unlike today, when women are pursuing careers and marrying at older ages, I was beginning to feel like an old maid at 24! Then all that changed. A man I had dated a little in high school and who was now a medical resident showed up at the hospital information desk where my mother was a volunteer. He asked to use the telephone and they recognized each other.

"How is Jane? What is she up to now?" he asked.

"Ask her yourself," Mom replied, giving him my number in Kingston, where I was pursuing my graduate studies.

He called me. I was surprised to hear from him but I did remember him as one of the nicer guys I had dated in high school. We agreed that we should meet on my next trip to Toronto. We met on a number of other occasions after that, although we never really spent any time together alone. Both of his sisters were engaged to be married and I was invited to their bridal showers. I always stayed with my family when I was in Toronto and it seemed we were always with one family or the other. We spent a pleasant few months this way. He always called me from the hospital when he was on call and I quite liked getting regular phone calls from the same caring man.

When in the summer of 1976 McGill offered me a spot in the first-year medicine class, he was considerably less thrilled than I was. What about him? he said. He was in the second year of a family medicine residency program at the University of Toronto. Did I expect him to wait four years while I finished my studies?

I asked him if he might do some studies in Montreal himself. (I later learned that it is common for medical students to do a year of postgraduate studies at different institutions around the world.) He made this sound like an huge undertaking. He liked U of T and he especially liked Toronto. This issue became contentious, but he eventually said he would come to do a year's training in Montreal only if I agreed to marry him at the first opportunity. He was prepared to put himself out for me but not without some guarantee for him. This seemed reasonable, and so I found myself engaged to a man whom I had never really referred to as my boyfriend. I have a tendency to agree to just about anything without considering the ramifications for myself in order to get out of difficult or unpleasant discussions. I learned the hard way that the decision to marry should be based on more than a way out of an awkward conversation.

From time to time I would think about my life. I was going to be a doctor, which had been a long-term dream, and I was getting married, which was also something I wanted. Why was I not more excited?

Medical school started with a bang. We were thrown into our studies. I did not get to Toronto at all during the first term. During the Christmas break, Mom told me I had to spend some time getting the wedding plans underway. Some parties were thrown in our honour. It seemed a little early to me, but it was true that I would not be spending a lot of time in Toronto before the wedding.

Three other women in my medical class were planning to be married in the summer after first year, and we had fun exchanging ideas for the weddings. The time flew past. Before long, I had moved back to Toronto to prepare for the wedding and my fiancé moved to Montreal to begin his next year of training. I found the prospect of setting up my own home exciting, but I did not want to spend much time with him in Montreal. My overriding sense of optimism went into high gear. I would go over and over all the reasons that this would be a good marriage. We had similar backgrounds. Our interests were complementary. He played hockey with my cousin and I knew and liked his two sisters. If our parents had been organizing an arranged marriage they could not have chosen better for us. And he was very pleasant. Still, I wondered why there were so many gooey love songs. I was in a good mood but definitely did not have any stardust in my eyes.

Following our disastrous honeymoon, I eventually discovered that my husband had a serious eating disorder. Ever optimistic, I told myself that this could not be true, that anorexia and bulimia were almost exclusively the domain of teenage girls. Surely this was some kind of stressful response to being married, a matter of nerves.

We did practically nothing together on our honeymoon. He would disappear for hours, running for miles and miles. Then he would do push-ups for half an hour at a time. Despite his having done such extensive exercise, I could never get him to eat a meal with me. My anticipated romantic meals, drinking wine and basking in the glory of the sunset, never happened. Meals became unbearable as our discussions focused upon my observation that he was neither eating nor drinking, or his observation that I was eating too much. Although he knew a lot about the medicine of diabetes, he seemed to have no concept of my need for regular meals and the consequences of moving away from my regime. He had phenomenal avoidance behaviour whenever I suggested a bite of breakfast or lunch.

Even at my optimistic best, I could not come up with a plausible explanation for my husband's odd behaviour. Within the first month of our return to Montreal I was weeping in the offices of the Student Mental Health Centre.

"My husband has anorexia nervosa and I don't know how to help him. What should I do?"

The answer was always the same.

"It is unusual for a man of his age to have anorexia, but it does sound as if he has a problem. You cannot help someone else with a serious mental health disorder. Your husband must want to change and come here himself. The only person you can help right now is yourself. Look at the impact this is having on your life."

I always told them I was a survivor and that I would be all right.

The first year of our marriage was a prolonged and pain-filled ordeal. I must have thought that my husband would be capable of dealing with his food phobia as a matter of will. I would make him breakfast. As soon as I left the room, he would hide the food and then say that it was delicious. This would make me furious. Sometimes at dinner I would serve him not only his dinner but also the breakfast he had hidden and which I had found. At other times, after exercising, he would eat 4000 calories at one sitting. I spent hours in the library poring over the literature on eating disorders. These were not as prominent in the 1970s as they are now and there was little information on what to do about them.

Advice for spouses or family members was completely lacking. It was inconceivable to me that he could not consume any calories. Eating and drinking seemed like such a normal activity.

One night, we were invited to dine with two friends in my class. He had asked for Scotch as a pre-dinner drink. Three of us enjoyed our drinks and hors d'oeuvres. My husband kept turning the glass in his hand.

"Is there something wrong with your drink?" asked our concerned host.

"No," he replied. "It's fine, thank you."

I looked on, feeling sick to my stomach.

Eventually our host suggested that we move into dinner and that my husband could have his drink with dinner. Our hostess had prepared a lovely meal. My husband moved the food around the plate but did not eat a single thing. I was mortified.

I do not imagine for one moment that he enjoyed being so weird and anti-social but we were never able to address the issue. If I began to question him about what was going on he would respond that I was hurting his feelings and demand that I back off. I said that he did not have to talk to me about it, but asked him to please get psychiatric help. He always said that it was his business, and his business alone. Eventually I stopped trying to share meals with him altogether. I would make two dinners and leave one on the hot plate for him to eat whenever he was able. Sometimes this could be at 2 a.m. The house was more peaceful when I began feeding only myself, but there was a terrible tension in the atmosphere. After all, one of the reasons I had wanted to be married was to share meals with someone.

Because the textbooks all said that anorexia/bulimia was rare in adults and especially in men, I thought that perhaps my diagnosis was wrong. I began to focus on the relentless push-ups. My husband must have done a thousand push-ups a day. One day I heard some nurses laughing about tripping over a doctor who had been doing push-ups in the clean utility cupboard. Another said she had heard he did that in the operating room. I myself had come across him working out on the landing of a busy public stairway. Back I went to the Student Mental Health Centre.

"I think I might have made a mistake," I told them. "I think my husband might have an obsessive-compulsive disorder. How can I help him?"

The answer was the same.

"You cannot help him. He must come here himself."

So, I did my best to hold my tongue as my husband embarrassed me in front of my classmates and colleagues at the hospital and in our neighbourhood as he continued to do push-ups in the most extraordinary locations. I eventually spoke to him about my visits to Student Health and their recommendation that he consider going there himself. Perhaps the most tender moment of our marriage was the moment he admitted that he had a serious eating disorder and said that the best thing that had ever happened to him was our marriage.

"Those doctors are wrong," he told me. "The only person in the world who can help me is you."

Tenderness wrapped in a devastating implication.

Somehow, we managed to live as co-habitants, some might say co-dependents, in the same apartment until the middle of my third year of medicine. At this time I learned that I was developing severe diabetic retinopathy, which required laser treatments. I began having retinal hemorrhages, which appeared as ugly black splotches in my visual field. Perhaps because he had more medical experience, my husband knew better than I the significance of these bleeds. In my usual optimistic state, I thought of these treatments as a tedious nuisance, but it never crossed my mind that my condition might be serious, that I might be losing my vision. As it began to sink in that I was probably losing my sight, my husband became very angry with me. Looking back, I am sure he must have had many things to make him angry. The prospect of his new wife becoming blind was an additional challenge for which he had no coping mechanism. Perhaps he was afraid of my role changing. It seemed as if I could no longer be the strong one, the only one who could help him. Blindness would mean I would become dependent. I was hurt and confused by his response; the tender hugs I needed so badly never materialized. Telling him about additional bleeds only made him angry; I felt that I had no one to talk to. The only encouraging thing on my horizon was my increasing passion for practising medicine.

I have asked myself many times what I would have done if the shoe had been on the other foot and my partner had become disabled instead of me. I hope that if I had been the healthy one, I would have been able to share my anger with my partner and together be outraged at the hand of fate.

The atmosphere in our home became even more frigid and hostile. I depended very heavily on my friendship with Ron Shepherd, the rector of my church. I was plagued by the vows of marriage my husband and I had taken so solemnly such a short time before. I could feel the life being drained from me by this relationship. Yet, a promise made before God seemed untouchable. Perhaps some of the best advice I have ever been given came from Ron.

He asked, "Does your husband know how unhappy you are?"

I told him that no one in their right mind could think our household was a happy one.

"Have you told your husband exactly what is bothering you and that it is a serious threat to the marriage?" he persisted.

"No."

"You must have that conversation and then go into marriage counselling. If, after that, there is no improvement, you may begin to think of dissolving the union."

I felt the need to speak with the priest who officiated at our marriage. I felt like such a failure and a fraud. He told me that God did not ordain marriage so that one person may suffer due to another. It was quite clear to me that I was not bringing any joy to my husband. His own medical problems prevented him from looking beyond himself. After a rancorous period of separation, I sought divorce from my husband. We were divorced in November 1981.

Twenty years later I still struggle with this most cosmic error of my life. How could I have failed for so long to see the signs of impending disaster? I must hold myself back from using my highly polished retrospectoscope. In hindsight I see everything very clearly and continue to chastise myself for not having known so much 25 years ago. This line of reasoning does not get me anywhere; part of my journey has been to learn to stop this self-flagellation. I have also had to learn that just as the lens of the retrospectoscope provides false clarity, the lens of unbridled optimism distorts reality.

Perhaps it is a sociological change, perhaps it is a more mature perspective, but today I do not know any marriages that seem to be easy. The crashing and burning of my marital dreams and all the associated hopes and expectations remain among the saddest losses in my life. My life went down a completely different pathway from the one I looked forward to in my younger years. And yet, this is a path I have learned to truly celebrate. Because I have not had one deep and all-consuming personal attachment and no child-rearing responsibilities, I have been free to develop an extraordinary number of intimate friendships. My life is not sparse and empty as I imagined the life of an "old maid" would be when I was 24 and was sighted. Today, as I face my impending death, I am reaping the benefits of those years of close friendships. I am more enveloped in love and support by my network of friends and family than I could ever have been had I become just another North Toronto housewife.

Rouse yourself! Why do you sleep, O Lord?
Awake, do not cast us off forever!
Why do you hide your face?
Why do you forget our affliction and oppression?
For we sink down to the dust;
Our bodies cling to the ground.
Rise up, come to our help.
Redeem us for the sake of your steadfast love.

Psalm 44:23-26

Chapter 3: In Sickness and in Health

A Deepening Shade

I learned to hate opening my eyes in the morning. For reasons no one understood, retinal hemorrhages seemed to occur during sleep. That had certainly been true for me. My theory was that it came from the jerking motion of the eyes during Rapid Eye Movement (REM) sleep. What did it matter? Each morning I awoke fearing that I would be blind. I had not been able to decide if it was better to flash my eyes quickly open to observe the carnage or to wait a moment to collect myself a little.

Today, as the alarm clock rang, I wished that I had never opened them at all. The left eye was crystal clear as usual. There was little sign of disease there and I had been told that it was quite safe. Many people function fully with one eye, I always reminded myself after seeing my ophthalmologist. Too often, recently, he remarked that the disease was very resistant to all treatment. This morning was living proof of this fact. There were several new and extremely ugly splotches in my visual field. I had to move the eye through its entire range of motion to survey the damage. The good news was that the central vision was preserved and I could read the clock with my good eye closed. I lay there quietly trying to gather myself together.

The new year, 1979, brought with it the start of the final phase of medical school. After several days of working in a team, it was my turn to be on call alone for the first time in my medical career. I remember waking on that first day, not concerned about my eye, but with a vaguely anxious feeling about would likely transpire later that day. I tried to ignore the queasy feeling in my stomach, but it increased as the day wore on. I was one notch below full-blown hysteria as each person on our team "signed out" to me, going through all their patients, listing all the possible disasters that might happen overnight. I remember wanting desperately to run off the ward as the last intern left.

"Who's on call tonight?" called out the charge nurse.

"The clerk!" called out another nurse, somewhat despondently.

As I was sitting at the nursing station writing myself a list of things to do after dinner, a reddish-black furry-looking frond suddenly appeared in my right eye field of vision. I had become somewhat used to the black dots that continued to harass me from time to time and had learned to look past them. I had not had anything new for the past week and had chosen to believe that the laser treatments had begun to stem the tide of the disaster brewing inside my right eye. This frond was a completely different story. I shut my eye so I did not have to look at it. I hoped that in a minute it would be gone. Instead, when I opened my eye the background was a rosy pink colour rather than clear.

I decided to go down to the cafeteria for dinner. The one fun thing about being on call at night was the camaraderie between the house staff. We all ate at the same table. This was in the days before all the cutbacks and this particular hospital was well known for its treatment of the house staff on call. The kitchen prepared a snack at midnight and at 3 a.m., and all who could make themselves available would find their way to the cafeteria. We did not need the food as much as the collegial fraternity. I listened to their entertaining conversation, but as I sat there the lower aspect of my visual field intensified in colour. Although I usually enjoyed dinner with "the team," tonight I could not engage in the discussion since I was too caught up in the affairs of running my ward single-handed.

"I was about to call you," said the nurse upon my return. "17A blew her I.V."

I would have to replace the patient's intravenous line, a procedure that was not on my list of potential overnight disasters. It seemed as if every patient in my unit blew their I.V. line that evening. I could not see well because of my eye; with each subsequent line change, I tried to ascertain if it was easier to use blurred binocular vision or monocular vision while starting lines. The procedure required depth perception to judge the depth of the puncture.

I began to need reassurance that I was all right, so I started my long history of taking advantage of my position within the medical system to cut through red tape. I knew that my eye doctor was married to one of the radiologists at this hospital. I phoned the hospital operator, who had the list of the staff's private home phone numbers. The operator sounded skeptical that a clinical clerk in medicine needed to speak to a radiologist who was not on call. Nevertheless, she gave me the number. My eye doctor answered the phone. He was puzzled about how I had found him at home, so I told him where I was and why I was calling. He quickly forgave me and then sounded quite concerned. He told me that the only thing I could do to help the bleeding was to avoid high blood pressure. Being on call did not make this possible. Another stroke of luck for me was that my endocrinologist was the physician-in-chief at the hospital. My eye doctor phoned him and told him what was happening. He called me and told me to return home immediately; he would speak to the senior residents to tell them that I had been sent home for medical reasons.

The next morning, I presented myself at my ophthalmologist's office. He examined my eye and confirmed a major bleed. He reassured me that the type and location of my bleed meant that it would surely clear spontaneously over the next six weeks, but I would have to take two weeks off. I immediately began to wonder if this would affect my chances of graduating. When I returned two weeks later, I was excited to see that the blurring had cleared quite a bit and that I could look at radiographs with both eyes. The major drawback was that half my visual field was rose coloured and fuzzy. Warm, fuzzy things are usually comforting. This was not.

I awoke one morning about three weeks later to find that my right eye had blurred into an opaque rose-coloured screen. I could tell that there was light shining at my eye but I could not see anything. I went directly to my doctor's office. He examined the eye and confirmed that the retina had detached itself almost completely from the back of the eyeball. There was nothing to be done. I did not need to take time off if I did not want to. I thought about how it would feel sitting at home alone contemplating my lost eye, and decided to carry on. I appeared on the ward only slightly late.

The tiny sliver of my right visual field through which I could perceive light and colour was a small haven for me. I took great delight from using this tiny window, even though my left eye could see well. I would frequently close my good eye and hold an object in my hand. I would examine the object with my little slit and attempt to identify its colour. For many months I managed to do fairly well with this little window of vision.

Miss D

I rapidly adapted to life with one eye. I could read well and drove carefully. In August, I did a month of internal medicine at the Montreal General Hospital to make up for the month I had missed in the spring. About halfway through the month I admitted a 23-year-old woman, Miss D. Her body was so grossly swollen, she could not walk. The diagnosis was not at all clear – all we knew was that she had had diabetes since childhood. I did not tell her that I shared this problem, nor did I tell anyone on my team. We determined that she had severe kidney disease because of the diabetes. The ensuing volume overload had caused heart failure. What troubled her most, however, was that she had lost the sight in one eye – her left. I cared for her intently, working with both the nephrology and cardiology departments. She lost litres of excess fluid and was delighted when she was able to walk in the hall.

One day I had lunch with my senior resident in the hospital cafeteria. Her tray was loaded with a plate of spaghetti with meat sauce, cake, and a glass of Coke. Halfway through the meal, she pointed to the soup, salad and milk on my tray.

"Look at your lunch compared to mine! You always eat such healthy food," she commented. "Don't you like cake?"

I hesitated and said that I did like cake but tried not to take it too often.

"Why?" she persisted. "You're not fat."

An awkward moment passed, then I told her that I had Type 1 diabetes.

"You what?" she exclaimed. "Why was I not told about this?"

I told her that I did not think that it was policy for team members to review each other's medical backgrounds. I had never told any of my seniors. Then she started asking me specific questions. I eventually told her about my eye. She became quite agitated and said that I should not be caring for Miss D. I reassured her that I was fine with it. She permitted me to continue caring for Miss D, but advised me to tell each of my future seniors whenever I started a new rotation. I was on call again the following weekend when Miss D had a cardiac arrest in my presence. We were unable to resuscitate her.

Tight Control

I began my next rotation, Pediatrics, with those words of warning from my senior resident still ringing in my ears. I told the next senior about the diabetes and my eye. She seemed to have a "What does that have to do with me?" attitude. "Well, thanks for telling me," she said, after ascertaining that she would not have to adjust her call schedule because of me.

I thought that would be the end of it, and I felt foolish. I made a note to myself to withhold this information the next time around. I only had one more rotation coming up: Psychiatry. I anticipated enough trouble there without telling them that I had recently become partially blind.

To my amazement and mild annoyance, my senior asked to speak with me several days later. She explained that she had taken the liberty of telling the endocrinologists on staff my story. They were starting a study and thought that I could help them. Always wanting to be helpful, I called one of the specialists, even though I was very nervous about speaking to her. When I had been doing my pre-clerkship surgery rotation, this endocrinologist had been a surgical intern. She appeared older and far more mature and wiser than the other interns. She was an internationally recognized pediatrician who had recently moved to Canada with her equally renowned husband, who had taken up a position at the university. Because all her training had been outside the country, the Canadian medical authorities required her to do an internship before she could be given a licence to practise medicine here. She had literally skated circles around the rest of us and as if to protect ourselves, I recall that we tended to give her a wide berth. Now, here I was, about to make an appointment to speak with her alone. I could not imagine how I might be useful to her.

I could tell right away that she did not remember meeting me. What a relief – she did not remember me as that pathetic little medical student who had not had a single useful suggestion that night when we had both been on call at another hospital during our training. My stomach was nonetheless in knots as she described her current project. She had acquired a prototype insulin infusion pump and hoped it would improve on standard diabetic treatment. Until then I had required one injection of insulin each morning. This usually acted for 18 to 24 hours. The level of insulin in the blood rose gradually through the first 0 to 12 hours and gradually declined thereafter. The trick was to give enough insulin to last through the entire day without giving too much for the maximal point. The most serious issue was that current insulin therapies in no way represented physiological conditions. Normally, there is a steady low level of insulin in the blood. In response to the ingestion of food, there is a short burst of insulin released from the pancreas. This insulin deals with the rise in blood sugar resulting from the food. As the sugar level begins to fall, the pancreas shuts off insulin secretion.

The purpose of her study was to approximate more closely this natural cycle with her little pump. It was set at a basal infusion rate; a mechanism released a bolus of insulin with meals. It was proposed that this would provide tighter control of blood sugars while reducing the likelihood of patients having episodes when the insulin level was too high and the blood sugar too low. One of her problems was finding suitable candidates to study. Each was required to have frequent, if not hourly, blood sugar determinations. Furthermore, if her research projections were accurate, she hoped to ask subjects to eat meals of different carbohydrate content and assess the bolus size to keep the sugars within the normal range. I was the best subject she and her team could have wished for. I was a captive subject, present for study and analysis at any moment. If the pump failed or caused unexpected problems, help was only minutes away. I was intrigued by the theory and signed up for the study. I thought it might be good for me, as more and more literature suggested that tighter control of blood sugars reduced the likelihood of complications. Up to this point, tight control of sugars had not been possible because of the limitations of available insulins.

The pump turned out to be tedious and cumbersome, but I was amazed at how marvellous it felt to have a normal blood sugar level. I felt light and energetic, and it was wonderful. I had not felt normal since I was 13. I immediately became addicted to feeling like that. It was like what I had always thought it would feel like to be in love. I wanted to tell everyone I met about it: "Guess what? My blood sugar is normal!"

I floated in to see the ophthalmologist two weeks into the project. In my mind, this pump had come along just in time for me. Sadly, I would have to go through life with only one eye, but I could learn to adapt to that. The vision in my left eye was excellent. I could read easily and was still driving my car. From now on my blood sugars would be normal and my vision would be saved. I was ebullient as I gave him my report. He looked into my eye and kept saying, "I can't believe this. I can't believe it."

I assumed that he was seeing a huge improvement in my eye already. This confused me because I had been under the impression that the left eye had remained quite healthy. I was wrong. His news was bad:

my left eye had deteriorated more than he could have imagined since my last examination. I was stunned and convinced myself that he was mistaken. The eye looked so bad that he began the first laser treatment that same day. For the first time ever, I had less than crystal clear vision from my beautiful left eye – the eye upon which hung my career and my future.

The deterioration of my left eye advanced stealthily. I began having dot and blotch hemorrhages in the left eye field. The endocrinology people wanted me to consult with a retina specialist at another hospital. I did, but he had little that was positive to say after peering in. He felt that a relatively new surgical procedure was indicated. Because the stakes were so high, he wanted two visiting American retinal specialists who were scheduled to give ophthalmology grand rounds at McGill in early January 1980 to take a look at me. This coincided with the end of our clinical clerkship. I agreed to see the specialists; I needed their help and I did not want to lose any more time than I already had. But in addition to medical support, I sought help of another kind.

Who Is Walking with Me? Ronald Shepherd

When I reach out for help in a time of crisis, it can be oblique, indirect. In Kingston, all through the uncertainty of my career in graduate school, I felt a persistent, nagging and undeniable force tugging me. I was inexorably drawn to cathedrals, churches and chapels during those two years. Sitting in them, alone, brought me a sense of peace and serenity. The air felt different inside the calm and protective walls of these buildings. Worshipping in them with a full Sunday congregation left me feeling exhilarated and infused with a new energy.

I spent my two years of graduate school exploring not only different churches but also different faiths. I did this exploration on my own for the most part. Perhaps this search for a "real" home was part of the legacy of living next door to Cathy Ryan years before in Toronto. I found myself returning to St. George's Cathedral in Kingston again and again. But as much as I loved attending the services there, I never presented myself to the wardens or dean. I seemed to be happy engaging anonymously in my own developing sense of spirituality. It was amazing to observe this unrolling personal spiritual growth. At first I did not feel the need to talk about this experience with anyone else.

After moving to Montreal to attend McGill University, I once again began my practice of attending different churches, but I restricted myself largely to different Anglican churches. Even though it was relatively far from my home, I felt the strongest sense of my own spirit while inside Christ Church Cathedral. I initially sat in it, silent and alone. Then I began to attend Sunday services. I had found what was going to be my spiritual home for at least the next four years. I signed the forms asking to be added officially to the church roster.

Father Ronald Shepherd, the cathedral dean, had greeted me on several occasions at the end of various services. It felt not only essential but also completely natural to me to arrange to speak to him privately when I learned the severity of my eye problems.

I do not think I knew what I wanted or expected from him. I suppose I was taken aback by his directness and his sure sense of unsentimental compassion. I had not allowed myself to even think of the possibility that the surgery might not be successful. I had contemplated what it might feel like if the surgery was unable to arrest the vascularization problem in my retina, but that was as far as I had permitted myself to go. I would not let myself consider the reality of blindness.

I felt both scared yet oddly calm speaking in his office about these things that up to this point had remained trapped within me. It was too horrific to think of blindness as something that could happen to me. Yet, as we spoke, I sometimes closed my eyes. He asked me to consider what I could see, what I could not see, and what the difference was. His office was a lovely old octagonal room with tall windows on the outside aspects of the building. It was February and the leaded glass windows were slightly frosted. I could see columns of steam rising from the vents in the road outside. The smell of his tobacco smoke was rich and aromatic. The old radiators clanged and groaned in the background as they struggled to keep the room cozy and warm. Hundreds of volumes of books lined the floor-to-ceiling shelves. The warmth and slightly musty scent were so much more comfortable than the cold and sterile hospital environment. Although I knew it could not be so, he gave the impression that he had nothing more important to do than speak with me. As I left his study, he took the details about the time and place of my surgery the following week and promised that we would continue our discussions.

True to his word, he called me two days before the surgery. He asked if he could bring communion to me the following evening once I had been admitted to the hospital. I was slightly anxious at this thought, as I had never received communion in private. I agreed, and he arrived at the appointed time. It was such a great comfort to have him there and

I felt much calmed by his prayers. He surprised me when he did not pray that the operation would be successful. No, he prayed that I should know the peace and calm of the Holy Spirit within me. This became a very important incantation, almost a mantra, for me. Left to my own devices, I know I would have blurted out something more in the form of a special order than a prayer. "Please, God, make this operation a success. Make all my eye problems go away and let me focus all my attention on my medical studies. And while you're at it maybe you could also …." No.

The result of the surgery on my left eye was worse than anything I had imagined. They told me afterwards that the procedure had been much more complicated than anyone had expected. The retina detached during the surgery and there had been a lot of bleeding. A clot formed and drifted into the region of the macula, the point for central vision. They told me that I would not be able to see directly for some time. They also said that when the bandages came off, I would have blurred vision in the periphery but that this would clear with time. The good news apparently was that Mother Nature does not leave clots intact for a prolonged period of time, and as we spoke, my body was busy at work dissolving the clot and reabsorbing the blood. At least that was the theory. I would have to be a patient patient for some time after they removed the bandages. If the bloodied fluid in my eye did not clear itself up, they could repeat the operation, withdrawing the offending fluid manually and replacing it with clear fluid.

I was naturally very anxious to have the bandages off and assess the degree to which my vision would be impaired. Before the surgery, I had been reading an interesting article in a magazine. In the hope of encouraging myself and showing a positive attitude, I had reserved the last page of the article for the post-operative period. I hoped that it would not be long until I could finish the article myself. Perhaps as a form of superstition I asked the nurse to save that magazine for me in my locker so that it would not be thrown out by mistake.

This brand new surgical procedure was designed to interrupt the pathological process that was occurring in my eyes. I needed this surgery to be successful in order to preserve useful eyesight, as I had already lost the sight in my right eye. In those first post-operative days, I could not see at all as my left eye was tightly bandaged.

I thought wryly to myself that this experience of darkness was very different from sitting in Dean Ron Shepherd's office with my eyes shut. I was terrified. I suddenly felt very vulnerable and constantly felt as if someone had walked into my room and was standing there staring at me. I feared that I would be robbed or harmed in some other way. One evening I left my room in search of the nursing station, which I knew was close at hand. The hall suddenly sounded quiet: there was no one at the station. I turned around and then did not know if I had turned a full circle or perhaps a half or quarter. I could not find any doorways and stood panic stricken, groping about the hallway, until a nurse rescued me. "Don't leave your room again!" she admonished me. I felt demolished, shattered. One month earlier I had been officially at work in this very hospital, a free-wheeling individual making decisions that were sometimes quite important. Now I was being told to be a good patient and was confined to barracks.

Ron Shepherd came the afternoon the bandages were removed. My disappointment was palpable. I had been trying to prepare myself for losing my central vision, and had tried to think of the rest of my visual field being cloudy and pink in colour. In reality, there was reddish-black plaque in the centre of my field extending practically to the margins in most directions. At the very bottom I had a window where I could detect some light blazing through the muck, which was impenetrable everywhere else. Ron tried to find a place where I could see him. There was no such spot. We spoke of my disappointment and also how I might return to school. I was afraid that I would miss my final year of medicine if I could not return to the last three months of classes. Talking about how I might return to the mainstream of life while this clot cleared gave me some hope.

My eye apparently settled sufficiently and I was sent home to wait for Mother Nature to work a miracle and dissolve the clot in my eye. We agreed that if there was no improvement in six weeks, the surgery would be repeated. Six weeks have never felt so long. I saw the surgeon weekly and I detected his growing sense of disappointment at each visit. Still, I kept myself going by focusing upon improvement in the vision. Throughout these six long weeks, Dean Ron Shepherd spent much time with me, helping to keep my spirits up.

Six weeks passed but there was no improvement. In fact, the reddish discoloration had been replaced by a slate-grey film. I had more awareness of light in my right eye. There was still a tiny crescent of intact retina on the outer edge of my visual field in my left eye. I was grateful that the time had elapsed and that we could now do a definitive procedure to clear the rubbish left during the first operation. Ron Shepherd and I prayed together again before this procedure. What amazes me now, despite all the evidence to the contrary, is how strongly I believed that the surgeon would be able to restore my vision. I was sure that this surgery would remove the grey slate-like material and replace the fluid in my eye, and that I would be able to see again and concentrate on my final exams in medical school.

When I awoke from the anesthetic, I was aware of unusual activity in my room. I kept falling asleep; when I woke up significantly I was alone in the room. It was the first night of Passover and as I was in a Jewish hospital, most of the staff members, including my surgeon, were at home having their Seder meal. Eventually, my soon-to-be ex-husband came for a visit and I asked him what had happened in the surgery. I had a very sick feeling that there would have been more excitement had the news been good. He had not spoken to the doctor and was trying to get through to him at home. When they connected the conversation was very short. When he got off the phone, he told me that I would never see again.

My surgery had taken place on the Monday of Holy Week, probably the busiest time of the year for a cathedral dean. Nevertheless, Ron Shepherd had been in touch with my family constantly and knew the bad news. Despite his frantic schedule, he came to see me on the Wednesday afternoon. I was alone at the time so we were able to have a good visit. When he walked through the door and asked if he could enter, I turned and lashed out at him, saying, "I think your God is the biggest jerk I have ever known."

"I am sure He must seem that way sometimes," replied Ron.

We did not do a lot of talking that afternoon. I was enormously grateful that he did not try to convince me that God loved me deeply and that I was in the strong arms of the everlasting Saviour, which was something I had heard chaplains and priests say to patients. That was the very last thing I wanted to hear that afternoon. Just as in our first meeting I had not known what to say or what I wanted him to say, mere words seemed woefully inadequate.

What I do remember very strongly to this day is that Ron allowed me to express anger, frustration and despair with God. He did not try to defend himself or to provide any ridiculous and facile explanations for what had happened to me. I learned to bite my gums when people would explain to me that God was using me to teach the world, or that God would never send me more than I could bear. Had Ron used that approach that afternoon, I think I would forevermore have been turned off by religion. No, we sat and absorbed the dreadful news. As he left, he stuck his head around the door and said, "I am going back to the cathedral now to pray to that jerk on your behalf."

That was – and continues to be – Ron, a strong and constant supporter who walked beside me through all the trials that followed this terrible experience.

It was time for me to start learning how to be blind, and at the same time to find my place in the profession I so loved and was determined to pursue, my handicap notwithstanding. This is a never-ending journey for me and, like any important venture, it started with practical and immediate little steps.

O LORD, do not rebuke me in your anger,
or discipline me in your wrath.
Be gracious to me, O LORD, for I am languishing.
O LORD, heal me, for my bones are shaking with terror.
My soul also is struck with terror,
while you, O LORD – how long?

Turn, O LORD, save my life;
deliver me for the sake of your steadfast love.

Psalm 6:1-4

Chapter 4: Rehabilitation

This Is Not Relaxing

"Why is it so quiet?" I wondered. I was approaching the corner of Van Horne Avenue and Boulevard Côte des Neiges, a major intersection leading to the town of Mount Royal to the north and Outremont to the east. I was usually confused by the noise and suffocated by fumes at this intersection. I had stood here many times with my mobility instructor, who had been trained in how to teach the blind to move about independently using only a white cane for solace and defence. Together, we had stood at this very corner listening to the traffic noises as if we were studying music appreciation. Traffic noises were more than noise – they provided useful information about orientation. I listened to the noise as the cars ran parallel to me. This sound meant that I was relatively safe. (When the traffic was at right angles to me, I was terrified.) Small changes in angulation make big changes in the sound. My teacher pointed out repeatedly that the trick was to keep my head straight and then follow my nose. Until I had become blind, I had not known how difficult it was to do these seemingly straightforward things with your eyes shut.

I ventured forward and, breaking all the rules, turned my head left and right desperately searching for a clue to my position. I nearly leapt out of my skin when a hand came from nowhere and grabbed my elbow.

"Would you like some help?" asked a man as he dragged me out of the intersection. It turned out that he was the driver of the number 165 bus. I had wandered into the intersection and had stopped the traffic in all directions. We had only walked a few steps when the traffic revved up and the confusing cacophony began all over again.

"Have a good day," said the driver, cheerily walking back to the busload of curious onlookers.

"I wonder if I look as if I am having a good day?" I thought to myself. I dearly wanted to hurl my cane as far away as possible, curl up into a ball and weep. I could not. The bus driver had let go of me in front of a service station and a car honked to let me know I was blocking his exit. I dusted off my cane, turned my head in the direction I hoped was home and followed my nose.

After this traumatic experience, I quickly learned how it sounded when I was walking in the same direction, or against the flow, of the busy traffic of Montreal.

I Am an Island

Without a doubt, the period of my rehabilitation was the loneliest of my life. Everything I knew had been ripped from me. During the first weeks following the disaster, my classmates had rallied around me. They helped organize car pools to get me to class. People read to me and studied with me as we all prepared for final exams. They got together with various staff from the medical teaching office to buy me a tandem bicycle to replace my beloved green Raleigh. My biking days were not over, as long as someone was brave or foolhardy enough to take the front seat. Then exams were over, graduation passed and my colleagues moved on to seek their fortunes. What was my fortune?

The traumatic events of those last three months of medical school had produced an incredible amount of energy within me. This energy was directed at useful activities such as preparing for exams and graduation. Once these activities were safely behind me, this same energy began to threaten me.

I felt completely alone. With graduation, my faculty advisers wished me well and turned their attention to the incoming class. I was neither a medical student nor fully a doctor. No one could think of anything for a blind person with a medical degree to do. My family was devastated and many miles away in Toronto. My fragile marriage was in tatters. My then-husband could only come up with lists of things I could no longer do, and spent as much time away from our apartment as possible. My eye doctor had nothing more to offer. I was no longer a person with ailing eyes seeking help. My eyes were dead.

The people and the places in my world were the same, but a major sea change had occurred. Although I remained in the same place, I was no longer on the same path I had shared with my friends or family. We were all grieving, and shared a lot of rage at what happened. But people quickly returned to their usual routines. I was surrounded by the familiar voices of people trying to be helpful in their own way, but I felt as if I were adrift in outer space, no longer guided by gravity or other natural laws. No matter how much my friends and colleagues wanted to help, none of them could be with me in this new, hostile, desiccated, unwelcoming space. When I acknowledged this new reality, I felt a loneliness and despair more isolating than I had ever imagined possible.

Of course, professional help was available, and lots of it. I knew that it was a matter of asking for it and adapting it to my own needs when it didn't take the form I thought it should. I quickly discovered that in spite of my accomplishments elsewhere, I would not exactly shine in blind school. I must have made life very difficult for some people who were doing their best, but my personal needs and sense of professional urgency were too intense.

I Am a Blind School Dropout

Blind school is the only education program I ever flunked. I did not do well with the curriculum, which was geared to such a different set of needs and life experiences than mine.

The school was certainly expertly staffed and well equipped. One classroom was fitted with kitchen appliances and utensils such as irons and saucepans. I spent several exasperating afternoons learning how to develop a grid pattern on my floor to ensure that sweeping was done methodically and completely. Then I learned how to use an iron without scorching either myself or the wrinkled cloth. The teachers were confused by my lack of enthusiasm for learning to perform household tasks. I had to explain that I had no intention of wasting my precious time learning how to do domestic jobs for which I intended to hire a housekeeper.

I was not a star in Braille class either, although I did learn to read the alphabet in what is called Grade One Braille. Braille letters are composed of six raised dots set out in various permutations and combinations in two vertical lines. In Grade One, each letter is represented by a full, six-dot pattern. Any document written in this way would be overly large and bulky. In Grade Two and Grade Three Braille, multiple contractions are used. For example, instead of using nine separate Braille letters to spell the word "knowledge," it is identified by the letter "k."

There are key signs for commonly used prefixes, suffixes and other frequently occurring letter groups, such as "-tion," "-ment" or "-ing." Thus the word "acknowledgement" should be written with the signs for the letters "a" and "c," then the sign for the letter "k" for knowledge, then the sign for "-ment." It is all quite ingenious, but nothing else I have ever encountered matches it for aggravation. I repeatedly lifted my hands from the page to take a sip of tea or scratch my nose. When I returned to the page I had lost my place and it took me 10 minutes to find the spot to continue reading. I truly thought I would go mad.

I had what I can only describe as "My Big Braille Crisis" early in the fall of 1980, about six weeks into rehabilitation. I was in Toronto visiting my family for a few days. I had telephoned two of my med school friends who were working as interns in Toronto and had heard all about the travails of internship. I had my Braille workbook with me. I went upstairs to the study to work on Grade One Braille. This particular exercise was on the letter "t." I painstakingly made my way across the rows of miserable dots. I tried to remember to keep my fingers on the page so I would not lose my place. For 15 minutes I hunched stiffly over my work. At the end, the secrets of the page were revealed to me.

Tom is a cat.

He eats mice.

The mice hate Tom.

I wept, thinking of what my friends were doing as I sat reading about mice and the hateful Tom.

I told my Braille teacher that I did not see any reason for me to continue learning Braille. Her response was understandable as I had literally bullied my way into the school and had done nothing but scorn the curriculum since my arrival.

"How are you going to read and write in your charts if you do not learn Braille?" she demanded.

"Well, that is just it," I replied. "No one else in my life will be using Braille, so I do not think it is worth my time learning it."

So I dropped that course.

I knew I needed help with certain aspects of the written word. As a doctor I needed to be able to write charts and fill in forms and to do so relatively quickly. Twenty years ago, the medical profession was in the dark ages when it came to the production and management of words. We were still very much in the era of handwriting when I lost my sight.

I figured that the woman who had tried so hard to teach me to do kitchen and other household chores could teach me handwriting. When I asked her to teach me how to write straight, she said, "No blind people ever use handwriting."

"But I must!" I cried.

She was amazed at my tenacity when I wanted to learn something. And learn I did. In fact, by the time we had finished we both had learned something.

The Common Room

As much as I despised learning Braille and floor-cleaning techniques, what I dreaded most were the periods of organized free time and recreation. There was a spacious common room on the ground floor where all the clients relaxed at lunch or between classes. Several blind people lived in the neighbourhood because of its proximity to the school. The traffic lights buzzed as the lights changed to allow safe passage for those who could not see the changing of the light. Many of these people had attended junior school here and felt very much at home in the common room.

The shelves contained games adapted for use by the visually impaired. I had never been a big game player, but I did enjoy playing Scrabble, cribbage and solitaire. "No problem," said the recreation director. "We have playing cards with both large print and Braille markings. Here is Scrabble with Braille markers and depressions so that you do not move the squares as you touch them."

I felt a sudden rush of faintness and nausea, thinking that she might arrange for me to join a game of Scrabble with the regulars who gathered here for lunch. Perhaps they could sense my extreme discomfort. A terrible silence fell in the room. Fortunately, none of the silent onlookers offered to play with me. They all knew that this awkward and demanding new client said she was a doctor. They knew that I had fast-tracked myself because I would be returning to work in several months. They also knew how hard it was for the visually impaired to find suitable jobs.

Slowly, as I tried to make myself invisible, the conversations resumed. I pretended that I was not listening, which was difficult as I was sitting in a circle with them. They laughed at a tale of one of them nearly getting on the wrong bus. Suddenly a new voice joined in the conversation and I realized that I had no idea how many people were in the room. The thought of being in a room and not knowing who else was there gave me a chill. Alone, awkward, frightened, and so angry about my new circumstances, very much alone in this crowd in the common room, I knew that I would never fit in with this common-room crowd. I was a fish out of water. I was gripped by panic. Why? Because it was here in this place, in this common room, surrounded by people who, like me, were blind, that I was suddenly hit with the crushing reality of my circumstances. I was, like them, truly handicapped. I was now a blind person among the blind. I was not only like "them," I was one of them.

I suddenly became aware of the image I had imposed on this common room in Montreal. This institutional room, filled with blind people, had suddenly become my world, one I was afraid to enter. In this protected space, we had two experiences in common: blindness and the need to find our own way. This room had become for me a metaphor for the world at large, where even greater risks and challenges awaited me. Beyond the safe confines of this room, in the world out there, we have only one thing in common: the need to find our own way. Blindness, the defining characteristic in this room, is rare in the world beyond the walls of the common room. And it was beyond those walls that I had to learn to be blind in a sighted world.

Walking Step by Step

I became determined to learn how to walk by myself. I wanted to walk fast and in a straight line. I wanted to go up and down stairs. I wanted to use the escalator. I wanted to walk through a revolving door. I wanted to get onto the correct elevator when the bell rang. I wanted to walk on the sidewalks even if the pavement was cracked. I wanted to avoid falling into manholes if someone forgot to cover them. I wanted to walk in the park in the sunlight. I wanted to listen to the birds and the children playing, not the traffic sounds, to figure out my position. I wanted pleasure and relaxation from walking. I did not want to experience something as basic as walking as a terror-filled, monumental challenge. I wanted independent mobility and a mind free to wander and enjoy as I walked. And I was determined to achieve this.

I thought back to our childhood games of blind man's bluff, when we used to wriggle our noses the make the scarf over our eyes shift in position. Surely if I kept moving my eyes around I would eventually find a little window of light or see my toes. Desperately I clawed at the invisible bands over my eyes. No sparks of light were permitted entry. Inwardly, I prayed for an end to this. Outwardly, I stood compliantly tapping my cane on the ground, listening to the difference between concrete and wood. Wooden planks were sometimes placed over the manholes. Covered with wood or not, they were usually not level with the concrete, so I had to keep my stick right on the ground or I would trip. Despite the crippling rage within me, I looked calm, cool and collected to the curious onlookers who would stop to watch my lessons. I passionately hated those people who I convinced myself were entertaining themselves watching me grope.

The techniques for mobility and orientation are different for indoor and outdoor travel. I learned my early stick-handling techniques indoors. In order to travel in a straight line, I had to hold the cane exactly in the midline and gently arc the tip from side to side in symmetrical sine waves. If the arcs are done asymmetrically you gradually walk towards the side of the larger arc. If you are walking in a corridor you eventually smash into the side wall. Out of doors, you step off the curb, either twisting your ankle or falling in front of an oncoming truck.

The rehabilitation staff did not like my language in walking school. They were not fond of my descriptions of encountering furniture or walls as "smashing crash-ups." The correct terminology, which they made me use, is "contacting an obstacle." I referred irreverently to my cane as "a stick" and spoke of "walking lessons" rather than "mobility" and "orientation." They felt, and I think they were right, that my choice of language reflected a certain attitude. Did my use of apocalyptic language reflect a bad attitude? Yes, it did – real bad.

Eventually, I learned to walk along the city streets. I did not enjoy it, but I could do it. I advanced to crossing the road, first with a stoplight fitted with a buzzer for the blind. Then I learned how to cross a side street. Finally I learned how to cross at a stoplight with no aural assists. You know that you are at such a place by listening to the traffic sounds. Even if you do not want to cross the street, it is useful to recognize that you are at a stoplight as these are good clues for orienteering. My street address in Montreal was two streets north of the stoplight at Van Horne Avenue. The grocery store was one block south of the lights at the top of the hill.

I learned to navigate the region near the institute. I learned to listen for clues, like one-way only traffic or certain smells. I knew that I was going past The Body Shop by the delicious fragrances that wafted into the street. I learned that I could not count on the mobile hot-dog stand to be in the same place every day. (It is a very foolish blind travel-ler who makes decisions about position based on information gleaned from moving rather than fixed landmarks.) I learned to use the buses in the neighbourhood and, on a special assignment from my mobility in-structor, I even took the bus from the institute to a designated depart-ment store. I had to count the stops and get off. Then I had to listen for the location of the main door into the store. My assignment was to meet my teacher at the checkout.

Hating every minute passionately, I gradually progressed through the various steps of mobility training. Some exercises were fun – like the one where I had to find my way to meet my teacher at a coffee shop for lunch. Many were not fun at all. At the end of a meal or coffee break, my teacher would suddenly get up and walk away, saying that she had an errand to do. She would meet me at such and such a location in 15 minutes. The further along I got in the course, the more unpleasant it became.

Inevitably she would leave me in the back corner of some café. This would lead to a series of "smashing crack-ups" with about 10 tables before I even made it out onto the sidewalk to begin the search for my teacher. I often thought that I should just take a taxi home, for this "game" was no longer entertaining. The only thing preventing me from doing so was that I was unable to identify which car was a cab. Maybe I could ask someone to point me in the direction of a cab. But what if they were a handsome and charming serial killer? No, this "game" was not a game. The ultimate goal was to give me the confidence to know that I could travel alone, but I hated it. I kept wondering when this mobility and orientation course would end. Then it would hit me. The course would never end. This was my life.

My teacher knew that I was not nearly as calm as I tried to ap-pear. She could read me well. On very bad days, we would travel to a park and just sit and talk. We talked about our experiences at university. She explained how she had become a mobility instructor. She asked me what path I had taken into medicine, but never asked me how I in-tended to do the impossible: pursue my career as a doctor and medical researcher. I told her all about the atmosphere in a teaching hospital.

I eventually learned from these conversations that the staff at the institute was concerned because no one from the hospital or univer-sity had called them. One of the services the institute provided was teaching sessions for colleagues in the workplace about how to help a blind person. They would learn things such as specific arm positions for the guide and how to transmit information such as upcoming stairs. I told her that I had no permanent group of colleagues at the hospital and that I would not be working in a single specified area of the hospital, either.

My mobility teacher taught me lots of little things. Because of anxiety I had developed several odd mannerisms. Holding my cane with my right hand, I would cock up my left wrist, extending my thumb and index finger. I suppose this gave me some warning of obstacles on my left. After executing some configuration that she had concocted, I would be quite pleased with myself – until she pointed out my hand motions. Initially, I was put out by these observations. I asked her why it mattered. She replied that it looked weird and I would be causing enough of a stir as it was. She also taught me simple survival tricks, like how to approach a tabletop with the back of my hand and from below the level of the top. In this way I was less likely to injure my precious fingertips if the surface was hot or caustic or to knock over something on the table. I continue to be thankful to her for giving me these little tips for the rest of my life.

Winter brought my outdoor mobility classes to an abrupt stop. The morning after the first snowfall, my taxi was late and we slipped and slid all the way to the institute. I was too naive to anticipate the true impact that the snow would have on me. First, I was wearing boots for the first time. This changed the sensation of the ground under my feet. Second, I was wearing gloves, which changed the feeling of the cane in my hand. Suddenly, this stick felt much less worthy of my trust. The road was well cleared around the institute, so I crossed the street quite easily. It took several minutes more before I learned the truth about walking blind in the winter. My cane did not move as smoothly in its arcs on the sidewalks. The tip would hit patches of ice and snow and move me off course. Wham! My right foot hit a patch of ice and I nearly fell. I stayed upright, but I had lost my sense of direction. There were piles of snow at the curb so I was unable to use the curb for alignment. I made it as far as the corner. Cars were slipping and sliding all around me. The sounds were all different than they would have been on dry pavement. There were snow-clearing trucks all around me making very scary sounds. They had special beepers on them that wailed when they reversed. It sounded as if I was in the centre of a circle of snow trucks that were all simultaneously reversing towards me. I had to get hold of myself. There were other people outside; surely they would not let me be scooped up by snow trucks. I used my stick to try and find a clear place for crossing. I was wrong and found myself climbing out of a drift into oncoming traffic on Sherbrooke Street. Someone grabbed my arm. It was my mobility teacher, who had witnessed my efforts through the window. Sensing danger, she had run out into the cold, taken me by the arm and guided me to safety on the sidewalk.

"Take me back inside!" I screamed. "I will never go out alone in the winter again."

I am utterly spent and crushed;
I groan because of the tumult of my heart.

O LORD, all my longing is known to you;
my sighing is not hidden from you.
My heart throbs, my strength fails me;
as for the light of my eyes – it also has gone from me…

But it is for you, O LORD, that I wait;
it is you, O LORD, my God who will answer.

Psalm 38:8-10, 15

Part II: 1980 to 1985

Chapter 5: Putting It All Together

Practice

Blindness was very close to a lethal blow for my self-esteem and my sense of myself as a medical professional. I could not face the fact that I had worked so hard for 10 years straight at university and had nothing to show for it. As I had progressed through the senior years of medical school, I had begun to think of myself as someone with a good set of skills and a vocation to a profession I wanted to pursue more than anything else in the world. A stroke of a surgeon's scalpel snatched all this away from me.

I decided not to attend my med school graduation ceremonies, but my family contested this decision. At the ceremonies I felt like an outsider, as if I was an extra in someone else's drama. Had I been able to see a garbage pail in the vicinity of the stage I would have deposited my certificate directly into it. I took the certificate home but could not bear to take it out of its scroll protector.

I did not recognize the person who was enrolled in the rehabilitation program. I loathed each new thing I had to learn how to do. I hated myself for being able to walk straight in a corridor and then enter the third office on the left. I wanted to strangle the instructors who were congratulating me on making it down a set of stairs safely. Nothing could break through the thick layer of anger, fear, loathing and resentment that enveloped me during those dreadful days. Nothing, that is, except for the kindness and wisdom of my mentor and friend Dr. Robert Gardiner.

Like the Hound of Heaven in Francis Thompson's poem, he had been after me – to get back to some clinical work – and would not let the idea drop. I had been blind for seven months. I had managed to finish my academic studies and graduate from medical school. My marriage had just broken up and I felt overwhelmed with the events crashing around me. My peers were deeply involved in internships while I was languishing in a rehab program. But most of all, I had lost all sense of myself as a practising physician.

Dr. Gardiner would not let the idea drop. Each time he mentioned that he had not seen me in the hospital I found some excuse. Finally I confessed that although I had graduated from medical school, I had not had an opportunity to work as an intern. I had had no real opportunity to discover whether I could continue to practise medicine.

"Problem solved!" he said. "You may work in my endocrinology clinic whenever you wish. When can you begin?"

I started out cautiously. I continued with my rehabilitation program every morning and several afternoons each week. This enabled me to go to the endocrine clinic for a few hours at a time to rediscover my physical examination skills and other clinical skills and to figure out how these might be applied now that I could no longer see the patient.

The Doctor Will Not See You Now

I found out how much my world had changed with the very first patient I saw in the endocrine clinic. The nurse read me the chart and I listened – attentively, I thought. The patient was in the hormonal phase of a sex change. As the patient was walking into my office and the nurse was walking out, I found that I could not remember if the patient was a male here for estrogen en route to becoming a female, or a female here for testosterone en route to becoming a male. The patient gave their name: "Michel" – or was that "Michelle"?

The voice was somewhat husky, but mid-range, which did not clarify the picture for me. I desperately thought about what question I might ask to trigger my recall of the information. Somehow it seemed inappropriate to use as my opening question "So, how are your breasts doing?"

My mind was paralyzed by this predicament. No doubt to the patient's surprise I began groping in the direction of the door to leave the room before I had even told him/her that I could not see.

"Someone is looking for me," I said to the bemused Michel/Michelle.

I both laughed and cried with the nurse as she reread me the pertinent information. Then, armed with the correct information, I went back to the patient and had the appropriate discussion. Michel/Michelle turned out to be Michel with an appointment for estrogen injections en route to becoming a female. Fortunately, he left the clinic having been given the correct injection and seemed to be unmoved by the drama we had enacted.

This was the first of thousands of encounters of its kind. On one level it was hysterically funny, yet at the same time it was profoundly agonizing and wounded me very deeply. It was always painful to have such graphic examples of the extent of my impairment. Philosophically, I had to make a choice. I could either see the humour in these situations or I could drown in my despair. Laughter has been one of the driving forces in my life; fortunately, I was able to spend most of my energies laughing at the predicaments in which I found myself. This approach also, it turned out, eased the tension and insecurity that other people had about my blindness. Knowing that I was always looking for the funny side of any situation and that I could laugh at myself readily made people less anxious about how they should interact in order to be helpful. Some people, it seemed, thought it would be hurtful or insulting to refer to the fact that I could not see what I was doing. I always mentioned my blindness first, and usually in a light-hearted way, which gave everyone notice that it was all right to speak to me about it.

I felt strongly that these early clinical days were like learning to ride a horse. If you fall off you have to get on again quickly or you lose your nerve.

Getting Started

My few hours in the endocrine clinic sparked in me the energy to get myself organized. It was time to stop moaning and complaining. It was time to stop talking about how hard it would be to go back to work and time to do something concrete about it.

At first, I relied on the energy and courage of a medical colleague in the United States. Shortly after I lost my sight, a friend told me about a letter to the editor in *The New England Journal of Medicine*. It congratulated Dr. Francis Salerno of Reading, Pennsylvania, for having passed his Medicine Fellowship examinations despite having lost his eyesight partway through his medical residency program. I could not believe my good fortune. I wrote to the editors of the journal and asked them to forward to Dr. Salerno a letter I had written describing my situation. He replied immediately and we corresponded by cassette tape for several weeks. I arranged to travel to Pennsylvania to observe how he worked. I wanted to speak to his department chief and his colleagues. I wanted to be forearmed with as many answers as possible. I returned from that trip aware of the huge job I had ahead of me, but with a deep sense that my goal was attainable. Dr. Salerno clearly loved his work and was beloved by those who worked with him.

I began to accumulate a set of personal aids to help me get over some of the practical problems that others might interpret as barriers. Dr. Salerno's hospital was slightly ahead of mine from a technological perspective; he was able to dictate all his notes, and so handwriting was not a problem. I had to write all my charts and fill in all test requisitions by hand. What was I to do? My rehabilitation teacher was full of great ideas.

We looked at various models of writing guides. I settled for one that was a modified clipboard. It had a vertical, graduated rod attached to the left side of the board. A pair of horizontal rods were attached to the vertical rod. These horizontal bars were attached to each other and could be moved up or down on the vertical rod. There was enough space between the horizontal rods to write in. There was a small slider on the horizontal bar to mark your space.

I brought hospital chart paper to my lessons to practise getting the spacing right. I also brought hospital requisition forms. In order to be an intern I would have to be able to fill in test requests. Now, all this is done using computers, and in my case, voice recognition software. I had had the misfortune to lose my sight in the Paleolithic age of computers. Each test had to be requested in handwriting. And each test had its own form. My teacher helped me to make a cut-out for each of the forms we used at the hospital. She placed a cardboard stencil on the different forms. Each had spaces cut out at the appropriate spots for filling in the required information. Fortunately, each form had a different shape. I practised my writing on these forms until I was confident that I could request any test in the hospital. Although it is not easy to write when you cannot see, my friends tell me that my handwriting is no worse, and is often better, than that of most of my medical colleagues.

Please, Sir, I Want to Be a Doctor

Armed with all my gadgets, I made an appointment to meet with the program director for medicine at the Montreal General Hospital, who had been one of my teachers during medical school. I told him what I wanted. "Are you serious, Jane?" he asked. After telling him that I was deadly serious, he said that he could not take responsibility for making such a decision. He went next door to the office of the physician-in-chief, Dr. Phil Gold. Fifteen minutes later I packed up all my little stencils and clipboards and joined them. I had never met Dr. Gold, the author of one of the foremost texts in immunology, a subject in which I felt shaky. I was terribly nervous. Fortunately for me, my personal response to stress is to become quiet and calm. Although sweating furiously inside, I can usually appear calm on the outside.

"So, what can I do for you, Dr. Poulson?" he asked.

"I would like to do my internship in medicine at this hospital, sir," I replied.

"Have you any idea what a huge undertaking that will be?" he asked.

Sure and calm, I told him that I was very much aware of the challenge and was both prepared and determined to work very hard.

"Okay," he said. "You're on. I just have to check it out with the Dean of Medicine at McGill. Just because this has never been done before does not mean that it cannot be done."

I am eternally grateful to Dr. Gold for this attitude. Within two minutes of entering his office filled with doubt, I found myself out in the corridor shaking like a leaf and wondering what in the world I had just signed myself up for. Ten minutes later he passed me in the hallway and told me that he had received the go-ahead from the dean and that I could start my internship whenever I was ready. Dr. Gold and I have become close friends and we continue to laugh about our first encounter. He once told me that it was lucky I could not see the look on his face when I first told him of my plans.

I now turned all my energies to preparing to learn how to be a blind doctor when I scarcely knew how to be a regular doctor. One thing was certain, there was practically no one to whom I could turn for advice, apart from Dr. Salerno in Pennsylvania. Most of the local physicians thought my chosen course impossible. Some were enthusiastic and supportive, especially when I was discouraged, but most stayed quiet. Most thought that it would be a matter of time before I discovered that my ambition was foolish. I knew that I was being driven by an unshakeable need to prove something to myself, but at the same time I knew that I would never do anything that might risk harming patients. I promised myself that if I found it impossible to do, or if the cost to me of doing it was too great, I would not pursue the internship.

To the horror of my instructors at blind school, I dropped all courses except those that directly applied to my current plan. I started an orientation program at the hospital. This required learning a set of cues that would identify for me exactly where I was in the hospital. I had to construct a mental map of the entire building and plan in my head how I would get from one place to another unassisted. A medical residency program requires that interns and residents sleep at the hospital whenever they are on call, as they are frequently called in the middle of the night to come and attend to a sick patient. I could not ask an exhausted colleague to accompany me from the residence to the ward.

I think that observing me struggling to learn how to do simple things like walking straight in a busy corridor or taking the stairs to the cafeteria created a kind of bond between me, my fellow residents and the other staff members. It made people notice how many things they take for granted. For me, the challenge of presenting a seminar began not with preparing my notes, but with finding the correct amphitheatre. Until I pointed it out to them, no one had noticed that the stairwells at either end of the main corridor rotate in different directions. Remembering such details became essential for me to ensure that I did not fall down the stairs thinking that I was putting my foot out to climb up.

As I walked the corridors, people would call out encouragement to me. Initially they let me tough it out on my own. Later, as I became better known in the hospital, people would ask me if I wanted assistance with travelling. I always said yes, preferring a human arm over a white cane any day. My guidelines were simple: I would like to be accompanied as far as they were going, but I did not want them to go out of their way to guide me.

One of the most difficult aspects of blindness is the loss of friendly eye contact with others. Here I was in a huge hospital with several thousand employees all running about. So much communication took place in the hallways without anyone talking. It is incredibly lonely to walk down a crowded corridor with no contact with other people. Many came to recognize this fact and would call out "Hello!" and identify themselves by name as they went past. I have developed excellent voice recognition and have learned how to look people in the eye judging by the direction of their voice. Many eventually forgot that I could not see them and took it for granted that I knew to whom I was speaking. I usually did, but sometimes, especially when I was dog-tired,

I found myself in a conversation with someone, only to find partway through that they were not the person I thought they were.

This early phase of my medical career taught me that each day I have to be prepared to spend phenomenal amounts of energy on simple tasks, such as remembering to look into the eye of the person to whom I am speaking or concentrating on where I am at every point in a journey. I always have to think of where I am going, how I am going to get there, and what reference points I will use along the way, as well as to remember the landmarks I have already passed and those that lie ahead.

Which Bump Is a Lump?

As budding medical students, we were all thrilled to finally make it onto the wards and start learning how to examine patients. Up to this point we had learned (rather laboriously, we felt) how to take a detailed history of an illness. Every tutor reinforced the concept that in medicine, the art is in the history taking. You will only find something in the physical exam if you know what you are looking for.

I have discovered that one of my greatest skills as a physician is in taking a clear and ordered history. I have been blessed with a computer-like brain which I only partly used while sighted. When I lost the ability to look something up or read notes, I trained myself to be deadly logical, accurate and precise. This not only improved my capacity to take a history, but more importantly helped me to use the information that I gathered and organize it into a short and concise piece of data that I could relay to others clearly and succinctly. This ability is critical for doctors wishing to work in academic medicine. In a private office, one is not frequently called upon to give a synopsis of a patient's case and relay that material to someone else, but in a teaching environment this skill is essential. Because I could not read notes, I had to organize everything clearly and logically in order to remember it all.

Even skilled history-takers must do a good physical exam to complete a consultation. Having just completed medical school, I found it odd to be breaking out and developing new ways to examine a patient when I had scarcely mastered the time-honoured approaches. Perhaps it was easier to learn new skills before the old had become routine.

The physical examination consists of four distinct portions: inspection, palpation, percussion and auscultation. Inspection refers to looking at the patient, observing such things as colour, rash, scars, shape and form, or general self-care. Palpation requires touching the patient to determine the position of certain organs and to detect masses or lumps. Percussion is the part of the exam when the doctor taps out patterns on the chest, abdomen and back. Auscultation is using the stethoscope to get auditory information about what is occurring internally. I will ever be grateful to two senior residents at the Montreal General Hospital, Drs. Christiane Côté and Kenny Berris, who offered to help me work out how to approach the physical exam without being able to see the patient. I had not met either of them before, but both were superb clinicians and were known for their teaching skills.

One part of the anatomy course is called "surface anatomy," referring to the fact that many internal and skeletal structures can be felt on the surface of the body. We are required to know for certain what each bump represents and whether it is in the appropriate position. For example, we can feel the lower edge of the liver just below the rib cage on the right. If someone has a disease of the liver, it is often enlarged and we feel the liver edge further down in the abdomen. We must then know the normal limits of where organs should be felt. When I studied surface anatomy, I could see clearly with both eyes. It did not seem so apparent to me how many bumps one can feel while running one's hands over the surface of a human body.

One of my first challenges was to develop an intimate knowledge of how bodies normally feel when you run your hand lightly across them. This was a major tool for me to replace the skill of inspection. Palpation, percussion and auscultation are all non-visual skills that use the senses of touch and sound – all doctors could do them with their eyes closed. I have developed a quite accurate touch in noticing bumps that are abnormal lumps and ought not to be present, either at all or in that position or size.

Christiane and Kenny were senior residents on consultation services all around the hospital and so had information about various patients who had conditions that could be detected by physical examination. They arranged with patients they knew from all over the hospital for me to come and take the history and do a physical examination and try to detect the problem. I would have to find the abnormality and then they would come by and ask me to demonstrate how I found it. Both were great to work with because of their sense of fun and the way they encouraged their patients to be part of this learning experience. We would often spend much more time than usual at a patient's bedside while trying to figure out a particularly thorny approach. The patients were laughing with us and some even made some excellent suggestions about approach. This "seek and find" methodology is standard practice in medical training, but usually the students go to the charts first before talking to their tutors. They want to be sure that they have found everything that is present. Christiane and Kenny used to say that they loved teaching me because I was the only one they could be sure had not looked at the chart before case presentation. I learned to relax about asking patients questions about things I would otherwise be silently observing. "Have you noticed any change in the colour of the whites of your eyes or your skin? Do you have any rashes?"

For six months I worked on redeveloping all my skills – walking freely through the hospital corridors, finding specific rooms and particular patients in that room, using my writing tablet and stencils to write up histories and lab requisitions. I had to practise writing legibly as well as quickly, as there was a lot of writing to be done. I went to rounds on many of the different medical services and attended seminars and other presentations to help myself feel as if I belonged in the hospital.

After six months of rehearsing, we all decided that it was time for me to jump in. In April 1981, less than a year later than I was supposed to start, I officially began my internship at the Montreal General Hospital. With the benefit and perspective of time and maturity I can now congratulate myself on what an incredible transformation had taken place during those nine months. At the time, my excitement was mixed with a good dose of terror. For six months I had been doing histories and physicals as a kind of game, but now the patients were my responsibility to care for. Dr. Côté was my senior resident for the first three months, so both she and I knew what to expect.

I made strategic liaisons all over the hospital. I was responsible for knowing the results of the radiological and other investigations of my patients, so my dear friend Dr. Cynthia Withers, a radiology resident, introduced me to the other radiology residents. They agreed that after lunch each day, I would call Cynthia to give her my patient list and any studies that needed reporting. Each of them would look at one patient's studies for me. Cynthia would call me later in the afternoon before our rounds with the results I needed. This worked very well as it was not a lot of extra work for any one person, for I found it difficult to ask for help if it would be a burden for others. There was always a cardiology resident in the cardiac intensive care unit. The residents were always pleased to read my patient cardiograms for me. I spent a good deal of every day walking around the hospital seeking these aids, but my patients did very well by me. Everyone understood that I wanted them to say they could not help me that day if it was difficult for them.

I had friends and helpers in all the different departments of the hospital. The security guards would often walk me out safely to a taxi at night; the orderlies, porters and housekeeping staff were faithful guides who helped me to feel safe when walking around by myself. Eventually the secretaries of the different labs got to know me and I was allowed to phone the labs for an oral report of daily tests. I kept a small pocket tape recorder with me to record all my notes and information during the day. When it came time to write my charts in the evening, I had to play back the tape.

On the wards, everyone knew when there was something that I would need to read. Ward secretaries, charge nurses and others would ask me if there was something they could look at for me when they had a free moment. This worked out to be easier for everyone than if I asked particular people to look at something for me. The extra work in reading to me was spread across many people and did not appear to be too onerous for anyone. I think I made many people realize how much we take things like the ability to read for granted.

Working with the staff became easier with time. At first, many people did not know how to speak to me. I never understood this but had to accept it. People seemed afraid that they would hurt my feelings if they pointed out that I was doing something wrong. One time during my internship I was admitting a patient in the middle of the night. It was after 2 a.m. and I was exhausted. It was a complicated problem and my write-up was several pages long. I sat at the nursing station laboriously writing out my findings. The nurses were working around me. Just as I was nearly finished, my intern partner came over to say hello and asked me what I was doing.

"Writing this admission," I said.

"I was afraid of that," she said. "Your pen is out of ink."

The nurse sitting beside me started to cry and said that she had not known what to say as she watched me writing in vain.

"Look," I said, "next time just say my pen is not writing, okay?"

Another time, I was writing on top of something I had already written on. I always try to remember which side of the page I am using, but in my exhaustion I had turned the same page over twice. Again, a nurse looked on in horror and did not stop me from my mistake, and I had to redo the work. After a while, people learned that I would more likely laugh if they pointed out my mistake and would never be angry with them. Exhaustion and frustration often led me to cry myself to sleep in the interns' residence at night, but I rarely, if ever, lost my composure on the wards or in the hospital at large.

Interns are required to do many technical procedures while on call at night. It was clear that I could never start intravenous lines or draw blood, so throughout my residency I was always paired with a partner at the same training level and we shared the work. Close friendships are struck between comrades working side by side in a combat zone. My first intern partner was Dr. Carol Murphy. Carol had spent the first three months of her internship on maternity leave. She came back to work anxious about her new baby at home and feeling woefully inadequate as a mother and a doctor. During our first night of work together I knew that we would be good friends. One of our patients had taken a very serious turn for the worse during the evening. We went in together and I ventured the opinion that she needed an intravenous.

"Good idea," said Carol.

"What are you going to hang?" I asked.

She turned to me and said, "Listen, this job is fifty-fifty. I start the lines, you choose the fluids and drugs."

We worked well together and both profited enormously by the partnership. Our personal and professional collaborations endure.

Reading with My Ears

The amount of written material that has to be acquired, processed and then filed in a way that is easy to retrieve during a five-year medical residency training program is phenomenal. Textbooks are thousands of pages long and each week hundreds of journals publish reports of up-to-the-minute thinking about a huge range of subjects. There are examinations internal to the institution twice a year. At the end of the third year there are university-level exams. At the start of the fourth year, residents write exams set by the Royal College of Physicians and Surgeons of Canada. Successful candidates go on to do an oral and clinical exam at the end of the fourth year before they can be certified as internists. Part of the learning process is to be constantly presenting academic rounds – hour-long presentations on a specific topic to all interested persons in the community. On average, each resident does at least six of these annually. Then there are journal clubs. These are monthly gatherings of a certain group of doctors who discuss interesting papers that have appeared in the medical journals during the past month. The required reading is enough to put many people off the idea of doing specialty training in Internal Medicine.

Perhaps the most monumental task of the entire residency program was acquiring, maintaining and organizing my printed materials in cassette format. I had literally hundreds of people who read for and to me. (My dear mother, a physiotherapist by training, read the entire standard textbook of Internal Medicine onto audio cassette for me. This book is over 2000 pages long, with two columns on each page.) I kept all my cassettes in shoeboxes. The first cassette in any box said which cassettes were contained in that box. As people read to me onto cassette, I had them label an outer envelope with what each track on the cassette contained. Most of the time I used a special tape recorder that was developed for use by the visually impaired. The cassette both recorded and played back at two speeds – the commonly used speed, so that standard cassettes could be used, and a half-speed, so that twice as much material could fit on one cassette.

Some machines record on four rather than the usual two tracks. This again meant that twice as much material could go on that cassette. In this manner I could put up to 360 minutes of recording on a 90-minute cassette. This was both advantageous and aggravating. Often I wanted to look up a certain fact or small bits of information. In those days there was no way to index material on tapes. My machine had an indicator mark on it so that when I wanted to highlight something I could add an indicator tone. Still, I had to listen to a lot of stuff that was of no interest to me before finding the material I was after. I developed a system of three beeps for a new chapter, two beeps for a new heading within the chapter and a single beep for something I wanted to highlight. Each of my shoeboxes was labelled with a large-print letter made out of cardboard by my sister, Anne. I kept the shoeboxes in alphabetical order on rows and rows of bookshelves. Sometimes I worried that I had developed an obsessive-compulsive personality disorder along the way: I seemed to use so much energy organizing things. I soon found that being highly organized was not crazy. If I got behind in my organizing and had to find a specific textbook on tape and it was misfiled, I lost valuable time searching for it. My "obsessive" organizing allowed me to acquire a huge amount of information.

I had a good sense of community from my readers. They came from all over. I would make an announcement at the start of each of the first- and second-year medical classes. The students were keen and they all had to read the same materials at some point. It was all voluntary and

I did not ask students to make a commitment to a specific number of hours of reading each week. Some preferred to read onto cassette and others to read to me aloud. Colleagues, including many nurses, took part in journal clubs and would read for and with me. I made many good friends through this process.

One of the consequences of my situation was that I was able to remain outside the continuous but unspoken war of one-upmanship that reigns in most university hospitals. Each time we admitted a patient with an unusual disease, or had a strange lab result returned to us, or used a new methodology, or listened to a visiting professor who specialized in an esoteric idea, everyone would race for the library or book collection found on each ward. You could be certain that ward rounds that day would feature a "learned" discussion of a topic that no one had heard of before. By the time rounds took place, everyone was able to discuss this rare case or subject as if it were their own area of expertise. I had reliable access to printed material but never quick and immediate access. For example, *The New England Journal of Medicine* is a weekly publication. Each edition usually included at least one article that had everyone talking. I always felt that I was miles behind everyone else I was working with as it would be several weeks before my readers could read the journal for me.

I was very hard on myself during that residency. I knew very well that my colleagues had all been boning up in the library minutes before rounds. I knew that if I could read, I would have been doing the same thing. The fact that they could discuss case X in some depth and I could not reflected my limited access to immediate fact finding rather than a lower ability in clinical medicine. Still, I felt very strongly the sting of standing in the corridor not being able to discuss the meaning of variations in the values of the serum rhubarb level. It was also difficult for me to reconcile myself to the fact that I could not do any technical procedures. As med students, we had measured ourselves in terms of our ability to draw blood, start intravenous lines and do arterial blood gases. We seemed to value being able to collect biological material more highly than knowing what to do with the information about the sample. This sense carried over into the residency for me. During rheumatology rotations, I felt overwhelmed by the sense that I was not doing joint aspirations. It was irrelevant to me that I could describe the joint fluid findings in all the different arthritic conditions, and could make good suggestions about how to deal with the condition that led to the joint effusion. I tried to remind myself that in daily practice physicians were not starting central lines and Swan Ganz catheters unless they were working in the intensive care units. I already knew that my career was not in Emergency or ICU. Still, I wasted a lot of emotional energy thinking of what I could not do, rather than the extraordinary amount I was doing.

My residency finished in June 1985. No blind person had ever requested authorization to do the examinations from the licencing body for medical specialists in Canada, the Royal College of Physicians and Surgeons of Canada, and they were in a quandary about how to proceed. I certainly met all the academic requirements, and the McGill staff were prepared to sign the affidavits that I was clinically sound and prepared for the exams. I persisted with my request to sit the exams and they finally came up with a formula that satisfied all concerned.

The exam consisted of two parts. The first, which was two days of multiple choice examinations, was written. (There was no precedent for how these exams should be administered to a blind person except my own during the licencing exams for the Medical Council of Canada [MCC]. They, too, had been at a loss as to how to handle an applicant who was blind.) For these exams, we arrived at a formula that I should do the exams orally and be allowed twice as much time as the other candidates to complete the exams. Each exam had to be finished on the same day as the other candidates to prevent any allegation that I had spoken to persons who knew of the test materials. This was not problematic for the Fellowship exams, as they were serial half-day exams, held in the morning. I took the morning and part of the afternoon to complete each exam. The MCC exams had been much harder to do for me as all candidates wrote exams both morning and afternoon. For me, that meant doing multiple choice questions orally for over 12 hours, two days in a row. For both the Fellowship and the licensing exams, the questions were read to me by Dr. Robert Gardiner. He was known to both bodies and was felt to be an appropriate reader by the examining committees. It was good for me to have someone with whom I felt at ease spending such long stretches of time, and I asked him on several occasions if we could stop for a mental break. Both exams were recorded on cassette to ensure that the proceedings could be reviewed if there were any questions.

I passed both sets of written exams. The Royal College requires that all certified specialists also sit an oral clinical examination, which involves history taking and physical examination of actual patients. Again, there was some concern about how this would be accomplished. Ultimately, we decided that my exam would proceed as I was proposing to practise in the future. If there was something that could only be accomplished by visual observation, I would have to ask someone trustworthy to observe it for me. The college assigned one of its examiners to follow me around during my exam day. He did not initiate any comments, such as "Your patient is jaundiced." If, however, I asked him to describe the colour of the patient's skin, he would comment upon the jaundice. For the cardiogram recordings and the X-rays, the doctors described the salient features to me and the discussion went from there. To everyone's surprise and my delight, the clinical day went extremely well. The Board of Examiners had been skeptical at the start of the day but left convinced that a visually impaired physician could, in fact, practise as a specialist.

Make me to know your ways O LORD;
teach me your paths.
Lead me in your truth, and teach me,
for you are the God of my salvation;
for you I wait all day long.

Be mindful of your mercy, O LORD, and of your steadfast love,
for they have been from of old.

Psalm 25:4-6

Chapter 6: Go Straight – No, Go Left!

The Doctor Takes Direction

When I was a sighted cross-country skier, the trees were my friends. I loved to ski through forest trails looking at the trees in their beauty as they were weighted down with snow. My relationship with the trees changed after I could no longer see their beauty. Now they resembled poles on a downhill slalom course. There were several differences, however. Poles on a slalom course generally fall over when skiers crash into them. My experience with trees while skiing has been that it is generally I who yields, tumbling to the ground unceremoniously following contact. Skiers contacting slalom poles generally lose points on their performance, while I risk losing consciousness or integrity of my limbs following contact.

My first return to cross-country skiing was with Carol Murphy and Duncan Anderson, two medical friends who felt it was far more difficult to be an unsighted physician than an unsighted skier. We had decided that there was no reason why I should not be able to ski on a wide-open space, so we made a plan to ski on Lake Memphramagog in the Eastern townships of Quebec. The conditions were perfect, they said. How could I go wrong? I thought. I must have been focusing far more on the après-ski end of things. Often the small details of any adventure render it far more difficult than the main event. In this case, the challenge was getting to the lake in the first place.

We put on our skis in the clearing around the cottage. It was a pretty cottage set back nicely in the woods, out of sight from the lake. Therein lay the difficulty. I was given a detailed description of how beautiful was the scene that lay before us. Last night's snow was pure white and the tree branches were bowed down with the weight of the fresh fall. The sun was shining brilliantly from a clear blue sky. Smoke from the chimney was going straight up as we set off, filling the air with an incredible aroma. That was the end of the idyllic scene for me.

As soon as we reached the end of the clearing around the cottage, the beautiful trees suddenly became the enemy. The first overhanging branch ungraciously dumped its fresh fall of snow directly down the crack between my ski sweater and the skin at the back of my neck as I gently brushed the branch with my hat. My friends had described very clearly a straight trail between the trees on either side. "A nice, wide trail," they called it. Right! Wide for them, perhaps. It was a not so gentle downward slope to the lake's edge. Whoosh! They pushed off, one after the other. "You can do it," they said. "Just go straight!"

Something within me prevented me from pushing off and going straight: I am not sure whether it was prudence or cowardice. I stood there feeling the melting snow trickle down my back. There was now a matching stream trickling down my face: my own sweat.

"Come on, Jane. Just go straight!" they called again encouragingly. I chickened out and decided I would go straight but it would be walking, not skiing. I took off my skis and took several steps in their direction, only to find myself hip deep in snow. The two of them had to come back and haul me out. I felt it had become a matter of pride now, so back on went the skis. I shut my eyes tightly and pushed off. I felt as if I had stepped off the edge of Mount Everest, although I am told that this lakeside grade was somewhat less steep than that. The trees, it seemed, had decided to step back out of my way and to my surprise I found myself on the flat surface of the frozen lake. Our ski was invigorating, but I assure you, no one enjoyed the après-ski part of our day more than I.

Lest I make it seem as if going straight on solid ground is the hardest thing you might ask me to do, let me correct that notion and tell you that maintaining any sense of direction in or on the water is far more challenging.

I had no intention of going waterskiing. I merely went down to the dock, albeit in my swimsuit, where my nieces, nephews and cousins were doing their thing. Eventually I moved from dock to boat, and thus it seemed a natural progression to move into the water. My stated intent drove peril into the hearts of assorted aunts and a virtually speechless mother. They pleaded with me to change my mind. What on earth was

I trying to prove? My cousin who was the same age as me stated categorically that she had no intention of trying to ski and she could see. This sport was meant for agile young people, not stiff, aging old ladies who could not see where their arthritic frames were being pulled.

The opposition was quite vocal. Eventually, a large number of the fainthearted left the dock in protest. I calmed the fears of those who remained by promising that I would stay directly behind the boat and would not attempt going out over the wake, at least not on my first outing. I reasoned that a boat pulling me along with a straight rope meant that I could only go straight if I followed the lead of the boat. What I failed to calculate was that when the boat began to turn, I would be affected by centrifugal force. Unless I corrected for this I would indeed go flying out over the wake and into rough waters. Skiing while sighted always seemed like such a natural thing; it never occurred to me that one had to make adjustments for physical forces.

One false start sent me hurling through the air and ending with an enormous belly flop and a nose full of water. The second time I pulled myself up out of the water as if I had been skiing every day since losing my sight. What an exhilarating feeling! From the moment I had lost my sight, all my movements had been done in slow motion. If you are expecting to slam into a doorway or sharp object at any moment, you learn to move slowly. There is less chance of falling down an entire flight of stairs if you walk slowly enough to detect them before you leap off unknowingly. This, then, was the first time in 15 years that I had moved at more than a snail's pace. All was going well until the boat began its slow curve to the left, which of course sent me blissfully heading towards the right wake. Horrified choruses of shocked cousins looking on from the boat began shrieking, "Go left! Go left!"

Realizing the effects of my miscalculation, I attempted to correct the error. I gradually pulled myself gently to the left and back into safe waters. "Go straight! Go straight!" they shouted in response to my action. I had overcorrected and flew out over the left wake. The huge bumps caught me off guard. I valiantly fought to make my way back into the relative security of the smoother waters of the interwake space. I nearly made it back, but one last vicious wave spewing out from behind the boat caused me to do a complete and somewhat ungraceful pirouette before being thrown head first into the middle of Lake Muskoka on a busy Saturday morning. I tried to forget about all the boaters who were spinning through the waters without looking where they were going. I soon found one of my skis and held it up as a symbol of my helpless marooning. A quick rescue resulted and I triumphantly returned to the dock where I was greeted with a mixed chorus of people shouting "Hurrah!" and "We told you so!"

My arms and chest muscles were so sore the next morning, I could hardly bring a cup of coffee up to my mouth. It was worth every ache.

Go Right! Go Right!

Sailing remains a great delight for me. Following the loss of my sight, I developed quite a bit of motion sickness. When sighted, one fixes the eye instinctively on the horizon, effectively eliminating the effects of motion on the vestibular system. I remembered studying "Ocular Vestibular Reflexes" in first-year physiology. For some reason I remember thinking distinctly at the time, "What a silly reflex!" Having lost the ocular end of it, I had to learn the hard way, years later, that it was indeed a very useful reflex. Driving in cars or sailing in boats can now produce profound motion sickness in me if I forget to think about not being dizzy.

I love to sail, however, and I was able to indulge this love with Carol and Duncan at their summerhouse on Lake Memphramagog in Quebec's Eastern townships, the same lake we had skied on together. This is a perfect lake for sailing. The Eastern townships contain a number of mountain ranges, making them excellent ski country. In the summer, these mountains can produce a strange effect on weather passing through and around them, and summer storms can come up amazingly quickly.

One day we were enjoying a sail in their 26-footer when some clouds suddenly appeared. Carol and Duncan had a long think about them and eventually decided that there was nothing to be concerned about. The sky darkened within 10 minutes and we figured we were in for it. We beat a hasty retreat back to the mooring, arriving as the full force of the storm hit. We were moored, but still out in the bay in the midst of a violent summer storm with fierce lightning and unceasing thunder. Huddled inside the hull of the boat, we were carrying on a learned discussion of whether we were more likely to be electrocuted huddling around a 30-foot mast that was inviting the lightning to strike, or swimming for it to the shore about 200 feet away. I felt that the mast was likely grounded and we would be safer remaining inside until the storm had passed. My hosts disagreed, believing that water was a poor conductor of electricity so the voltage was quickly dissipated if lightning struck the water. The waves were so high that we would never be the highest objects in the water. I pleaded my case against them but they were not dissuaded, stating that I could remain aboard if I wished. They were going to jump in and swim for it. Grudgingly, I decided to tag along. We rushed out onto the deck, which was wildly pitching with the force of the waves. "Jump!" shrieked Carol, and so I did, not having the foggiest notion of where I was going or how deep the water was.

On the shore, their horrified children watched tearfully as they saw their parents and godmother jumping into waters they had always been warned to avoid. With the force of the waves I felt like a cork bobbing fretfully in the mid-Atlantic. The thunder was deafening; the only other sound I could hear was the howling wind. I valiantly struck out, not certain that I was swimming towards shore. Then I heard a faint little voice over the wind calling, "Go right! Go right!" I went in the direction I thought was right. "Go straight!" the voice said now. "Go straight!" Shortly thereafter I again heard a voice: "Go left! Go left!" I had to assume I was at least heading towards shore. I was very grateful 10 minutes later to feel the lake bottom under my feet and to reach a relatively calm space of water as we made it into the shelter of the bay.

Relax, Jane

I had a lovely weekend visiting a friend's cottage in New York state. She had met me at La Guardia airport and we drove out with her family to Bellport, Long Island. From there we took a tiny ferry boat across the bay to Fire Island. We ran on the sand dunes and swam in the frigid waters. Their old family cottage was quite primitive, with no electricity or running water. The weather was perfect and, with the exception of brief visits from her sister and family, we did not see one other person except the ranger making the rounds in his dune buggy.

My friend's brother offered to drive me back to New York as he was returning to the city and had to pass by La Guardia on his way. As it was a holiday weekend and we could not be sure of the traffic, we left in plenty of time. We beat the crowds and made a fast trip into the mainland, arriving at the check-in gate about two hours ahead of time. Brian was anxious not to wait around and I bravely said that I did not see any reason for him to stay at the airport. He told the airline personnel that he was leaving me there to wait for the flight. The agents said that they were going off shift before that flight but that they would pass the information on to the next shift.

Two hours is a long time to wait in an airport on your own when you cannot walk around, go for coffee, read or people-watch. I have developed an active imagination and am able to entertain myself within the confines of my head, but I was still lonely and a little anxious. As the time for the flight drew nearer, I was not entirely certain of the flight number and wished I could look at my ticket to verify it. The waiting area filled with people speaking of destinations all over the place, but not Montreal. I went over the details of how Brian had left me there. He had verified that this was the correct gate and that the airline personnel would come for me at the correct time. There was nothing to be concerned about. Surely the rest of these travellers were all at the wrong gate.

I felt marginally reassured when several different flight numbers were announced over the PA system. Every flight seemed to be leaving simultaneously. There was tremendous movement in and out of our waiting area. I heard them call a flight that I felt was mine, although a number of the different flights had similar sounding numbers. I decided that the airline staff was no doubt waiting for the area to clear before coming for me. That was it. Just relax.

More flight announcements. Last call for Philadelphia. What did I care about that? I was not going to Philadelphia. Just relax, Jane. The airline staff said they would come for you. Another announcement. This time they said the flight was bound for Montreal. Good, I was in the correct area and I had my flight number right. The airline staff would soon come for me now. They were boarding the front half of the plane. There were many fewer people in the waiting area now. Any minute someone would be coming for me. I had better not move because no doubt they knew where I was sitting and if they saw my chair empty they might assume that one of their colleagues had taken me aboard. Last call for my flight.

Gosh, I wish they would not leave me until the last moment. Just relax, Jane. They said they would come. I could no longer overcome my anxiety when the waiting area was nearly empty. I called out to a passer-by that I needed help. I in no way fit into the stereotypical picture of a severely disabled person. I do not look blind and at that time did not carry a cane. To an uninformed passer-by I do not look like someone needing help. Given that I was in New York, I could just as likely have been trying to trick someone into coming closer to me so that I could pick their pocket or catch them out. Or, perhaps I might be a psychiatric patient out on pass calling out to people walking by. Fortunately for me, I must have had enough panic on my face for someone to come over to me. They took me over to the gate, where an imperious gate agent told me that I was late for the flight and that I should never sit there without informing the gate agents that I needed pre-boarding assistance. I did tell them that, nearly two hours ago, I pleaded. No one told us, she said as we stormed onto the plane. They shut the door behind me and took off about 30 seconds after I had been seated. Just relax, Jane, the airline staff said they would come and get you.

Be gracious to me, O LORD, for I am in distress;
my eye wastes away from grief, my soul and body also.
For my life is spent with sorrow, and my years with sighing;
my strength fails because of my misery, and my bones waste
away...
I have become like a broken vessel.

Psalm 31:9-10, 12

Chapter 7: Mind Games

Seeking psychiatric help was not my idea. A great friend from medical school days, Dr. Jane Skelton, first proposed it. She said that she had observed me carrying out my daily activities without one external sign of stress. She knew that I was not only trying to do my internship having lost my sight only a year earlier, but that I was also dealing with the consequences of a failed marriage. She believed that it must be taking unnatural forces to keep me on such a steady course and she feared a sudden and massive breakdown. I discussed her feelings with my friend and personal physician, Dr. Robert Gardiner. To my dismay, he agreed with Jane that unless I created an outlet for all my stresses, I could face great difficulty in the future. Although I did not want to believe them, I felt that I had no option but to at least have a consultation. Dr. Gardiner arranged an appointment for me with Dr. Fred.

I was very nervous before my first appointment. What would I say? I did not see that I was having any difficulties. The doctor was a very kind and gentle person, however, and I did not object to returning a second time for further discussion. Our visits were pleasant enough and I thought that if this would prevent future problems, perhaps I would do this for a while.

At a certain point, I had seen Dr. Fred about eight or nine times. We had covered very wide-ranging topics. I quietly wondered to myself how this could prevent future breakdowns, but it was not unpleasant and I was getting over my anxiety before each visit.

This session started off like most of the others. He asked me how my work was going, how my presentation had gone and whether there were any new developments on the divorce scene. "No," I said, "everything is fine. Thank you for asking."

Then he took aim and fired at me right between the eyes. "Do you ever get angry?" The question was different from any he had ever posed, but seemed harmless enough.

"Everyone gets angry at some time or other," I said.

His response was firm and unequivocal. "I am not asking you to quote me line 14 in the chapter in Kolb, on mood." (Kolb was our textbook of psychiatry.) "I want to know about *your* anger."

This exchange launched me on a journey of self-awareness that has led me to heights and depths I had never known before.

Maybe I Am Crazy

In the beginning, it had been my intention to see Dr. Fred a few times. I had hoped that he would concur with my view that I was doing very well. Because my friends had been so concerned, I did not wish to appear to be taking their advice lightly. If I had known then that I would be in relatively serious psychotherapy of different kinds for the next 20 years, I might have thought more carefully before embarking upon this course.

Dr. Fred took me by surprise again several months later. With no warning at all, he told me that he thought I was suffering from depression. I was shocked by this statement. I had held strongly to my waiting-room opinion (i.e., I was completely normal and did not need to see a psychiatrist). I was terrified at the prospect of having a psychiatric diagnosis. When I had studied psychiatry in medical school, we had had two basic classes on depression: endogenous and exogenous. Exogenous or reactive depression was described as a mood alteration resulting from a reaction to some external circumstance. Endogenous depression was a state of mood alteration resulting from internal derangements. Dr. Fred and I spent a great deal of time discussing this classification.

From his perspective there was little useful purpose in attempting to classify depression in this way. Current research was demonstrating that there was no difference in treatment or outcome between these two distinctions. For my part, it was critically important to know that there was nothing wrong with my brain or persona, wherever that dwelt within me.

Dr. Fred was surprised at my concern. We spoke about the possibility of depression for several sequential visits. Often, our discussions would end with me in deep despair because of the material we had been discussing. He often suggested that we try to meet a second time that week to try to minimize my despair. Before long I found myself attending sessions twice a week.

In the earliest phase of my psychotherapy, our discussions mainly focused upon the disaster of losing my eyesight. What did this mean to me? What did vision represent for me? What did physical appearance mean to me? Could someone who was blind have good self-esteem?

Much material for discussion was generated as I worked through the years of my residency-training program, when I was plagued by feelings of inadequacy. Many times I had been virtually blinded by my own interpretations of my blindness. During a medical residency, the trainees measure themselves by their capacity to perform specific tasks, such as starting intravenous lines in peripheral blood vessels and sticking a thin needle into the radial artery at the wrist to sample arterial blood. Second-year residents were required to start more complicated intravenous lines into the neck and shoulder regions. Senior residents performed still more complicated plumbing tasks. Interns learned how to insert tubes into the stomach for feeding or lavage. More specialized tasks included inserting larger tubes lined with mirrors into the stomach for direct observation of stomach ulcers. I was plagued by the fact that I could not do even the most simple technical procedure, such as withdrawing fluid from a swollen joint. Dr. Fred would argue that it was the interpretation of the biochemical tests done upon the fluid rather than the extraction itself that was important. I was as good as the next resident at interpreting test results.

A second subject of our discovery was looking back on my sense of family. Dr. Fred was interested in exploring why I held such high and often unattainable standards for myself. Where did this come from? Why did I persist in replicating these difficult patterns of behaviour? We also spent hours discussing the effect of my having developed diabetes at the age of 13. I had suppressed all my feelings of anger and despair around this issue for many years. I held myself in disdain if I ever whined or complained about my lot. I had spent my important teenage and young adult years holding on to a disfigured and wholly unacceptable body image for myself, and had felt I was too disgusting to have a relationship with a man. The fact that I had had few if any social successes was proof that the whole world shared my view. These discussions were extremely difficult. I spent months on anti-depressant medications. In a wry but not inconsistent view, I saw my need for medication to keep a level mood as further evidence of my physical inadequacy. With Dr. Fred's assistance, I saw that I had been suffering from depression since my diagnosis of diabetes at age 13.

I waited patiently for the LORD;
he inclined to me and heard my cry.
He drew me up from the desolate pit, out of the miry bog,
and set my feet upon a rock making my steps secure....

Do not, O LORD, withhold your mercy from me;
let your steadfast love and your faithfulness keep me safe
forever.
For evils have encompassed without number;
my iniquities have overtaken me until I cannot see;
they are more than the hairs of my head,
and my heart fails me.
Be pleased, O LORD, to deliver me;
O LORD, make haste to help me.

Psalm 40:1-2, 11-13

Part III: 1985 to 1992

TORONTO

Jane, 3 years old

Anne (7 years old),
David (2) and Jane (9)

A wedding portrait
without the groom

The Poulson Family (circa 1970)

TRAVELS

With Tom Fitches

Florida

With Paul Geraghty in the Caribbean

Georgian Bay with John Fraser

Barbados with Elizabeth MacCallum

DOCTOR POULSON

Dr. Poulson takes leave of Montreal General Hospital, 1992

Dr. Poulson's Toronto office,
1998

Dr. Poulson receives the Havergal
College Hall of Distinction
Award, 1994

A CIRCLE OF FRIENDS

Toronto, 1988

Massey College Christmas Party, 1998

Berry

THE LAST SUMMER: 2001

Muskoka – The last photograph of David, Anne and Jane together
taken before Jane's final swim and her return to Toronto
for the last time

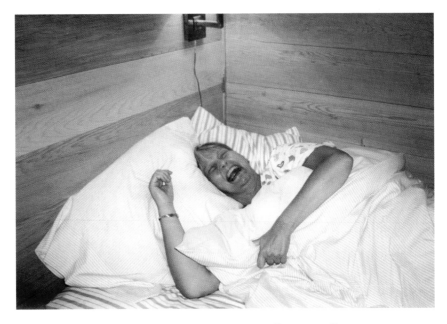

One of the last mornings on Georgian Bay

Chapter 8: The Doctor Is In

A Tough Transition

As senior residents, we felt that the hardest thing we would ever do in our professional careers was the fellowship exams. They loomed large, almost insurmountable hurdles that we had to overcome. It was a surprise, then, to find myself so forlorn when they were over. We all celebrated our successful completion of them, but then felt as if we had stepped into a vast empty space. Colleagues ahead of me had warned me of this phenomenon so I was not totally dismayed. What did discombobulate me was becoming a member of the attending staff. We had had a lot of responsibilities as senior residents. We had always discussed our opinions with an attending staff and reported our actions after treating a patient. There was rarely a problem with our action plan. Now that I was an attending, the buck stopped with me. For my first month I felt more nervous than I had ever felt as an intern. Now I was a real doctor, legally responsible for my patients' health and safety, I seemed to think that every case would have a hidden trick to it. I was very upset by my first death as an attending. Surely I could have done something to prevent this disaster. No, it turned out to be a case of a very sick person who died while I was in charge. Gradually I began to relax and know that I had made the transition from resident to the attending staff.

The most difficult part of the transition for me was losing the infrastructure I had set up for myself during the residency. My radiologist friends had also passed their exams and had moved on to jobs elsewhere. My fellow senior residents had all moved on to seek their fortunes. I no longer spent my time rotating from one ward to another building helpful relationships with ward clerks and nurses. The staff was always turning over and after about six months many of the staff were unknown to me. Certainly the relationships with the support staff change after the transition to the attending staff.

One of my big challenges was to set up my private office. I had to figure out new methods for acquiring the information I needed. Through the generosity of the Edward Dunlop Foundation I had a grant to hire a nurse to work with me. Together we would go to the radiology department and review the films that required one of the radiology staff. She would review charts with me and help with parts of the physical exam.

Margaret

Shortly after beginning my new position I met a nurse named Margaret de Chazal. This began what has evolved into one of the most significant professional relationships of my career. Margaret was the ideal person for this job. She was similar to me in age, energy level, personality and interests. We became fast friends and I would not have considered making any decision about anything without consulting Margaret. She had vast experience and a wonderful ability to generally assess patients. If Margaret told me that a patient looked better, I knew they were. She never told me that someone looked better to bolster me. Because I was blind, I could not look at a patient to get a sense of whether they were sick. This skill is known as "eyeballing" a patient. Margaret was as skilled an eyeballer as any of my colleagues. I trusted her implicitly. She became a favourite in our department and an asset all round. One of the hardest parts of leaving Montreal for me was discontinuing my working relationship with Margaret. We have remained close friends since the move. When the time came to consider hiring a nurse in Toronto, I prepared a job description based on my experience with Margaret. I specified the five most important qualities that she brought to her work: having a good sense of humour, loving a good laugh, being interested in all kinds of non-medical things, being level-headed, and being someone with whom I could spend five hours every day. I could teach anyone else the basic skills required to do my work.

Margaret and I had much natural non-spoken communication. One day I was examining a patient. He had been sitting on the table in front of me and I asked him to lie down. He asked if he should lie on his back. "Yes," I said, "lie on your back." I stood by the bed and he was lying down in a fraction of a second. He was a very thin-chested man with no chest hair. I did my cursory sweep of his chest and did not find my usual landmarks. I did another cursory sweep, more tentatively, and with no more success. "Oh, well, Jane, carry on with your exam," I thought. I located his shoulder and from there, I placed my stethoscope where his heart ought to have been located. Very faint heart sounds for such a thin chest wall. I moved my stethoscope across his chest and to my surprise the heart sounds became louder as I moved to the right. Totally perplexed I began thinking of a triumphant moment in medical school. Our tutor had asked us all to examine the patient and determine what we thought was wrong. I was the only student in our group who found the abnormality: a condition in which the position of the organs of the body is all reversed. I felt a familiar surge rising within me. Could I be making that rare diagnosis a second time? I started looking for his liver on the right and sure enough, it was not there. I thought to myself, what an odd thing! I was beginning to search for the liver on the left side when Margaret entered the examining room. I heard her draw in her breath with amusement. She came over to the examining table and said, "Hello, Jimmy. Now if you will turn over and lie on your back, Dr. Poulson will examine your stomach."

With that she stifled her laughter and beat a hasty retreat. I could hear her laughing outside as she told my other intern friends of my folly. I barely made it through the rest of the exam. After the patient had left, Margaret and I laughed for half an hour.

Mrs. G was a patient I had looked after since the early days of my internship. She became a private patient after my residency was finished. I had then known her for many years. She was a lovely, gentle woman with a cultured British accent. One day she had a number of issues concerning her. She had read a magazine article about the health problems of middle-aged women and had only just realized that she suffered from them all. I was reassuring her as best I could that she would be all right. Her last concern was varicose veins. Her legs were smooth and slender with no sign of veins. Still, she persisted that she thought she was having trouble with her veins. The article had stated that you could have circulatory problems without seeing distended veins exteriorly. I told her the early sign of this sort of problem was discoloration around the ankles. "Look here," I said. "Is there any brownish discoloration to your skin here?"

"What do you mean?" she asked. It was the end of a longish day and I was tired. I wondered why she was asking me such silly questions and having difficulty answering my clear questions. Finally I traced the area out around her anklebones and said, "Is the skin in this area any darker in colour that the rest of your legs?"

In a tentative voice she said to me, "Oh, Dr. Poulson, do you know that I am a black woman? I come from the West Indies." Fortunately we had known each other long enough that she too saw the humour in the situation and we shared a good laugh. Margaret and I again howled with laughter at the situation. "See," she said, "I leave you with one last patient to see on your own and look what happens!"

My internal medicine colleagues were very proud of me and very supportive of my work. We ran a large teaching clinic and during the day there were always competent doctors around. The most important thing for me to remember was what I could not do. If something I could not do was essential to the examination then I would not let the patient leave until one of my colleagues had done that piece of the exam. If a patient had been having chest pain and required an electrocardiogram in the office, then that study needed to be read before the patient could leave. I always wanted to examine a new patient's eyes. If they had normal blood pressure, no headaches, and no visual complaints, then I would let the eye exam go until the second visit if my colleagues were all too busy. This compulsive insistence that my patients had all necessary testing completed by me or one of my colleagues gave me the confidence that my patients were receiving as good care from me in my blindness as they would have received could I still see.

What Do the Patients Say?

One of the things that has kept me going throughout the years of stress and hardship has been the interactions I have had with my patients. My relationship with them is the most rewarding feature of my work; losing the doctor–patient relationships I have known would be a great tragedy for me should I ever stop working.

I am often asked about the patients' reactions to my blindness. Many anxious colleagues advised me when I was starting out to wear dark glasses and tell people that I had poor vision rather than no vision at all. This suggestion never appealed to me. I had to be completely comfortable with myself, knowing that I was providing good quality care to my patients and not being ashamed or feeling that I was offering second-class care. If I was giving good care, then there was no reason to pretend that I could see a little.

The first time we meet, I always tell patients and families my name and that I am unable to see. I do not make a prolonged statement about the facts, nor do I apologize. When we sit down to talk, I ask everyone to say where they are sitting so I can look at the person I wish to address. (I try to make eye contact with them when I am speaking, but I can't always sustain it.) I have rarely had any difficult interactions with patients or families. My practice style has always been to spend more rather than less time talking with them and explaining things, which seems to make up for the fact that I cannot see the person. Only one person I know of said she would not go to a blind doctor. I was working in my office in a residents' clinic in my second year, and I heard her making a fuss out in the corridor. I was crushed. I felt hot tears fill my eyes. Shortly afterwards, as I was pulling myself together, I got some perspective: she refused my colleague because of her gender.

There must have been other patients who had doubts about having me as their physician, but these doubts were seldom verbalized and after the initial visit most of the awkwardness dissipated. Margaret was a great favourite with my patients and people felt well cared for. I had a steady stream of regular patients throughout my four-year residency; many of them asked to continue on with me when I went into private practice. My practice was at first smaller than those of most of my colleagues, but it grew steadily. I was aware of the extra energy it took to compensate for my blindness and took on only as many patients as I could handle.

My success with patients went beyond my calm, open and assured presence. In fact, I believe that my disability reset the balance in the doctor–patient relationship. For the majority of patients this had a positive effect. Those who were looking for a physician to be completely "in charge" and dominant in the relationship were less likely to find my approach suitable to their needs.

Even the most self-assured people are apprehensive at best in a hospital situation, and some people are terrified. They are anxious about their symptoms and the implications for their health. Medical terminology is foreign. Many tests are performed in a high-tech environment, which can increase the patient's anxiety. The patient is lying down, clad only in an inadequate hospital gown. In swoops the fully dressed physician, or worse, "the team." The physicians feel at home in the environment and confident in manner, and use words the patient does not understand.

My disability reformatted this entire scene. I cannot swoop anywhere; I walk tentatively and carefully. I had to be certain that I was in the correct room and that my patient was in the bed. After introducing myself, I always asked the patient to draw the curtain and find me a chair if he or she was able. I could do this myself, but it was faster and more efficient to have the patient do this. This act started our encounter with me asking the patient for help. The short discussion about my eyesight always influenced the subsequent interaction. I believe it gave the patients the sense that they were not the only ones who had to divulge information about their bodies.

When working in our patient clinics, the nurses usually did tasks such as blood pressure readings. Very often, however, we were short-staffed and the physicians did them. I taught my patients how to read a pressure manometer. I pumped up the mercury and showed them the column rising. I asked them to indicate to me when the column had risen above a certain level. Then I explained to them that I was going to be listening for certain sounds with my stethoscope and would ask them what number the column of mercury was beside at that moment. Most of my patients became very good at reading the numbers. I did a lot of quality control readings with nurses or other physicians taking the same pressure readings, and my patients and I developed a good degree of accuracy. If a reading made no sense to me, or if the reading was critical in determining a course of action, I would have the pressure verified by a trained observer. To my surprise, the majority of patients enjoyed being part of this process. They were interested in the principle of how blood pressure readings were taken and felt more involved in the process of seeing the physician. They were subjects rather than objects in the doctor–patient relationship.

I had very strong relationships with patients who were struggling with irritating chronic illness and pain. In the traditional medical model, the patient is the consumer of medical advice and expertise and the doctor is the provider. There is an implicit understanding that the patients are "the sick" and the doctors are "the well." I shattered this image for my patients. Often, I was more apparently "sick" than they were. My patients knew that I understood what I was saying when I told them that they would have to modify their lifestyle and activities. They knew I understood it when I told them that it was difficult. And yet, I was living proof of the power of the human spirit to adapt to great adversity and carry on with a productive and rewarding life. Patients sometimes resent receiving this kind of advice from a doctor whom they perceive as having no personal, financial or health problems. Somehow this image of omnipotence and omniscience is embodied in the white coat the doctor wears. It seemed easier for patients to hear bad news and tough advice from someone who had been there.

Ethics, Theology and Palliative Care

There is an inevitable letdown period following the completion of the fellowship exams. The entire third year is spent in intensive study to acquire the millions of small facts one needs to pass the written exams, which take place during the fall of the fourth year of the residency term. No sooner are the written exams finished than the push for the orals begins. At the end of the oral exams, there is almost a feeling of "Is that all there is?" For two years, I had lived, slept and breathed exams. Now what was I going to do with all my time? This situation is magnified for people like me who do not go on to do a sub-specialty program. Following the fourth year, those who sub-specialize have another year of training and another set of both written and oral exams. I had intended to go into Oncology – the field dealing with cancer. I had applied to and been accepted into the McGill program. I was fascinated by the disease, but I also liked cancer patients. The stakes were particularly high for them and I liked working with people who were very sick. The only problem with my plan was that it meant acquiring whole new sets of information and skills. There would be still more exams to sit. My friend Laurence Green, who had been the very supportive chief resident when I was an intern, approached me one Friday afternoon. He and Tim Meagher, who had been chief resident the following year, had joined the Department of Medicine in the new division of general internal medicine. They asked me to reconsider my decision to do Oncology, proposing that I do another year of general medicine and then join them on the staff of the hospital. I was very flattered and accepted their offer. Thus I became the first resident in the general internal medicine division at the Montreal General Hospital.

On July 1, 1985, I found myself with both a hospital and a university appointment, but nothing to do. As medical residents we had gone to the assigned service and started to work. Now I had no patients. Gone also was the entire hospital infrastructure in which I had worked so well. It was no longer appropriate for me to expect the nurses to go out of their way to help me. I did still work in some clinics, which kept me busy to a certain extent, but I had a lot of time on my hands. It takes time to build a private practice. Fortunately, both Tim and Laurence had warned me of this period, and had told me that it happens to everyone.

As it turns out, I was relatively lucky. About six months after I started, Laurence went to Ethiopia to work at a hospital with which McGill had some ties and asked me to look after his practice while he was away. This was an excellent way to break into private practice. During the year, many referrals came from a doctor Laurence had met who worked with the Inuit community in Quebec, and from this doctor's colleagues. Eventually, I was asked to set up an official program with the Ministry of Health. This became a major and extremely interesting part of my practice. I was designated as the contact person for all the northern nursing stations and hospital facilities. I would give phone advice or arrange for patients to be seen in Montreal. I also taught groups of nurses who were leaving to work in northern nursing stations. I eventually made several trips north to the very tip of Quebec. I loved my work with the Inuit people and was thrilled to travel to the Arctic.

I also became more and more interested in medical ethics. I was on the hospital ethics committee and was an active member of the clinical ethics team. This team was designed to help the different areas of the hospital with difficult ethical questions encountered during the course of patient care. Most of the staff did not want to take the time for such work and tried to avoid ethical problems as much as possible. I loved the work and took as many consults as I could. I began to feel that I ought to pursue medical ethics in a more focused way. In the mid-1980s, this area of medicine was blossoming into a separate and well-recognized field, and a new department of medicine, ethics and law was established at McGill. I enrolled there to do a Master's degree in 1988.

I was able to enrol in graduate studies because of the major advances in computer technology during the 1980s. There were now some software packages that made access to information possible for the blind. The Edward Dunlop Foundation provided me with my first talking computer. It revolutionized my life. I could now write presentations or papers and edit them as I went along; during the residency it had taken ridiculous amounts of time, energy and patience to produce a small amount of work. Acquisition of printed material was still difficult, and was a major stumbling block in my pursuit of formal study of the humanities. Now I could produce acceptable written work. I found that I liked researching a subject and then writing about it.

The ethics program was housed within the department of religious studies. I was enjoying graduate work so much that I transferred into a Master's program in theology. I did this for one year, then decided I had insufficient background to continue. There is a whole language and ethos in any field such as theology. You gradually become comfortable in this milieu as you study. If I had wanted to pursue graduate work in theology, I would have wanted to start at the undergraduate level. My interest in ethics, medicine and theology found expression in the field of palliative care after I was approached by the palliative care group at the Royal Victoria Hospital in Montreal. I agreed to work part-time on the palliative care unit, and found the work professionally challenging and personally fulfilling. Over the next three years I was to spend ever increasing amounts of time and energy in this field.

Palliative Care and Me

I never would have thought I would enjoy myself as much as I did in palliative medicine. There are doubtless many reasons why this should be so, but in particular there was a very strong correlation between the skills required and my skill set. There were fewer invasive investigations in this field, so I did not feel I was unable to care fully for my patients. More than medically invasive investigation, my patients needed a doctor who had compassion and good communication skills. I found it professionally satisfying to achieve good symptom management, and I found that persons with terminal illness endured much unnecessary suffering as a result of standard medical care.

I looked at my own life quite differently after working in palliative medicine. I began to have a sense of my own mortality. I did not dwell on it, but I became aware of the concept of death. We had a disproportionately large number of young patients on our ward. Death no longer remained the realm of older people. I was not too young to die.

My work in palliative care did not make me think so much about dying as about living, and about what was important in life. My dying patients fell into one of two groups. Those in the first group were sad and angry about their impending deaths because they had never had time to do what they wanted and were dying unfulfilled. Those in the second group were sad to be dying because they were so enjoying living. I came to realize that one cannot know about one's mortality. We have only the present. We are each responsible for our own happiness; we all have time and how we spend it is our own call. It became increasingly clear to me that now is the time to "follow your bliss." We have to determine what is important to us, then examine our lives to see if they reflect our priorities.

"You're Not Going to Like This, Jane"

Our hospital, like all the others, was chronically short of funds. In April 1986, it launched a campaign for a huge sum of money for a worthy cause. There was a lot of hype about it at the site. In order to engage as many of the staff as possible, the hospital arranged with *The Montreal Gazette* to publish a series of human interest stories profiling the hospital. I received a call from the campaign chair asking if they could write about my accomplishments.

"There is no obligation to take part if you prefer not to," he said.

Terribly shy of any publicity, I told him I would like to keep my privacy.

"Fine, then," he said.

I mentioned this to one of my colleagues in the medical clinic.

"You said no to the campaign chair?" she gasped. "You must be kidding. You have nerve to say no after all the hospital has done for you."

Others agreed that I did not have a choice, so I called the campaign office and told them I had had a change of heart.

Little did I know then the impact that this call would have on my life. When the journalist assigned by the *Gazette* telephoned to set up the interview, I told him that he could write anything he wanted about my work and the exams I had passed, but that my personal story was private.

"But this story is about you," he replied, "and because of my profession I am nosy."

I told him that I could see him between 12:00 and 2:00 the following day, as I had clinics in both the morning and the afternoon. I was in the middle of a busy morning the following day when the clinic secretary knocked on my door and told me a gentleman wanted to see me at the desk. To my horror the journalist was standing there, notebook at the ready.

"I thought I would follow you around at work today," he said.

I was dumbfounded. I appealed to the clinic director to pull rank and forbid him in clinic.

"I can't forbid it," he said, "and besides, it's for the hospital, remember?"

My last desperate ploy was to claim patient confidentiality as he approached the patient in my office; she readily agreed to his being present. This patient had mild schizophrenia. She was obese and used a wheelchair. Going to clinic was a real outing for her. Now the newspapers wanted her story.

He followed me around for about two hours. I heard him asking my first patient what it was like to see a blind doctor. She had such a fanciful mind that I cringed at what she might say. After he left I heaved a sigh of relief.

I had relaxed too soon. During afternoon clinic he reappeared, this time with a photographer. I did not know what a big story this was going to be when I started that morning. "Gotta get some pics," he said.

My current patient was only too pleased to have his picture in the newspaper. The angle of the shot was appalling. The patient was lying on his back with his head tilted. I was listening to his heart with my stethoscope. It looked as if I were administering last rites to a dying man rather than providing follow-up to someone with high blood pressure.

The reporter asked me the dreaded question. "What happened to your eyes?"

My shame was so deeply ingrained that I could not say aloud that I had diabetes and this disease had cost me my sight. This was somewhat perplexing to my colleagues and peers. They all knew my situation, but played along with my storyline. I had told everyone that I had had an accident, so that is what they all said.

The next morning, my story appeared on the front page of the *Gazette.* "Montreal General's Blind Doc Has the Healing Touch," the headline read.

The public relations office took over my phone line for the following week. The journalist had managed to spell my name incorrectly so I was once again the subject of his column the following day. He was a syndicated columnist, so his article was picked up across North America, with each publication giving the story a different headline. I have the somewhat dubious honour of having appeared on the pages of *The National Enquirer,* with the headline "'Being Blind Makes Me a Better Doctor,' says gutsy MD." Mail soon arrived from all over the continent.

The fuss in the newspapers died quickly and I retreated into the comfort of my little cocoon. My solitude did not last long, however; the article had spawned much interest in me and from then on, I received numerous requests to do interviews with magazines such as *Chatelaine* and on radio and television shows. I laughed in retrospect at how I had cringed at the arrival of the newspaper's photographer. Now I had television trucks arriving with lights, cameras, makeup and the whole works.

I had mixed feelings about those years of "celebrity" status. I wanted nothing more than to return to my private little world and get on with my beloved job, but the media exposure did a lot of good for people with disabilities. I received many letters thanking me for my example. Mothers of blind children wrote expressing appreciation for showing them new possibilities for their offspring.

In October 1987, I was awarded the Order of Canada for my accomplishments. Once again, there were articles about me in the local newspapers, and I received numerous accolades. It was agony for me to speak about it since it meant I had to acknowledge what I still saw as my grossly deficient body. I hated the publicity, but felt guilty if I declined an opportunity to be interviewed.

Would I Do It Again?

As I work with young residents during their five years of fellowship training, I often think to myself that I could not do what they were doing. Long days and nights with little sleep and continuous pressures and stresses seem overwhelming. Then I stop and remind myself that this is exactly I did – without the benefit of eyesight. It is a mystery to me how I survived: I must have been in a state of denial. Then I remember that I was 20 years younger as well, and then I can reflect upon my years of practice and the pleasure this experience has brought me. I would not trade my work for anything else. Of course, I would love to be able to see. There are certain things I cannot do for patients that I would like to be able to do. It is hard to accept that there are limitations to what I can do, what kind of medicine I can practise and where I can work. Fortunately, I thrive in an academic atmosphere. I love being in a busy teaching hospital, and there are always lots of people around who can help me. There is a radiology department to look at my films. There are residents and students who do the first perusal of the charts and allow me to function in a more supervisory role. Seminars and rounds keep me aware of new developments in the field.

My dependence on the help of my colleagues has enriched my career and my life, requiring me to meet and know as many people as I can. Because of my situation, I have come to know people I would never otherwise have met, and I have benefited from these relationships. I believe that the traditional practice of medicine engenders in practitioners the sense that one person can and ought to know all the answers. From day one in medical school we develop an aura of always being able to cope, no matter how much comes our way. We are not encouraged to ask for help. We are made to feel that not knowing something reflects a personal deficiency. I have had the perfect built-in excuse for needing to seek help from colleagues. I have learned that one can require help and yet still make a valuable contribution.

I have known great satisfaction from my work and from my struggles . These experiences have been profoundly important and formative for me. Would I do it all over again? Yes, without a single doubt.

Yet is was you who took me from the womb;
you kept me safe on my mother's breast.
On you I was cast from my birth
and since my mother bore me you have been my God.

Do not be far from me, for trouble is near
and there is no one to help…

I am poured out like water,
and all my bones are out of joint:
my heart is like wax;
it is melted in my breast;
my mouth is dried up like a postherd
and my tongue sticks to my jaws;
you lay me in the dust of death.

Psalm 22:9-11, 14, 15

Chapter 9: The Dark Night of the Soul

Every year it is the same. My gut wrenches and I leave the church with my head reeling with old, familiar questions. The urgency of the questions never diminishes, nor do the answers seem more readily apparent: How can I reconcile the idea of a good and loving God with my life, which is full of distress? Why do I believe so deeply in such a God? Why do bad things happen to good people? These questions are never more pressing than during Holy Week. Year after year I repeat the same ritual, but no matter how painful it is, I feel compelled to participate in Holy Week services. The week between Palm Sunday and Easter is the most significant in my calendar.

Ever since learning that diabetes could result in blindness I had begged God to deliver me from that fate. Now, my lifelong struggle had become learning how to live faithfully with God when the answer to my prayers appears to be silence or an outright "no."

It was easier to be a person of faith when things were going well, when despite the diabetes, life was good. I had financial, family and social security. I was working towards a fulfilling career. My prayers were being answered, and I was aware of the Spirit within me. I nurtured this presence of God through worship, study and association with like-minded persons. Faith and worship came naturally to me then, but I only began to grow spiritually when I had to face difficult questions about faith and God, when my life was at odds with my hopes and prayers.

It's Easter Once More

On Good Friday 1980 I was discharged from the hospital following the disastrous eye surgery. It was as bleak and dreary as an early April day can be. Cold drizzle blew directly into your face no matter which way you were walking. My husband and I were still living together in our small student flat, but we provided no comfort to each other. My parents had come to offer support while I was in the hospital, but once I was able to go home, we all agreed that they should return to Toronto.

When I entered our flat, I tripped over snow boots in the hall, then fumbled and stumbled around until I found a chair that had been moved from its usual place. I sat there in the most profound misery I believed possible. My life appeared to be in total collapse. All I could wish for was that I would soon die.

I cannot remember anything of the next day. To my amazement, when I awoke on Easter Sunday I felt entirely different. It was warm. I could feel the radiant energy of the sunshine on my face through the window. The birds were chirping and the air was rich with the smell of the thawing earth. I felt energetic and resilient. I knew I absolutely had to be in church. My husband was much less enthusiastic, but agreed to accompany me to Christ Church Cathedral. I was completely transported by the beauty and mystery of the service. The music was fabulous and the scent of Easter lilies permeated this glorious space. I felt myself regrouping and was filled with the sense that I would be all right. On our way home, I asked my husband to stop and walk with me through a small park so I could drink in the feeling of the sun upon my body, smell the air and enjoy being in that space despite being deprived of the sight of its beauty. Twenty years later, this experience of Holy Week 1980 has not faded.

Holy Week is a graphic expression of all the conflict and contradictions I experience in my faith life. I know the agony that is quickly replaced by joy. I know the absence and separation from God that are rapidly followed by the enormous presence of God. I know human frailty and defencelessness and I know the strength, security and comfort of God. I have known God's silence followed by a resounding message of hope and joy. God has been both distant from me and deeply present with me almost simultaneously. The heart-wrenching call of the psalmist in the work our choir sings each Maundy Thursday strikes directly in my heart and gut:

My God, my God,
Why hast thou forsaken me?
Why art thou so far from my pain and the words of my distress?

I live in that agony each Good Friday and Holy Saturday. Each year I am lifted to lofty heights by the Easter experience, but I know both the agony and the glory of God.

As I examine my Holy Week experiences across the years, I am aware that cynics would say that what I feel is not an encounter with God, but a music lover's emotional response to a dramatic and moving liturgical presentation. One of the great legacies of the Anglican tradition is no doubt the rich music and liturgical traditions, and if I were an occasional churchgoer this might be a plausible explanation for what happens to me in church during Holy Week. My heart does beat strongly after a rousing hymn, but some of my most profound experiences of encountering God have occurred when I am participating in small, prayer-filled settings with no music at all. During these services, something connects profoundly within me; it is deeply comforting and beyond my ability to describe.

Why Do I Pray?

A woman in my former parish led me to explore the question "Why do we pray?" At the time of my surgery, my parish and several other spiritual communities were praying fervently, not only that the surgery would be successful in staving off any further deterioration in eyesight, but also that it would correct any previous visual loss and that the problem would completely go away. There was an awkward silence all round when I returned to parish life; not only was I not cured, I was permanently disabled. No comments were made about the prayers that had been sent heavenward and that were apparently either disregarded or delivered to the wrong address. No one spoke to me about prayer in those days.

About six months after my ill-fated surgery, dreadful accidents happened in two families in the parish. One child had a serious head injury resulting in a prolonged coma. Another child fell and broke her neck. Immediate prayer vigils were called. The parish community was very upset for about 10 days. Both children were restored to perfect health, and the parish rejoiced with the two families. A fellow parishioner was chatting with me about the traumatic events and the successful outcomes. Her parting comment to me was, "Well, it just goes to show the power of prayer, doesn't it?"

I was dumbfounded. What did that mean for me? Just six months ago we were praying for my recovery, and the outcome could not have been worse. Were we not praying hard enough? Were there not enough people praying for me? Would things have been different if we or I had prayed more fervently? I was astonished at how willing the parish was to take credit for changing the outcome of those accidents by their prayers. Everyone was congratulating each other; even the rector was praising the power of prayer. This was in stark contrast to the awkward and painful silence following my surgery. Is prayer not powerful and worthwhile if the result is not what we want? I asked myself. Can prayer alter the outcome of a physical injury such as head trauma? Should we even pray for a specific outcome in such cases? If our prayer is not answered the way we would wish, what do we say about God and our prayers? These are difficult but important questions.

These questions have not stopped me from praying, but have helped me understand that I need a model of prayer that values the act no matter what the outcome. I need my prayer practice to be affirmed despite inexplicable tragedies and pain.

What was I praying for as two young members of our parish community were dealing with serious head and neck injuries? I was praying that they would feel the love and support of God. I was praying that their families would be open to the love and support of the community and that they would have the strength to deal with whatever happened. I was praying that something positive would come to the community as the result of shared experience. I did not pray that they would recover fully, just as I do not pray that my eyesight will return. I continue to ask God to give me the strength to carry on when I feel that I cannot, and when things are going well I pray in thanksgiving for the feelings of joy and satisfaction. I experience tremendous power in prayer that connects me with the Spirit within me, but I cannot believe that my prayer will influence the outcome of a particular situation. Do I think that the prayers of the community were powerful? Yes, but I believe that their power lay in the comfort, strength and sustenance that the act of prayer offered to them and their families.

Images of God

As I wrestled with the concept of God and the practice of prayer, I found that I needed a constant image. I could not have a relationship with one kind of God when things were going well, and with another kind of God when things were falling down around me. I have found two images that help me on my journey of faith. The first, where I try to view my life as part of a greater tapestry known only to God, is particularly helpful in dealing with circumstances that defy all rational explanation. I remind myself that my life and my experience are only a tiny moment, a stitch in God's tapestry of life. Had I been present at Golgotha 2000 years ago, I would have been among the most outraged people there. Looking back today, it is clear that Jesus' crucifixion was a critical part of God's plan for us. Set in the broader context of God's tapestry, Jesus' death is filled with great significance. This does not diminish Jesus' suffering at the time, but reminds me that everything I know and experience is but a tiny piece of a greater whole. When I am railing away at God for what has happened to me, I try to think of the resurrection story. It is a great comfort to me to believe firmly that my life and the universe are cared for by a wise and loving God whose power is much greater than I can imagine. I do not expect to understand how my life and my suffering are part of God's tapestry, but believe that I in all my frailty am part of a greater picture.

The second image, which helps me relate to God on a day-to-day basis, is that of a boat. At a seminar I once attended, Dr. Fred Schmidt, an Episcopalian theologian at Messiah College in Pennsylvania, asked us to imagine ourselves in a boat. The first model was of a powerboat. He explained to us that many people like to think of themselves in a powerboat because they see God as a powerful engine and propeller in their lives. Being in a powerboat with a big engine and a rudder allows them to ignore challenges in their environment. They do not have to consider the currents or the winds, or if it is wise to pursue a certain course. They are tempted to think that they can dictate the course and outcome of a journey. This kind of thinking can lead people into great difficulty. If we think we are in charge, we will be very disappointed and may feel that God has let us down when our course is not what we would wish. Many people believe that they are at one with God during periods of their lives when things are going well. It is seductive to think that God is with us and is enabling and empowering the course we are pursuing, but how do we comfort ourselves with this model when our world suddenly shatters?

Perhaps a more reasonable image is to picture ourselves in a sailboat, with God as a constant passenger. In a sailboat we are subject to storms, currents and adverse weather conditions, and must keep them in mind. We could be becalmed or blown off course. With God as a constant companion, however, we have the resources we need to help us if our course or our plans change. I like the wind-powered craft image. More challenging to me is finding a way to nourish my relationship to God, the passenger in the sailboat of my life.

Another marine image for God's relationship with us was suggested to me by Christine Hamilton, a woman of profound faith who has Multiple Sclerosis, a disease that has left her progressively more disabled. I first met Christine through Ron Shepherd while visiting Salt Spring Island in British Columbia. By chance, we met again, this time through another Anglican friend, Archbishop Ted Scott. Christine later wrote to me, describing her image of God as the bedrock in a large, open bay. According to this image, we are born on one shoreline; as we traverse the bay in the course of our lives, we may sometimes feel as if God or the ocean floor is remote from us. The distance between us and God varies at different times in our lives. Sometimes there are small islands where we are again one with God. Sometimes we feel that God has deserted us and we are tossed around in a tempest at sea. But God is as faithful as the bedrock, even in the worst of storms. At the end of our lives we arrive at the other shore and are safe with God.

This model appeals to me, although it makes me more passive. I cannot control the depth of the ocean upon which I am sailing, but I can choose whether I wish to have God as a passenger in my boat and to live in a way that facilitates our passage.

Well-intentioned people of faith are constantly proffering their insights on why I have been stricken by various ailments in my life. Often these people have not faced a challenge to their faith or their comments would not be so shallow and insensitive. One man told me God had sent these trials to teach me humility. I found it hard to believe that anyone would even think that way, let alone express those sentiments to someone in my situation. Do I think that there is anything to be learned from suffering? Yes, I do. I have learned a huge amount about the world, about life, about love, about community and about God because of my experiences. But I reject outright the concept of a God who would inflict disease or suffering upon one of his creatures in order to teach anything.

Several people have said to me that God never sends us more than we can bear. I am supposed to feel encouraged that God knows I can cope with just about anything and continues to send me so much trouble. I refuse to accept any concept of a God who sends trials to challenge us to live up to our potential as persons. Learning to be crea-tive and to adapt in the face of adversity has been a valuable part of my life that has contributed to my personal development and has touched those around me as well.

Someone from my parish once remarked that I should be pleased that God had been paying attention to me. She felt that as she had never been challenged by God, God either did not know of her exist-ence or He thought poorly of her ability to deal with adversity. I was tempted to respond that I would gladly change places with her.

The story of Job holds infinite intrigue for anyone with faith or knowledge of this Old Testament character. "Do you feel like a modern-day Job?" people ask. "Do you feel that God is testing your faith?" "Do you believe that God is using you to teach others about faith?" "Do you believe that your faithfulness will be richly rewarded?"

No, No, No, and No. None of these concepts reflect the nature of the God I believe in. I believe that God created a complex world with many complex physical forces that interact with each other to produce life in many forms. My physical and genetic format has led to physical limitations; I do not think that God specifically sent me these disasters. Rather, I believe that it is God's wish for me – and for you – to engage in this life to the fullest. I have been given the character, nature and will to adapt to adversity and to enjoy life fully despite great sadness. God demands that from each of us.

Atheists ask me how I can believe in a loving, omnipotent God when I face so many hurdles each day. Some use the example of my life to refute the existence of God. Some ask why I pursue a God who has so clearly failed to protect me from adversity. My response is that I can only live in a world that I believe has been created by God. I prefer to live in a world where I cannot understand many things than in a world where I cannot perceive the presence of God everywhere. It took time to reach this place of faith and hope, and it was the result of years of hard work and spiritual inquiry.

Who Is Walking with Me? The Benedictine Community / Paul Geraghty

My spiritual life began to take on a new dimension in Novem-ber 1986, when I accompanied my friend Wilks Keefer to the Benedic-tine Priory of Montreal. Wilks had often spoken passionately about his time spent with this religious community. The Priory was started by

Father John Main, an Irish Benedictine monk living in England who came to Montreal to open a house dedicated to the teaching of Christian meditation. It started as a small community of several monks from England in a house on Vendome Avenue in Notre Dame de Grace.

Father John was a fascinating and very talented man. Years earlier, he had learned about the practice of meditation of the early desert fathers and had developed this tradition into a contemporary and very powerful form of prayer. He wrote several books and recorded many cassettes on the subject.

The community in Montreal flourished, and several more monks arrived from England and the United States. They quickly outgrew the original house and were fortunate to be offered the old McConnell family mansion. Built from the design of an Italian villa, the house had 18 bedrooms, a beautiful marble chapel, a large meeting room and a magnificent library. It was an ideal monastery and retreat centre, nestled into the side of Mount Royal Park, next door to the Montreal General Hospital. The community grew. There were evening classes in meditation and the public was invited to join the community's celebrations of the daily office. Over time, the monks established a large oblate community of lay persons who wished to be affiliated with the community, but who continued with their secular lives. Many of these people saw the Priory as their regular place of worship and spiritual nourishment. The monks also established a sister community of women Benedictines and acquired another large house for them across the street on Pine Avenue. Sister Christian Morris arrived from St. Benedict's Convent in St. Joseph, Minnesota, to lead the women's community, which thrived and shared in all the worship and teaching activities of the men's house.

Wilks spoke often and at great length about the impact that meditation and his association with this community had had upon his spiritual growth. At the time, I was nearly overwhelmed by my medical residency training and the adjustment to my recent blindness. I finally received my divorce papers in January 1982, and was still struggling with a host of associated feelings. As I said good night one Monday evening after dinner with Wilks, he told me he was going to the Priory for a teaching session and asked if I wanted to come along.

We walked quickly through downtown Montreal amidst the traffic, noise and fumes, deep in discussion about some troubling event. When we arrived at the Priory, we walked through the great oak door and into rich silence. I could feel myself descend into a deep and pleasing relaxation as I breathed the incense-laden air. We descended a long marble staircase into the common room, where about 75 people were sitting in silence. In the centre sat a monk, Father Paul Geraghty, playing a recording of wonderful chamber music. I could not believe that such an oasis existed in the middle of bustling Montreal.

Father Paul eventually stopped the recording and began an address about prayer. He spoke with grace and commitment about how the practice of meditation could bring us closer to the presence of God in our hearts. I was riveted. Following his address, we all sat and meditated together in absolute silence for 25 minutes. At the end of the meditation period, he quietly started the music playing again. We rose and filed out in silence. Wilks and I decided to join the monks for Compline. I floated out of the Priory afterwards, knowing that I had to return as soon as possible. The next time I wanted to go, Wilks was unable to accompany me so he phoned ahead to the community and asked them to look out for me. I was anxious about arriving without him, but did not need to be. I was greeted by different members of the community as if I were an old friend. They made it very easy for me to join in the worship that evening. Later, they called a taxi for me and saw me off safely.

I became a regular and soon discovered that a woman who also worked in the hospital attended Vespers at the Priory after work most days. I arranged to meet her so that we could walk over together.

The Benedictines believe that meditation must become a disciplined way of life. To engage in the practice, we were asked to meditate for 30 minutes twice each day, preferably first thing in the morning and just before dinner. My timetable at the hospital was already quite rigorous; I found that what worked best for me was to rise half an hour earlier each morning to meditate. I needed to be at the hospital by eight, so my days started early. These periods of morning meditation became an integral part of my life. Whenever I missed my morning session my entire day felt disorganized and unsettled. I attended Vespers most evenings after work, and found myself drawn to the monastery even on weekends. I also attended other kinds of activities there, such as musical soirees. I developed a particular friendship with Sister Christian, the Benedictine sister from Minnesota.

Despite my growing and deepening attachment to this Roman Catholic monastic order, I could not give up my strong ties at the Anglican cathedral and continued to attend Sunday services and educational events there. My family was concerned that I might be heading towards officially entering the Benedictine order. I could only reassure them that having witnessed the life of a committed religious, I knew that I was not called to this type of commitment. Still, my family worried about the depth of my association with the Benedictines and my practice of meditation, which I would do when I visited them in Toronto.

The Priory was the right place for me to be at the time – this period of great turmoil when I was longing for a rich, deep and silent space within myself. Meditation made this possible for me. I preferred contemplative prayer to petitionary prayer. In meditation I could imagine myself sitting at God's knee and being silent in the presence of the source of all strength and life. It gave me more energy and strength than continuously begging to be able to carry on with my life, which seemed so difficult for me. The peace I found within the Priory was a very powerful force in my life.

Sadly, nothing is ever as perfect as it seems. After Father John Main died in 1982, leaving behind a very young and inexperienced group of men and women, the fractious forces of human nature slowly started to threaten the peace within the community.

Leadership of the community was taken over by Father Laurence Freeman, one of the original monks who had accompanied Father John to Montreal from England. Disagreements about Father John's original vision for the community quickly ensued. Main had travelled around the world teaching about meditation and had established meditation groups throughout Canada and many other countries. He accomplished this mission without losing sight of the importance of a strong base community. Father Laurence continued the international part of John Main's work while Father Paul Geraghty worked to maintain a strong core community and teaching program at the Priory. Both men were too young to be able to see the necessary co-existence of both these ministries. The community began to suffer under this stress. Unfortunately, there was no wise person to advise these young people about the directions they ought to be pursuing. By 1989, there was such dissension and unrest at the community that it fell apart. Five members, including Sister Christian and Father Paul, withdrew. Those who remained struggled along for an additional year, but the heart of the Priory was gone.

The Loss of Sacred Space

When the Benedictine Community in Montreal collapsed, I felt as if the big oak front door had been slammed right in my face. That community had become an integral and irreplaceable part of my life. I meditated with them and attended vespers five or six days a week.

I had lost one of my sacred spaces. The ground floor chapel in the Priory was a jewel. The high ceilings produced fine acoustics and the smell of incense wrapped around me like a cozy blanket. My body could totally relax in that space. Even when I was somewhere else, I could imagine myself at the Priory, sitting in silence. This brought me a certain amount of peace. Now this sacred space was gone forever.

It was hard to imagine any good coming from this disaster. Because I was living on my own in a four-bedroom house with a large basement, my home became a storage depot for the Benedictines who had left the Priory community. They laughed as they piled all their worldly possessions in one corner of the basement. "You would never know that we had taken vows of poverty!" some of them said.

Over the next year each of them did what he or she had to do to get over the trauma. My home often served as a meeting place where we would gather on a Friday night to say vespers and meditate together. Then we would order in pizza or Chinese food and share a meal. It felt like a version of the Priory community. Gradually they moved off in different directions, but I became good friends with the two who remained in Montreal: Sister Christian Morris and Father Paul Geraghty. Christian did some travelling back and forth to Minnesota, but mainly lived in Montreal where she was pursuing her Ph.D in Theology at the University of Montreal. When she first came to Montreal, she spoke not a word of French. She worked hard on her languages and to my amazement selected a French-speaking university for her graduate studies. After completing the residency requirements for her doctoral work, she returned to Minnesota in the summer of 2000. We continue to keep in touch with each other by phone and e-mail.

Following a year in Boston, Paul returned to Montreal in search of a new focus for his life. Right away he took a clinical course in pastoral care at the Royal Victoria Hospital. He needed a place to live and my house seemed the perfect interim resting spot. The house was big enough that we could each have our privacy, since I was busy at work and he was busy with his chaplaincy course. I liked the idea of having the company and besides, he was a very good chef! (I am not.)

Paul is a good and sensitive listener, which is partly what makes him such a good priest and chaplain. I was still getting over the trauma of my marriage and was stressed by the responsibilities of my new job. I appreciated having such a wise and patient sounding-board close by. We both had a slightly quirky sense of humour, and he could always make me laugh. We shared a deep faith but, not surprisingly for an

Anglican and a Roman Catholic, we argued back and forth about many doctrinal issues. We exchanged views on many different topics and learned a lot from each other. Our backgrounds were very different. As a young law student, Paul had been captivated by Father John Main. Although he had finished his legal training and had worked as a lawyer for a short time, he had accepted Father John's request to come to Montreal to help set up a new monastery dedicated to the teaching of meditation. Living in a monastic community had worked well for Paul for a number of years, and he longed to become connected to another Benedictine community.

As soon as he was hired as a chaplain at the Montreal Children's Hospital, he rented a small flat in the house of another former Priory oblate and set up his own living space. I was sorry when he moved out of my home, as I had enjoyed his company. Fortunately, Paul's departure did not weaken our friendship.

After I moved back to Toronto I saw much less of Paul, but we continued to talk regularly on the phone. He would come to Toronto to visit and I was always happy for an excuse to travel to Montreal to visit old friends.

The true depth of our friendship revealed itself during my various illnesses. Paul's support became invaluable to me; I am sure I would not have managed as well without him. His monastic experience came in handy as he sat in silence by my hospital bed as I slept after surgery.

I treasure my friendship with Paul. He knows me well and is not afraid to tell me when he feels my thinking is out of line. We are soul mates. While we enjoy the intimacy of this friendship, we also respect each other's need for space. These boundaries have allowed us both to develop and enjoy many other intimate friendships. While I am sad not to have had the experience of a happy marriage, I am grateful for the many relationships I have enjoyed, which would have been impossible had I been happily married. These relationships have greatly enriched my life – perhaps none as profoundly as my relationship with Father Paul.

What now of my meditation practice? In the years immediately following the dissolution of the monastic community, I continued to meditate regularly, supported in this practice by others who had left. Following my move to Toronto I initially continued this practice, but without the support of a meditating community I have gradually lost hold of it. I continue to reap the benefits of having followed this discipline for 10 years and I still appreciate the value of meditation. I meditate when I feel drawn to it, but I no longer order my life around it. Being still in the presence of God continues to be a very powerful form of prayer for me.

Who Is Walking with Me? Douglas Stoute

On Good Friday 1987, I met a priest who, like Paul Geraghty, was to have great significance in my life. Douglas Stoute was the guest preacher at Christ Church Cathedral in Montreal. He had been invited to Montreal by Dean Andrew Hutchinson, who had met Douglas while working in Toronto.

The Good Friday liturgy calls for seven short sermons throughout the three-hour service. Douglas' sermons were spectacular; I was captivated by his words and his presence. It turned out that Douglas was about to be appointed rector at St. Clement's Church in Toronto, which Andrew knew was my parish in Toronto. After the service, Andrew invited me to dinner at his home. It was to be early and short, because there was another evening service. We had a great time at dinner. I learned that Doug, this deeply spiritual man, also had a terrific sense of humour. After dinner I told the dean that if he didn't mind, I had had enough church for one day and was going home rather than back to the cathedral with them. To my great surprise, Douglas announced that he had had enough church too. As he had no role in the evening service, he was going to beg off the evening's religious activities. Andrew's wife seemed taken aback at this announcement. What would her house guest do for three hours while he waited for his flight home? She was even more taken aback when I said, "He can come to my house."

Ten minutes later I found myself walking through Westmount Park with this eminent visitor. Doug immediately asked me about the spiritual journey of losing my sight and carrying on in the face of desperate circumstances. I was still in the full bloom of my Benedictine experience, so we spoke about meditation, prayer, grace and many other things that had nothing to do with religion. I promised to send him some of John Main's books, as it was hard to explain the power of meditation to him in my own words. I thought at the time that I had never met anyone who was capable of such deep thought yet was so much fun. When he left to catch his plane, I felt as if I had known him for much longer than three hours.

That Good Friday was the start of a wonderful, enriching friendship for me, one that endures to this day. Doug never feels he has to say how good I am or to paint a picture of a blind wonder-woman. He has been a rock-solid support at times of great need and has helped my personal growth. In 1987, I spent a year reflecting upon a possible vocation to ordained ministry. When I had formulated my thoughts, I asked him what he thought. To my amazement he told me I could never move forward with my life until I had accepted my blindness. I was stunned. What did he mean? I had a satisfying medical career. I was a good teacher, had an interesting social life, and had recently been awarded the Order of Canada. What more could he expect in fewer than 10 years following the loss of sight? I had accomplished more in my career to that point than many people accomplish in a lifetime.

"That is exactly my point," he replied. "You have spent a huge amount of energy carrying on with your life as if nothing has happened. You have lost your vision and you must acknowledge this before throwing yourself into new projects."

This encounter precipitated for me an intense period of reflection. I had to learn the difference between active and passive "letting go." For many years, I valiantly struggled, doing all the things I had always presumed I should do. I pursued clinical medicine. I taught at the university. I bought a house. I travelled. I had achieved a lot of things, but in many ways, my pursuit of all these activities allowed me to pretend that blindness was not such a tragedy. I started running so fast so soon after the loss of my vision that I had not allowed the emotional impact to sink in.

I am not sure that my approach was all bad. Had I dealt with all the depression initially, I am not sure I would ever have been able to get back on my feet. I would not have been able to do my residency without the help of my hospital classmates; I would most likely have returned to Toronto where I did not know the medical community. Looking back now, I do not think Doug meant I had made a big mistake. He was telling me I needed to consolidate all the things that I was before going on to other things. I was a doctor, a teacher, an aunt. But I was also sick, lonely and blind. I eventually had to engage the pain of all of this before I knew myself.

The period of this engagement with deep pain was complicated, at times very difficult, but not as dreadful as I expected. I should not speak of this experience as being complete or in the past; to be fully alive I must continue to face these feelings every day of my life. Initially, I thought letting go meant saying the words and then carrying on as if nothing had changed. While I acknowledged the fact that I was divorced, I held tightly to the notion that the only way I would find happiness would be to marry again. By actively letting go of that thought, I have opened myself up to the rich friendships that are so important in my life. By letting go of the thought that the only satisfactory way to live was to be completely "independent," I have been able to explore different ways of doing things and stay open to the warmth of helping relationships. I could both help and be helped.

Active letting go is not easy. Many aspects of me must work together. I pray for the strength to go forward and the wisdom to notice when I have grown. I need my periods of meditation for peace. My family and my inspiring friends such as Paul and Douglas are an integral part of the process. They are always there for me, pointing the way and picking me up when I fall down.

In Memoriam – Dad, 1987

Perhaps the saddest legacy of my diabetes was the impenetrable barrier that developed between me and my father. While I never really spoke to any of my family about the diabetes and its impact on me, we were able to develop good relationships in different aspects of our lives. For some reason, I could never be honest with Dad.

It was not a problem of insufficient love. If anything, I think he loved me too much, or expressed that love to me in such a way that it was a burden rather than a warm and safe place to nestle. I was stricken by the sight of my father crying as we sat in the vice-principal's office all those years ago, telling him that I had diabetes. That was how I knew what a big deal my diabetes was: until that moment, I hadn't known that men could cry. Something about me had made my father cry in front of my school vice-principal. I must not let this happen ever again.

In those first few years I kept my emotions to myself. I made my mother cry once, which upset me, but did not have quite the impact that my dad's tears did. She was a woman so it was less shameful; besides, we were in the privacy of our home. No one saw except me. I wish I had had an outlet for all that emotion. Overall the medical world was not as attuned to the psychological aspect of disease then as it is now. As I was not acting out, no one questioned me about my feelings. I was probably inconsolable, but dealing with these feelings might have helped to prevent the major assault I launched against myself and fostered for most of my life. I find it ironic that despite all my medical training, I did not begin to respect my body and congratulate myself for tenaciously pursuing vibrant living until I developed life-threatening illness in my 40s.

My relationship with Dad sustained a mortal blow in 1970, when he developed diabetes himself. Unlike most adults who develop diabetes in mid-life, Dad was neither overweight nor underactive. He resisted taking insulin injections, but none of the oral medications would control his blood sugars. I was terribly confused by my mixed reaction. Secretly I thought, "Why should he be exempt from taking injections?" I also hoped that now someone close to me would finally see what I had been going through. At the same time, I was upset seeing my father struggle. Rather than bringing us together, diabetes drove us farther apart. Maybe my inconsolability caused this to be so. Dad tried to have several conversations with me about how awful it was having diabetes. I remember lashing out at him once, saying: "At least you are 55 years old. I was thirteen!" In his hurt, he replied that his life was not over at 50. It always made me furious to hear him speak aloud about the rigours and aggravations of being diabetic. Looking back, his response was clearly healthier than my own, but it made me even more silent. Dad followed the doctor's advice and wore a Medic-alert bracelet, in case of an accident. I refused to wear a bracelet and resented the fact that it said "Diabetic," which felt like a slur against me, rather than "Diabetes."

The other aspect that troubled me about Dad's diabetes was the question of culpability. The genetic basis of this disease remained an unspoken topic in our household. Because of my grandmother, we had all presumed that my disease had come through the maternal line. With the development of Dad's disease, this opened a whole new option. As the research in diabetes revealed that Type 1 and Type 2 diabetes appeared to be two separate diseases, he would mail me newspaper clippings reporting research of a possible viral connection with Type 1 diabetes, or the lack of correlation between juvenile diabetes and family history of Type 2 disease. I always felt that he sent me these mainly to clear himself of any responsibility for my disease. For some reason this infuriated me.

The irreparable blow to our relationship came with my loss of eyesight. Dad was devastated. Once again, I witnessed raw and naked emotion in my father. He could not even pretend to accept what had happened to his beloved first born. I felt as if the tables had been turned. It was now my parents who were inconsolable. They were so distraught, I took on the role of parent and comforter. During this terrible time I sometimes stopped to ask myself why I, the afflicted, was forced into the concurrent role of comforter. Now, an older and wiser observer, I suspect that I snatched this role myself. I preferred playing the part of the strong one. I also had the part of the grounded-in-science, non-emotional family member down pat. Whatever my role was, Dad never progressed in his emotional response to my worsening health. No one in my family accepted or became hardened to my distress. They did, however, develop coping techniques and were always open to suggestions about how they might be most helpful. Dad and I remained in a hopeless standoff fuelled by our individual agony.

He was incapable of assessing what information was critical to convey to me and which situations could be downright dangerous. I was always frightened to walk with him. One time he picked me up at the airport. While we were walking to the car I suddenly found myself on a down escalator. I shouted, "Dad! What in the world are you doing?!"

In all innocence he replied that the car was parked on the lower level.

"You didn't tell me that we were going onto an escalator," I said angrily. "Think what it is like for me to be suddenly dragged onto a moving staircase – especially one that is going down!"

I had stepped perfectly onto the escalator without breaking pace, but this was merely lucky. It probably looked quite simple to do. Dad did not see the danger and was hurt and confused by my strong response.

Another time I hit my head on a piece of metallic pipework hanging as a decoration in a hotel lobby. Although I was not seriously injured, I was embarrassed and surprised.

"Dad," I said sharply, after making painful contact with the metal.

"Watch out, sweetie," he replied.

I rode up the elevator with him in icy silence. When we entered our room, Mom asked if there was something wrong. To my amazement and undoing he said to Mom, "Oh, nothing. Janie just knocked her little noggin."

Livid, I replied, "I did not! You smashed me into that pipe display in front of a crowd of people."

My response hurt my father deeply. Mom asked me if I was hurt, trying to defuse the scene by focusing on the minimal physical injury.

I gradually withdrew from placing myself at risk with him in this way. I specifically chose to walk with anyone else but him. Not surprisingly, he viewed this as a personal rejection. It never dawned on him that he had a high record of near and not-so-near misses with me.

I tried to explain that things like escalators and overlying structures at head level were serious hazards for me. I told him that doorways were easy as long as the door was either open or closed: doors that are partly open are the real hazard. I called these the "in-between doors" after I crashed into one, hitting the bridge of my nose. Dad did try. One day he proudly told me to be careful coming out of the bathroom because the door was half open. Rather than congratulate him on his keen observation, I expressed disapproval that he would report a danger rather than correct it.

Our strained relationship was the source of both profound sorrow and conflict for the rest of my family. My sister said our tortured interactions were the most difficult things she had ever had to watch. In a kind but very real way, my family came down on my father's side. After one of our contretemps he withdrew, crushed. I, on the other hand, appeared to be strong and resilient in anger and disdain. My family constantly asked me to let go of my angry reactions. He could not help being nervous and absent-minded around me, they said. They thought I had the inner strength and fortitude to withstand almost everything, it appeared. None of them understood how tightly stretched my coping coils were being pulled. Whenever someone said or did something stupid to me, they expected me not to react. "You have to forgive people for being nervous around you now that you are blind," came the chorus. I felt as if I were being struck twice; not only did I bear the burden of my disability, I had to relieve everyone else's embarrassment and discomfort.

The last chapter in the saga of my relationship with my father is strange, possibly macabre, but very moving. It is a moment between us that leaves me with a certain sense of peace.

In August 1987, Dad underwent surgery for removal of a malignant tumour of the bowel. As a result of the surgery, he would have a permanent colostomy. Dad was devastated; he was fastidious about personal hygiene and found it difficult to accept help. I was terribly worried about how my parents would cope. Although Dad appeared to be fit and healthy, the 15 years of diabetes was taking its toll. He also had angina, which he could not accept. To prove to me that there was nothing wrong with his heart, he would insist on carrying all my bags whenever we travelled together. His hearing was rapidly deteriorating and he had not been able to find a suitable hearing aid. He was also showing the beginnings of decreased circulation to his feet, which were always cold. I was dreading the development of severe vascular complications, which often lead to amputation of a limb. Dad lived to play golf, but now he was beginning to slow down. Nine years younger, Mom remained the dynamo.

Dad did not do well in the post-operative period. He had continuous low-grade fever and such confusion that one of my medical friends who had stopped in to see him called me to tell me that he did not look at all well. She was right. By the time I arrived back in Toronto the next day, it was clear that Dad was septic. He was very frightened but crystal clear mentally. I spent a lovely afternoon alone with him. We spoke of many things. He was so pleased to be able to speak about cancer, his colostomy, dying, God, heaven, and many other important things. I knew that my presence was a great comfort and a great joy for him. I was so happy to be with him, even as his condition deteriorated later that evening and he was moved to another room for closer observation. He made it through the night, but the following afternoon he required intubation and respiratory support. He was afraid, but I was there to calm him and explain what was happening.

He spent the next two weeks on a ventilator; he deteriorated gradually. I was at his side constantly and spoke to him a lot in the event that he could hear even though he could not respond. On day 15, he had a cardiac arrest while I was with him. The medical staff resuscitated him and told me that he would have to go on a special jet ventilator. I asked them not to do this. I then had a difficult meeting with Mom, Anne and David. I told them that Dad could not possibly live much longer. I thought it best not to torture him any further. He had initially asked that extraordinary measures be taken to prolong his life, but I told them what Dad had told me: he was not afraid of death; it was the process of dying that he feared. My family tearfully considered what I told them and eventually agreed that to put him through anything more was not in his best interests. I conveyed this information to the surgical team who, it turned out, were not fully in agreement. I suspect that they were keen to try out their new vent. The nursing staff supported our decision. During lunch, they moved Dad into a small private room in the unit. When I returned that afternoon, the nurse said that the team had left orders for them to "discontinue any interventions that Dr. Poulson wanted discontinued."

"You've got to be kidding!" I said incredulously. "They want me to discontinue my father's life support."

It seemed that there had been a difficult discussion around this point in the team meeting. There was no doubt about what was going to happen when adjustments were made to the supporting machinery. Every possible button had been set at maximum, yet still he was slowly deteriorating. Someone would have come eventually, but they were so busy on this unit that Dad would have been a low priority. I took a deep breath and went to tell my family what was about to happen. I asked them to come for whatever part they wanted but they found it too difficult to watch.

One of my friends came with me. In a strange way, I found it easier to do this without a lot of people watching. Dad was so sick that the dying process was fast. I knew that we were doing the right thing as soon as we touched the intravenous line that was delivering a medication to maintain his blood pressure and heartbeat. This tiny adjustment caused his heart rate to plummet. In effect he had been dead for several days. While we were clearly doing the best thing for him, it still felt strange to know that the last nice thing I would do for my father would be to discontinue his life support systems.

I am eternally grateful for those few hours my father and I spent together before he lost consciousness. All our familiar defences were down. He was my dear old Dad and I was his treasured daughter, comforting him in a way that no one else could.

Create in me a clean heart, O God,
and put a new and right spirit within me.
Do not cast me away from your presence,
and do not take your holy spirit from me.
Restore to me the joy of your salvation,
and sustain in me a willing spirit.

Psalm 51:10-12

Part IV: Welcome to the 1990s

Chapter 10: Living and Working in a Sighted World

My Arctic Adventure

While at McGill, I co-ordinated a native health care program for Northern Quebec. The Montreal General Hospital served as the base for providing the majority of tertiary care for Quebec's Cree and Inuit populations; I was the physician responsible for co-ordinating this care. I spent a lot of time on the telephone to northern nursing stations giving advice about how problems might be managed locally. I spoke to regional physicians and arranged for special blood testing to be done in Montreal when they sent down specimens.

We thought it would be a good idea if I travelled up north from time to time to meet the physicians and nurses. I could also do some regional consulting work, bringing the doctor to the patients rather than the other way around. I was intrigued by the idea of becoming familiar with where my patients came from and what their lifestyle entailed. So, in mid-January 1990, I made my first trip up to the Arctic. Another doctor from the pediatric hospital was supposed to be accompanying me, but when I met him at Dorval airport, he informed me that there was an outbreak of some description at one of the nursing stations half-way up and he would only be going as far as Great Whale River that day. Panic! How was I supposed to find my way up to the north end of Hudson Bay by myself? I tried to appear calm as I casually expressed to him my concern about the three flight changes I would have to make on my own. "Oh, don't worry," he said. "I am sure they will help you." Right. Just relax, Jane, I tried to convince myself.

We parted company at Great Whale. "Enjoy your trip," he said cheerfully as he walked away from the airstrip. Right, I said. Inside, I had to admit I was hoping that he would be caught out on an ice floe somewhere. The people from the Great Whale Nursing Station had my tickets for the subsequent legs of my journey and they popped me onto the next flight. The original plan was that one of their nurses would be going on up north and would accompany me that day. Unfortunately that plan changed. Their advice was: "Get off at the next stop. Someone from that nursing station will see that you make the right connection."

The plane sat on the airstrip for a long time. Eventually someone came with a message that we had been rerouted and would stop off at the Belcher Islands in Hudson Bay. I was to remain on board for two additional stops, after which a nurse would join me for the final leg of this complicated journey. The nurse would see that I made it to the right plane. Anyway, they said, it would be hard to miss it, as the airline had such a limited number of planes and flights that I could not make a mistake. "Right!" I thought. "How do you think I am going to find the plane even if it is the only one in the airport?" Relax, Jane, I said to myself. You have a mouth. You can ask someone. Relax. Just relax.

I followed instructions and stayed aboard the plane. Fortunately, whatever errand we had been on was short and we quickly took off. We eventually landed again and everyone, including the pilot, got off. He knew that I was to disembark and helped me into the airport. I use the term "airport" loosely; it was a tin hut crammed with people from the area waiting for the arrival of a plane bearing their local hockey club. From the sounds of it I was the only English-speaker there. For the first time, I had a sense of what it must feel like to be a refugee arriving in a foreign land, knowing no one and not being able to converse in any local language. Relax, Jane, I told myself. That pilot was surely waiting for the next plane to come and he knew you had to get on it. The victorious hockey team arrived to great and noisy adulation. Then the airport suddenly emptied and I felt terribly alone. There were no signs that the plane that had just arrived was going anywhere else.

I heard some women speaking French and tried to get their attention in the hope that they were the nurses who were looking out for me. They were not, so I asked what time the next flight was scheduled to leave. "Scheduled?" they laughed. "There is no schedule here!"

By now, I could no longer remember the name of the next outpost where we were to change over. I asked them where they were headed. It sounded like the right place, but all these stops had Inuit names and I was having trouble keeping them straight. "It's the only one leaving here today," they said, so I assumed it was the one I was supposed to take. I asked if I could go with them when the plane arrived. "Sure," they replied. "What are you doing up in this neck of the woods, anyway?" they asked. I was beginning to wonder myself.

Eventually a small plane arrived. We ventured out into the freezing cold wind. We had to climb a ladder to get into the plane; I hit my head trying to enter the tiny door. What if I get an epidural hemorrhage, I wondered? Who would know who I am and where I come from if I lose consciousness? Relax Jane, you have hit your head much harder than that many times and besides, you were wearing a thick hat.

I strapped myself in and wondered who was piloting this plane. It is pitch black up north for most of the winter, so these guys must have experience finding tiny airstrips in the dark. I assured myself that these planes must have good radar and directional devices.

I was definitely feeling sorry for myself; by the time I made the last flight change onto an even smaller plane, I was inconsolable. I was quite certain that I would not be able to climb up one more ladder that day. Then I gave myself a shake and tried to think of how many 80-year-old grandmothers I had sent back up north on exactly this trip – and they had just had their gall bladders or something removed at my hospital a few days before. Some nurses I had met left me at this stop, but fortunately for me another got on. She told me that because of the weather conditions at our final stop, we could not land at the airstrip, but would be using the frozen river instead. "Great!" I said. "Thanks for sharing that with me."

I wondered if the people who were to meet my plane knew about this latest change in plans. I fought off dreadful images of myself frozen on some glacier in northern Quebec. I reassured myself by thinking of all the stories I had read about how nice it was to fall asleep in a snowbank and never wake up. Would there be wolves or polar bears circling around, licking their chops? I had to give myself over to fate and presume that someone was expecting me and would meet the plane. No one else had been expecting me, but at each stop someone seemed to be going in my direction.

I arrived safely and the medical officer of health and his wife were there to greet me. An hour later, I was warm and comfortable, sipping a glass of red wine. After a delicious dinner of Arctic char, I fell into bed exhausted and relaxed. But not for long.

Looking Around the Local Museum

This Arctic adventure became one of the most interesting things I have ever done. I did not think it could be as cold as it was up there. Each morning I would ask about the temperature but they said they did not need thermometers up there during the four frigid months of winter. "It's cold enough to be dangerous," they would say.

The native people I worked with were amazing. I had seen a number of them in consultation in Montreal and they were delighted to have me visit in their community. They were fascinated by the fact that I could not see. Many people came to the clinic over the time I was there to verify the rumour that they had heard about a blind doctor.

The woman who was acting as my interpreter told me that the people of the village had decided they would like to open their nature museum, which was generally closed in the winter, and give me a tour as a special sign of their hospitality. We proceeded into the freezing night wind and trudged over to the museum, which was housed in an old wooden building shaped like a large beehive. The interior of the building was quite sparse. There was no heating and they were using live torches for light. Once we all got inside, I met several of the local dignitaries. After a small discussion, they asked me to sign their guest book. I wrote my name in English; the interpreter then wrote something beside my name. When I asked her what she had written, she replied that the others had asked her to put in brackets beside my name "Blind doctor from Montreal."

I felt claustrophobic inside this building and was anxious for the tour to get underway. It turned out that the main display was on the second floor, which the guide told me we could reach by climbing a ladder and crawling through a trap door in the ceiling.

I was feeling very panicky as I climbed up a wooden ladder whose rungs were not placed at regular intervals. My boots were especially thick soled and I had two pair of socks on, so it was hard to feel exactly where my foot was on the ladder. I stumbled several times as I climbed up, wondering where the hole in the ceiling was and how I would climb through it when I arrived. Fortunately I had been a good athlete in my sighted days and managed to scale the ladder and climb through the hole in the ceiling as if this were something I did regularly.

The upper room was even smaller and more enclosed than the lower level had seemed. The men and their torches in this dry wooden building were terrifying me. "Put out those torches!" I pleaded with them in my head. "I can see as well in the pitch black as I can with dazzling light!" I imagined the building going up in flames as we looked at their artifacts. How would I ever find the hole in the floor to climb back down the wooden ladder? I worried. I felt a strange sense of calm when I realized that if one of those torches caught the building, none of us would be climbing down the ladder. We would be charbroiled on the spot. I directed my attentions to two endeavours. The first was taking in the amazing display of native history and realizing the incredible experience I was being offered. The second was trying to avoid stepping through that gaping hole leading down to the first floor. I kept making a mental note of where I thought the hole was relative to our movements through the gallery, then realized that I had no idea where it was. I stepped gingerly, expecting to go crashing through open space with every step.

After the tour ended, we crawled over to the hole in the floor. Somehow I lowered my feet, legs and heavily clothed body through this opening, madly reaching with my feet for what felt like the rung of a ladder. I hoped that my wild movements would not knock the ladder over and leave me hanging out of a hole in the ceiling of a building thousands of kilometres from my familiar life in Montreal.

The many thick layers of clothing made my body feel strange. Clearly I had come to depend upon my sense of touch to locate my body in space. Years of gymnastics as a child and scaling rickety ladders into and out of tree forts stood me in good stead, and somehow I made it down the ladder, although I must admit it put me in mind of the first breech birth I witnessed, as a tiny human came into the world. My guides dropped me off at my lodgings where I fell into bed exhausted but exhilarated by this unique northern experience.

Helpers, Please Read This

Back home, I was the perfect project for my colleague's pouty 14-year-old daughter.

"Kids are so self-centred these days. It will be good for her to do something for someone else," declared her mother. This ought to have been a warning to me to somehow take back my question about finding a helper. I had been asking if there was an older sister or some friends. At each step along my long journey I learned another lesson. There is nothing less helpful than an unwilling teenager who has been roped into helping a friend of her mother's.

In the early days of my blindness, everyone was upset and everyone wanted to help. I was not only flooded with offers, but also with acts of kindness. Most of these were helpful, such as bringing casseroles and other nourishing food. Eventually, they trailed off and I could no longer count on prepared dinners. Then, when various people would call to see if they could be useful, I would ask them to pick up some margarine, or fruit, or whatever I could think of at the time. I always forgot something and was constantly in a position of need and therefore frustrated. What we all needed to appreciate was that this was not a temporary situation. I needed to work something out for the long run.

I had many such arrangements, all of which worked for a time, but which were all flawed in some fatal way. All were, to my mind, tedious chores being done for me by someone who was being kind. This meant that I was constantly at the mercy of a friend or neighbour. No one complained but I found myself constantly saying thank you, thank you, thank you. When I was not saying thank you, I was asking another favour. My food shopping lists were at least in part based on what would be the least amount of work for my shopper. Regular rolls would do, since I did not want to ask her to go to the bakeshop in addition to the grocer's. I was always concerned about the volume of my shopping and how heavy it might be. Often there was not a convenient place for parking and the trek with groceries was not easy, particularly in the winter. (I am no help in carrying groceries, or anything else for that matter. I always need to hold on to someone, which reduces my carrying capacity.) I found it awkward to say that I preferred a different brand than the shopper had selected. I always felt inhibited asking a friend to buy items that went against my diet: "Is there any sugar-free chocolate fudge almond ice cream?" It was as if I had asked them to deliver chocolate-flavoured rat poison.

I moved from asking my friends to paying their children to help me. This worked fairly well, but the kids were not always available when I needed them. I could not very well ask a friend's child to miss soccer practice in order to do my shopping. In any case, very few of these young assistants were enthusiastic about being perpetually available for good deeds, and it was difficult to be directive or critical of a friend's daughter's lack of enthusiasm.

I was in a constant state of anger and didn't even know it. My chronic depression was fed by my feelings of being a burden, of always having to ask for help and say thank you. I also felt that I had very little control over the intricacies of my day-to-day life.

I was seeking help for depression at the time. I was weeping and crying the blues one day about not being able to go for a walk or to do some task I had wanted to do. I felt trapped and helpless. My counsellor, who was very wise, said, "Well, why don't you do it? Hire someone to walk with you and you can do all the walking and poking about that you want." He pointed out that plenty of people were looking for work. They were prepared to rake lawns or shovel snow, so they would probably be willing to help with errands.

This was a turning point for me. I began to pay helpers to accompany me on my errands. This reduced my sense of total dependency and the feeling that I was always the one being helped. It also increased my sense of being in control in my life. What a difference! In my first move from my Cote des Neiges apartment to my little Lower Westmount house, I had relied upon my friend Carol Murphy, a doctor and mother of three, to help me pack. Her time was at a premium and often came in small chunks. For my next move, I hired kids who might otherwise be babysitting to work with me. They knew what they were getting into and could say no if they were not inclined to do it. I felt no embarrassment as I asked them to make another trip to the basement.

Another "Sink Hole"

Many people want to be helpful. Why do we want to help others? It is part of our Judeo-Christian upbringing. Help your neighbour. It also makes us feel good about ourselves. We do not think about the feelings of the person being helped; we assume that he or she will be appreciative. This is an extremely thorny issue for me. For many people, once they have decided to be helpful, they cannot be dissuaded. This approach ignores or greatly diminishes the position of the recipient.

Here is an example. I sometimes arrange to meet people at a particular spot. If this happens to be on the street close to an intersection, I am amazed at how many people will take me by the arm without a word and shepherd me across the road. They expect that I will be grateful for their good deed. It is a very awkward scene when I am not grateful and am quite cross about having been kidnapped. I have to ask to be returned to my original position. How can this be avoided? Very simply. Helpers need to ask if they can help and how.

The act of helping someone is politically complicated, especially when someone is the chronic object of good deeds. A chronic recipient can easily start to feel like a supplicant. The helper can start to feel a sense of power. In the early years of my blindness, I felt that I was at the mercy of my many helpers. This added to my sense of hopelessness and helplessness and contributed in a major way to my depression. I was fortunate in many ways. I had a certificate – my medical degree – which proved that I had a good brain. I was highly trained in helping others. (Perhaps this was why I had such difficulty becoming a recipient rather than a donor.) My friends were invaluable to me. With the exception of the very earliest months, they frequently asked me for advice or for an opinion. At first I asked why they were asking me. They made it clear to me that I still deserved respect and dignity. I go ballistic when people use that tone of voice reserved for those who need help. The words are said slowly, clearly and louder than normal, in case I am also deaf or cerebrally challenged. Invariably, I am addressed by such people as "dear."

It is, of course, so much easier to be the helper than the helped. This may be hard to believe when you are caught in the middle of a traffic jam while doing a good deed, but it is true. Know that your actions make a difference and let this be sufficient reward; if you are thanked, this will add to your good feelings. My stomach always turns when I hear the comment "She isn't even appreciative."

Perhaps the most important thing I have learned is about the nature of help: everyone needs it. No one is completely a donor or a recipient. Nothing better exemplifies this notion of interdependence of members than the inspiring work of Jean Vanier. Everyone, no matter how apparently disabled, has a unique contribution to make to the life of a healthy community. As Vanier says in his book *The Scandal of Service*:

> People with handicaps are often discouraged. For years they have been regarded as disappointments, "misfits" with little or no value. In response to these negative attitudes, they tend to lose all confidence in themselves and to see themselves as ugly and useless. They can even feel guilty for existing. In order to help them, or others who are discouraged, we need to be attentive to them, to love them and to trust in their capacity to do things. To love someone does not mean first of all to do things for that person; it means helping her to discover her own beauty, uniqueness, the light hidden in her heart and the meaning of her life. Through love a new hope is communicated to that person, and thus a desire to live and to grow. This communication of love may require words, but love is essentially communicated through non-verbal means: our attitudes, our eyes, our gestures and our smiles. (*The Scandal of Service*, Novalis ,1996, pp. 4-5)

Toronto

With a mix of great sorrow and much anticipation, I packed away 17 years' worth of belongings and memories in Montreal and moved to Toronto, where I could be closer to my family. I had kept in touch with many of my Toronto-based friends, and my entire extended family lived within a five-mile radius of each other. I wanted to play a significant role in the lives of my nieces and nephews and spend time with my cousins and their children. I was an aunt and a godmother many times over, but I was not a part of the children's everyday lives. It was time to change that.

I grossly underestimated the impact that returning to Toronto would have upon me. I presumed that because I had been born, lived and attended school in Toronto, I knew the city. I knew that Toronto had grown in to a big and busy city, but I was not apprehensive. I thought that moving back to Toronto would be like putting on an old and well-worn pair of slippers. By the time I returned in 1992 I had lived away from Toronto longer than I had lived there. Perhaps it was not so much the city that had changed, it was me.

I was young and naive when I left Toronto in 1970. My personality had not yet gelled. In Montreal, I had successfully completed medical school and had experienced the simultaneous trauma of a divorce and the loss of my sight. What I failed to realize was that although I had spoken to family members by telephone several times each week, this was very different from living 10 minutes away from 39 cousins, aunts, siblings and my widowed mother. I had learned to reorganize my life to adapt to my blindness, but I did not realize how attached I had become to my new patterns or how much they would change given my new circumstances. In short, "home" was not the "home" I had imagined. It was like moving to a new place.

The surprises were not all unpleasant. Probably the nicest surprise was getting to know my brother and sister better. When I left home to attend Queen's, David was only 11 years old. We had had very little in common in those days; the gap in our ages had made us virtual strangers. When I came back to Toronto, he was a married man with a home and two small boys. It was fascinating getting to know him and appreciate his breadth of talent. It was a nice surprise to find someone in whom I could confide and upon whom I could rely for wise and considered advice. There was also much to catch up on with my sister, Anne. I had been so busy being jealous of her freedom from physical illness that I had not allowed myself to know who she was. She, too, had changed.

She was now married, a mother of two, and was very competent in the world of business. I marvelled at how my siblings had become successful in the corporate world. I became very attached to and dependent upon both Anne and David as my Toronto years rolled along. I think I also gained some insight into how hard it must have been for them to be my brother and sister. As one calamity followed another for me, it became increasingly more difficult for them to say if they were having any problems in their lives.

Proving Myself to Myself

Working in palliative care forced me to think deeply about my highest priorities and whether my life reflected these priorities. I had been very happy with my work at the Montreal General Hospital and the palliative care unit. My colleagues were good friends and we socialized frequently. I was content with my spiritual and social life at Christ Church Cathedral. I had a nice little house and great neighbours. It all was all very positive, but it felt somewhat temporary. The political upheaval in Quebec at the time, which resulted in a mass exodus of anglophones to other parts of Canada and to the United States, aggravated this sense of uncertainty. As I said goodbye to friends at church who had decided to leave the province, I knew that I was unlikely to see any of them again. We had been friendly, but most likely not enough to stay in touch once we lived in different cities.

My dearest friends, Duncan Anderson and Carol Murphy, also decided to leave Quebec when a superb job offer came along. This was the final blow for me, since they had been among the most supportive of my doctor friends. Their departure for Vancouver underlined the fragility of my sense of professional well-being in Montreal.

With all this personal uncertainty as well as the tightening of provincial licence rulings, I decided to apply for an Ontario medical licence.

Despite my decision to leave Montreal, I worried that I could not work in a hospital where no one knew me. I had proved myself in Montreal, but would other doctors believe that a blind doctor could be a valuable asset to their staff?

I knew that there were many good general internists in every region of the country. My work with Native people was good, but such programs were rare elsewhere. The only other experience that distinguished me from the rest of the pack was my blindness, and I did not see this as a particular asset. I decided to market myself as a specialist in palliative care, a field that I loved.

Palliative remains a medical specialization that is still very much in its developing stages. In the 1990s, the leaders in the field in Canada were based in Montreal at our hospital. All the international movers and shakers in palliative care visited our unit. As I attended national and international meetings with my famous colleagues, I became well established and well known because of my association with this important centre.

In July 1992, I "followed my bliss" and moved to Toronto. Leaving Montreal was like being torn from the womb. What was worse, I did not feel a thrill at re-entering Metropolitan Toronto. I felt like a visitor. Professionally, this foray into Toronto's medical community felt disastrous. I did not know anyone at the hospital or university who could help me with my goal of setting up a palliative care practice. I missed McGill very much.

I made appointments with the various people I thought I ought to be working with. It was very embarrassing explaining my situation. Eventually, I realized that my mentor, Dr. Phil Gold, might be able to do something. With his help I gradually made strategic alliances with people who, while they could not change my situation, were in a position to support my cause with those who could.

Just when I felt that I was making no progress at all, I was offered a chance to take over an internal medicine consulting service. This was the kind of work I had done in Montreal. I would be required to do the medical consultations on patients admitted to various hospital departments. For example, I would see patients who were experiencing chest pain while in the surgery or gynecology units.

A major component of my job was to clear patients for surgery if they had medical problems such as hypertension or diabetes. No patient could be admitted to the cardiac unit, the intensive care unit or the department of medicine without my order. I spent a great deal of time in the emergency room assessing and caring for the sickest people in the hospital. If the emergency doctor asked me for a consult, the patient became my responsibility until he or she was safely delivered to the appropriate department of the hospital.

After all my years of avoiding emergency or critical units, I found myself in this extraordinary position. During my residency, I had told myself that it was more important to know what to do, than to have had the experience of doing it. Despite my most convincing arguments with myself, I had never persuaded myself that I was a good doctor. I believed initially that my friends Laurence Green and Tim Meagher had arranged a comfortable spot for me to prevent me from anything particularly challenging. Now, here I was on the front lines, dealing with sick and highly unstable patients. My capacity to remain calm under extreme stress made me a great hit in emergency. I did well and I eventually realized that I had done it myself. In the move from Montreal to Toronto I had done more than change my address. I had overcome some extraordinary hurdles and had reached an awareness of a certain unavoidable truth: despite all my doubts, I was a good doctor.

Cognitive Behaviour Therapy

I learned in a painful way that I had underestimated the emotional impact of moving from Montreal to Toronto. Somehow I had been lulled into complacency, convincing myself that going to Toronto for good would be like going to Toronto for a weekend, only longer. There was some truth to this line of thinking. I had an existing group of friends, family and a church community in Toronto. I knew the layout of the city and knew how to access information about such things as entertainment and culture. I knew the difference between Etobicoke, Mississauga and Markham. I knew the major highways into and out of the city and I knew what people meant when they talked about "cottage country."

Unfortunately, I had not accounted for my total naïveté about the medical and university infrastructure in Toronto. I had "grown up" under the McGill medical system; whenever I needed to know something, I knew exactly who to call. When I spoke to someone, they knew who I was. I knew all the porters, doormen and housekeeping staff at the hospital. All the locating operators knew me, knew I could not see and went out of their way to be helpful. I knew the phone numbers for radiology and all the labs. I did not realize how much comfort and assurance this knowledge provided until I had to start over.

When I started working in Toronto in September 1992, I walked into a hospital whose geography I did not know. I knew no one and no one knew me. Worst of all, people did not seem to be at ease with my disability. This difficult initial period happened in Montreal as well, but I seemed to have forgotten that part. Perhaps I was so focused on returning to work after losing my sight that I did not notice the awkwardness of people who were learning how to help me. I got used to grabbing the nearest arm, and my colleagues learned to walk with me. Here in Toronto, every move seemed strained. People tried to act as if they did not notice anything, while at the same time cautiously asking how they might help. It was exhausting.

To make matters worse, there had been some misunderstanding about my arrival, and the appropriate preparation for integrating a new staff member had not been done. This would have been bad enough for a regular newcomer, but it was especially difficult for a blind and somewhat anxious one. I knew that the only way to break the ice was to take charge of introductions myself. I made a point of meeting most of the medical staff individually to introduce myself and to fill in some of the background information. I had a nurse working with me; she introduced me to many of the other nurses. Although they were initially aghast at the thought of a blind doctor working in the hospital, she did a lot of PR work on my behalf. The whole experience was stressful and tiring. The administrative problems around my appointment were complicated and long lasting, and I feared there would be no resolution. For two full years I felt very uncertain of myself.

Musing about the wisdom of my move eventually led me down a familiar and disastrous path. I began to doubt myself both as a physician and as a person. I wondered if I had been a successful physician in Montreal. Maybe everyone had made exceptions to allow me to pretend that I was succeeding. Rather than thinking of myself as part of an interactive community both professionally and socially, I started to see myself as totally dependent upon everyone else. These doubts as well as the other adjustment reactions combined to tip my mental scales towards depression.

At around this same time, I experienced my first bout of coronary artery disease. My angina was not typical cardiac chest pain. Rather than sharp central chest pain with sweating, my angina took the form of indigestion and a sense of suffocated breathing. Most of the doctors I consulted felt that my symptoms were more anxiety than organic disease. The thought that my symptoms were all in my head did not help my tendency towards depression and low self-esteem. Luckily, I was referred to a doctor who did cognitive behaviour therapy. She helped cardiac patients deal with the anxiety component of their illness.

With certain reservations, I can say that cognitive behaviour therapy was very helpful to me. As time would tell, my symptoms were due to cardiac ischemia, or reduction in blood flow. Following surgery to correct blocked vessels in the heart, all my symptoms disappeared.

The cognitive behaviour therapy did not help my angina, but it did help me learn that I could control my emotions. I learned how to prevent myself from going down the path that led to feelings of hopelessness and worthlessness. Ever since losing my sight, I had experienced the sensation of waves of depression surging in my direction. I would see them in the distance and then panic, afraid of drowning. I had spent most of my therapeutic thinking-time working out that I was not a bad person for having these periods of darkness. I had worked on ways of surviving these waves but did not have the sense because I had any control over them. It was only during my last 18 months in Montreal that I had begun to learn how to take control over some of my problems. I learned that, rather than feeling depressed because I could not do my errands on Saturday mornings when my friends were busy with family responsibilities, I could take charge by hiring a student to go out with me and help me with my errands. In retrospect, this sounds obvious, even trivial, but at the time I had to learn how to become proactive in running the details of my life. I had lost that ability to take control in the process of moving to this new city and new job, and as a result spent much of my time feeling dependent, almost worthless.

The principle of cognitive behaviour therapy, at least as I understood it at the time, is that we can have a significant input into and thus control over our emotions. It is a very cerebral process and is well suited to persons who, like me, tend to be most at ease in the rational sphere. I learned the various trigger points for my dysfunctional feelings. For example, I knew that certain people or situations were very difficult for me. I analyzed what made these situations uncomfortable and then developed a strategy for coping with it. I learned to recognize certain feelings which, if left unchecked, would lead inevitably to despair, low self-esteem and depression. I also learned to observe very closely my reactions to different situations. For example, I have a tendency to allow the significance of a small event to increase in severity. Small misunderstandings can quickly grow into large misunderstandings with catastrophic outcomes. When I was not feeling well, there was no such thing as a small mistake. A small, but poor choice meant that I was stupid and clearly a poor physician. This grew into a belief that I had always made the wrong choice, that I had no clinical judgment and that I should not be doing clinical medicine or any kind of medicine. There was nothing I could do. I was worthless.

A small misunderstanding with a friend or colleague would grow into the certain knowledge that no one at work or home liked me and that I had no friends because everyone saw my many flaws. The cognitive behaviour therapist ruthlessly kept bringing me back to the details of the event that initiated this downward negative spiral. She asked me what exactly was said in the interaction. She wanted to know what the person had said that indicated low regard for my abilities. She wanted to know about my response at the time and why I chose to interpret this in such a negative light.

After analyzing each event in this way, I learned to see things quite differently. This therapy was not interested in diagnosing or treating the roots of my neuroses; it was directed at recognizing my flash points and then actively intervening to prevent myself from falling into anxiety and despair.

Although this therapy could do little for my angina, it opened up an entirely new vista for me because it required me to write about the inner workings of my reactions to various experiences. If I felt that something I had done indicated stupidity on my part, I had to write all the reasons why this would be so. Besides helping my therapeutic process, this put me back in the habit of journalling, a practice that continues to be very helpful to me today.

While it was good for my ego and my personal development, being responsible for this demanding work in the emergency room began to take a toll physically. Before long, it was clear that it was time to reduce the stress. In July 1995, after having established myself well at the University of Toronto, I started a new position with the Department of Medicine at the Toronto General Hospital. My job was to develop an academic program in palliative care. I was thrilled with this new challenge since it also meant maintaining my professional and academic links with the University. All that I had lost I had recovered. I had an academic position and an office in the hospital.

When my soul was embittered,
when I was pricked in heart,
I was stupid and ignorant;
I was like a brute beast toward you.
Nevertheless, I am continually with you;
you hold my right hand.
You guide with your counsel,
and afterward you will receive me with honour.
Whom have I in heaven but you?
And there is nothing on earth that I desire other than you.
My flesh and my heart may fail,
but God is the strength of my heart and my portion forever.

Psalm 73:21-26

Chapter 11: The Winds of Change

May 15, 1996

I arrived at the hospital early, hoping to get some catch-up work done before the day got underway. I opened the office window. My office was in an older part of the building which meant that the windows were unsealed. Fresh air and birdsong! The tree in the courtyard below attracted the small birds that lived in the downtown core. The birds thrived on bits of sandwich crusts that people left for them.

I had had a particular fondness for this little courtyard ever since I had a summer job in the labs at this same hospital following my third year at university. I wanted so much to enter medical school at that time that I was thrilled to be working in a hospital environment. I took everything in and daydreamed about what it would be like to be a doctor here. I had no idea what I would have to go through to earn the right to work here. I spent my breaks and many lunch hours in this little green space, imagining what the people in the offices were doing or studying.

It was a glorious spring day. Warm sunshine radiated through the glass onto my back as I sat at my desk working through the pile of papers that awaited me. I was filled with a great sense of well-being and contentment.

I had a number of phone calls to make; luckily, most of the people I had to phone were in their offices and answered in person. My final call was to the gynecologist at the hospital who saw me for my regular checks. I told her that while showering this morning I noticed that my left nipple had become inverted. There was a small area that felt gritty. Even though I had seen her just five months earlier and all had been fine, I wanted her to have a look. I had had multiple lumps in both breasts over the years and had been consulting a breast surgeon since I reached the age of 35. All my routine mammograms since then had been unremarkable. The lumps were related to my menstrual cycles and always disappeared as quietly as they had arrived.

"Come over right now if you like," she said. "I am doing some paper work."

Ten minutes later we were chatting in her office.

"Let's see what you have there," she said. She became more serious as I took off my shirt to reveal the source of my concern.

"How long has it been like this?" she asked.

"I am not sure, really," I answered. I had some pain in this breast last month and noticed some firmness. I was going to wait another few weeks to see how it evolved.

She asked me several questions and then sat down at her desk again.

"I think this one is beyond me, Jane. You are right, the nipple is inverted."

My training told me that this is normal for many women, but my nipples had never been inverted. We both knew that this could be an ominous sign suggesting malignancy. "I am going to call my favourite surgeon," she said. "I'll be right back."

I sat in silence, trying not to race to dramatic conclusions.

"We're in luck," she said as she breezed back into the room. "He is between cases. He said for you to come over to his office right now."

The breast surgeon's office was along the corridor from mine. Although I had not met him in the few months I had been working at the Toronto General Hospital, I knew he had a very good reputation.

Ten minutes later I was again baring my breast to one of my colleagues. He was a quiet and reserved man by nature; today I felt something ominous in his demeanour.

"How long has it been like that?" he asked.

"I have noticed a firmness and some intermittent discomfort for about three weeks, but I only noticed the nipple inversion today."

"I am going to biopsy this right now, Jane. But I must say that this is certainly malignant."

My nice, warm sense of well-being was instantly replaced by a dreadful and menacing sense.

"I will book you for a metastatic work-up before you go," he added.

"Okay," I said. "I can get my secretary to arrange it if you like."

"There is no need to wait for the pathology," he said. "We should get on to this right away."

"Yes," I said. "Time is of the essence."

"Is this the first time you have had a breast lump?" he asked me. I told him that I had had a number of them, but nothing serious. He said that he had several diabetic patients who had had multiple non-malignant lumps. He ought to write the cases up.

"I wonder what the pathophysiology would be," I said with interest. "I know that Type 1 diabetics get a lot of swelling and fibrosis in other soft tissues, resulting in different symptomatic lumps and bumps. Perhaps the pathology is similar."

"Maybe," he said as he sealed the biopsy specimen. "There is so much we don't know."

I was now fully dressed and we chatted away like colleagues.

"I will call you with the results," he said.

"Yes, thanks a lot," I said.

Passers-by in the corridor would have sworn that he and I were discussing a mutual patient.

Now What?

I had another discussion with a colleague whom I met in the hallway. Anyone observing our interaction would have described it as a perfectly normal discussion between two physicians. That conversation was to be the last one in this hospital in which I felt like a doctor.

I returned to my office and sat in my chair. Everything felt foreign. Had I ever occupied this office?

My shelves were lined with books about cancer. They were full of information telling me, the doctor, how to treat pain, shortness of breath, swelling, thrombosis and all the many medical problems that cancer patients encountered. I had many pamphlets on my shelves telling patients how to deal with the diagnosis of cancer. I had always thought that these pamphlets were excellent. Now I felt like throwing them out my open office window into the courtyard below. They seemed banal and grossly inadequate in the face of my personal crisis.

Pat, my nurse assistant, arrived with coffee and her usual enthusiasm for our work. I felt numb and stiff and not sure that I could make my mouth form the words I had to say.

"Pat, I have breast cancer."

"Oh," she said, shocked.

"What should I do?" I asked.

"I don't know," she said.

"I have to teach medical students this afternoon. Do you think I should do that?"

"I don't know," she said.

We sat there in disbelief and a very tense silence. We were used to being an effective and efficient team, accomplishing an incredible number of tasks each day. Now we were physically and emotionally paralyzed by my news.

Unable to even address the issue, I switched into an action-oriented mood.

"I have to teach the students this afternoon. Should I cancel that?"

"I don't know," she said again.

I was a tutor for a first-year medical course called Brain and Behaviour. It was a two-hour seminar; I could not imagine standing there looking and feeling professorial after hearing such terrible news. Neither did it seem appropriate to sit here at my desk in stunned silence all day. My lifelong propensity was to carry on in the face of disaster – to the detriment of my own self, my friends might say. What would a normal person do in my position? I thought. I did not know what to do next.

So I did what I always did when I found myself in a difficult position. I phoned my friend Douglas Stoute for advice.

"Douglas, I have cancer and it's really bad," I blurted out the moment he answered the phone.

"Oh," he replied after a short silence.

"I have to teach a two-hour seminar this afternoon and I don't know if I should do it."

Always wise, Doug then asked, "Have you had any lunch yet?"

"No," I said.

"Well, have some lunch and I will call you back in 15 minutes."

Pat went to get me a sandwich and more coffee. We ate lunch together in silence. True to his word, Doug called back in 15 minutes.

"Have you had something to eat?" he asked again. "Yes," I said.

"You have to take care of yourself first. I don't think you should do anything too stressful."

"Should I go home?"

I was afraid that he would say yes, but I did not want to sit alone in my apartment, frozen physically and mentally. I did not want to tell another person this horrible news. If I did not speak of it, it might never come to be. I decided to stay at the office. Doug and I agreed to meet for a drink after work.

Hello, I Am Dr. Poulson

Instinct eventually overpowered my paralysis. I called the undergraduate teaching office and rescheduled the afternoon seminar. Then I turned to Pat and said we had a lot of work to do.

We saw eight new consultations that afternoon. My inability to act had been converted into a frenetic kind of energy. I felt as if someone closely resembling me had possessed and taken over my body. My real self felt as if I were tumbling headlong into a bottomless black hole somewhere in the universe. The impostor in me walked out of my office into the main part of the hospital and carried on as if nothing had happened. I was able to have rational discussions with the various medical professionals I encountered. Despite the fact that one hour earlier I could not make a single decision myself, now I was making multiple decisions about many different patients. Douglas and I spoke several times that afternoon. I told him that I was doing well, very well indeed.

In fact, I was haunted by a very strange feeling. As I walked down the busy corridors it seemed odd to me that people did not stop to say they were sorry. I felt as if I were walking around with a giant aura that announced to one and all, "I have cancer. I used to be the doctor, now I am the patient."

My relationship with the patients I saw that day seemed different from usual. Although I talked to them as I always had, part of me wanted to say, "Hey, lady, I have it too. Please do not think that I am the doctor – I have a terrible tumour. I might well be dead before you."

I felt like a fraud presenting myself to staff and patients as a cool and confident physician.

Victoria Day Weekend 1996

Over drinks on the fateful night of May 15, 1996, Douglas persuaded me that our mutual friends John Fraser and his wife Elizabeth MacCallum ought to know of my situation. Elizabeth was in France, so Douglas called John with the news. This gave both John and Elizabeth some time to collect their thoughts before we spoke. Doug agreed that no one else needed to know until I had the confirmation call from the breast surgeon. Until then, I could hide in my interior world of magic-like thoughts, secure in the belief that none of this was happening to me.

The call came on Friday afternoon. To my surprise, the surgeon told me that the pathology report revealed that there was insufficient tissue to make a secure diagnosis.

"I must have hit an area of fibrotic tissue. Can you come by now so I can repeat the biopsy?"

I went to his office and he once again sampled the mass with a large needle.

"There," he said. "I am sure I got good tissue this time."

"You are quite certain of the diagnosis, aren't you?" I said.

"Yes, Jane, I am certain."

Douglas and John were both awaiting a phone call from me. Both were shattered that even an iota of doubt still remained. As it was the Victoria Day weekend, John invited me to join him and his three daughters at the ritual opening of their cottage at Go Home Bay. I said that I did not have the energy, but he wouldn't take no for an answer. I had a very cool reception from my mother when I told her that I was going to Georgian Bay with the Frasers.

"I thought you said Elizabeth was in France," she said.

"She is," I said. "I am going with John and the girls." There was disapproving silence on the other end of the phone, then we moved on to less controversial topics.

The weekend turned out to be just the tonic for me. The weather was glorious. My mind was completely off the topic of cancer, as it was occupied by cottage tasks, playing with the girls, and the annual Go Home Bay season opener of baseball at the Jackman's Island. We were all sad to leave on Monday.

We were on our way back to Toronto when I spontaneously started weeping. We drove the last 15 minutes in total silence. At my door, John said he would not leave me alone in this condition. We all needed showers and a change of clothing, so he took the girls home and returned for me in an hour, saying I must come down to their home at Massey College with him. Before we left my apartment, he made me throw stuffed animals at a pile of pillows until I had demonstrated a suitable amount of anger.

John wisely felt that part of my tension was the result of my decision not to tell my family. I had planned to have them all over for a drink at my apartment the following night after I had confirmation of the diagnosis. He felt that that would be too stressful; he called my brother, David, to come down to Massey right away. Half an hour later John, David and I were drinking scotch together. My brother has a very wry sense of humour. After hearing the bad news from John, he said, "Jane, Mom is going to be *so* pleased."

I thought this an odd response and asked him what he meant. He replied that she would be delighted that there was a legitimate reason for me to be away with John while Elizabeth was in France. The concept of me being so flagrantly indiscreet had ruined her weekend. We had a good laugh about that and then returned to the matter at hand. Both John and David felt it would be better if David told Mom and Anne without me being present. I agreed to this plan as I did not feel up to handling their emotional responses.

Treatment

For some strange reason, I thought that because I had spent so much of my professional time working in oncology clinics, I knew what cancer patients went through. How could I be so wrong? Viewing the entire cancer experience from the vantage point of patient rather than physician was a phenomenal experience. Had I not been so totally turned inside out, I might have said how interesting and educational it was. It took every ounce of physical, emotional and spiritual strength I possessed to come out on the other side intact.

My tumour turned out to be inoperable at this stage, so the plan was to do six rounds of chemotherapy first. How many times had I told chemotherapy patients about the new marvel drugs against nausea and vomiting? Why, then, did I feel so anxious in the waiting room? I felt nauseated already and I had not even started. I was terribly unwell on chemo. Each round severely affected my bone marrow. My white cells, responsible for fighting infection, fell rapidly to zero. Levels less than 500 put one at risk of serious infection. I was admitted with each infusion for treatment of fevers and low white cell counts. The longstanding diabetes made me prone to infection. One of the medications against nausea, a corticosteroid called dexamethasone, has as one of its side effects high blood sugars. Diabetics are advised to avoid this drug, but we had no option. I had to adjust my insulin to try to control my sugars. My doctor told me that they never saw patients with both Type 1 diabetes and breast cancer. There were no guidelines about how to deal with diabetes when the body was under attack from all sides. For over 20 years I had tested my blood sugars at least twice and injected insulin four times every day. This strict regimen had kept my sugar levels relatively normal. Now it appeared that I had gone to all that trouble only to survive long enough to develop premature breast cancer.

My entire existence was taken up with the treatments. My days were no longer called Monday, Tuesday or Friday, but chemo day 1, 5 or 8. Each day was medically significant and contained a different combination of pills or injections. Being blind did not make this process any easier, but I felt that I knew more about these meds than most other people and reserved the right to administer them myself.

At first, I thought I might be able to continue with my work, but I decided to withdraw from all of my clinical work while undergoing treatment. It did not make sense to me to be involved with patients who were suffering pain and other serious complications from the very disease I was fighting. I wanted to ensure that I had everything going for me. I did not think it helpful to see every day what could very soon be happening to me. I did continue going to the hospital to write, however. Eventually, I had to acknowledge that it was taking me hours to accomplish what would normally take minutes. Nevertheless, I finished many of my research projects and in 1998, I had six professional publications.

As my energy fell I was plagued by infection. I had great difficulty concentrating. I found that I was living in a smaller and smaller world. It often seemed that there was nothing more important happening than the decline of my white cells and the rising of my temperature. I tried to listen to the world news, but found it hard to engage in any normal activities. I have great respect for women who must continue caring for families or working to earn income when they are in cancer treatment. Fortunately, I had disability insurance, which gave me income and covered the cost of my medications and my many admissions. I am grateful that I have been able to direct all my energy to healing.

Following my fifth injections, I developed severe infections. I was seriously anemic and required transfusions of both packed red cells and platelets. The tumour was apparently quite resistant to the treatments as it had shrunk very little. My doctor decided to discontinue chemotherapy and go to surgery.

Doris

While I was working in the palliative care unit at the Royal Victoria Hospital in Montreal, I had a patient who confused me. She was a bright, intellectual and well-educated woman and she spoke clearly about a number of different issues. This patient had been admitted because of generalized failure from a lung tumour that had spread to her liver. As I was going through her admission history and work-up, she told me that she had been well until she got her "jujubes." She was francophone; I thought she was using vocabulary I didn't know so I asked her for more information. She described very clearly the metastatic disease in her liver. It became apparent that she could not say the words "cancer" or "metastases," although she knew what they meant in terms of her mortality. I spoke of her disease; she asked me to refer only to her "jujubes." I have always tried to provide patient-centred care, so we spoke only of "jujubes" until her death a few weeks later. Several days before her death, she told me that it was her "jujubes" that were killing her; I could only agree with her.

I finally understood in May 1996, when I faced my own tumour, her need to distance herself from hers. My breast cancer was of the inflammatory type. This means a rapid onset, with little warning. The entire breast is involved and becomes enlarged, red and hot. I found it disgusting. My friend Paul Geraghty immediately suggested that we name it Doris. It seemed like a good idea to me; indeed, this strategy carried me through the next six months. Inflammatory tumours cannot be removed until they are treated with chemotherapy. This meant that Doris and I had to co-exist until October, when the mastectomy would be performed.

My friends were very much involved in my chemotherapy and entire cancer experience. They were all familiar with Doris and spoke of her often. It was much easier for them to speak about Doris than to ask if my breast mass was shrinking. Doris gave us all a focus upon which we could direct our entire wrath.

Doris also helped with chemotherapy. I had to take five tablets of cyclophosphamide, a medicine which made my stomach feel queasy, for 14 days. As I complained to the person who was counting out my pills that they were poisoning me, the answer invariably was, "No, we are poisoning Doris." Strangely, this was a very comforting thought.

Doris also helped me prepare for the surgery. I thought at length about the upcoming traumatic detachment of a very special part of my body. I found images of a single-breasted body very distasteful and tearfully wondered what they would do with the breast after removing it. I had worked in the Pathology Lab as a young summer student, but I could not remember what we did with surgical specimens after they had been processed. I conjured up dreadful images of my precious breast being tossed into a green garbage bag along with the rest of the day's discarded tissues.

I had never particularly loved my body because of gross mental and emotional distortions brought on by the diabetes, but suddenly I began having mixed feelings about having ignored my physical self. I had never thought of myself as a sexual woman. In fact, my damaged self-image dictated that I was repulsive to men. If that had been true when I had two perfectly sound and nicely shaped breasts, what now? It was very disturbing to think of myself becoming the repulsive and disgusting person I had always presumed myself to be. Left unchecked, I found myself feeling guilty and neglectful of my body, as if I ought to apologize to my body and particularly my breast for never having acknowledged it. Fortunately, these severe self-reprimands were infrequent and did not last long.

I turned my thoughts to Doris. Rather than losing a precious body part, I was performing the ultimate attack upon her, cutting her away and discarding her in some waste disposal, which she richly deserved.

My Private Chernobyl

The surgery was fine, I suppose – as fine as any procedure that results in the removal of a breast could be. I have mainly blocked it out of my mind. Despite all my medical training I was shocked at the extent of the incision. I had been told it would be about six to eight inches. The wound extended from mid-sternum to the lateral edge of my underarm: 72 steel staples were required to close it. Only two things stand out in my memory. First, a young and inexperienced resident removed the dressing on post-op day two.

"Oh, it looks great," he proclaimed proudly.

"I am sure," I muttered sourly.

"No," he said, "it's amazing. It's beautiful."

"Right," I said. "Thank you." Then I turned away.

The other remarkable thing about the operation was the pathology report. They had had quite a difficult time with the surgery. There was a lot of tumour that had not responded to the chemotherapy, and there were a large number of nodes, with extensive local involvement. The news could not have been worse. I was recommended for urgent and extensive radiation therapy to the area.

For reasons I still do not completely understand, I developed a pathological fear of radiation. As fourth-year undergraduate students we spent enough time in labs to require us to wear tags so our lab coats could record our exposure to radiation. We had catchy posters warning about the use of radioactive materials. This was during the Cold War era, and the fear of radiation was not limited to lab students. As I willingly climbed into the linear accelerator to be blasted, I thought about my little radiation tag from long ago and wondered what it would register for me after this event.

I hated radiation, although no one would ever have known it. In my usual fashion, I overcompensated and appeared calm and relaxed. I required 35 treatments – five days a week for seven weeks. This seemed a little odd as I had been told that I was only expected to live for about three months anyway. Did they not think there was anything else I would rather be doing with my precious time?

Is That All There Is?

January 4, 1997, had been circled on my calendar for many weeks. This was to be my first day without treatment in over eight months. Rather than the great surge of energy and release I had expected, I awoke with a strange sense of emptiness and loneliness. For months, my main outing of the day had been a trip to Princess Margaret Hospital. This morning I rose and ate breakfast before taking my first rest. Then I bathed and rested again. Dressing was another great task for the day. Now what was I going to do? Through the treatment period, I had mourned for all the activities I was missing. It was time to get cracking again. Because my treatments took place close to the Christmas holiday, I had not seen my doctor for nearly 10 days. Marg, my nurse in the chemo clinic, often called to see how I was doing between my injections. I had not been speaking with her during radiation. Perhaps I should call her. I felt as if someone official ought to know that the treatments were over and that I would not be back to the hospital for three months. This odd state of mind persisted for many days. My "old" life had been completely supplanted by the rigours of therapy. I did not know where to begin picking up the pieces.

I was grateful for my many years of introspection and my ability to listen to my innermost being and to address my troubled soul. I felt like a radically different person. I had presumed that all would return to "normal" after the treatments were over; I had expected to feel tired but not to feel so unsettled. I felt very vulnerable.

I had convinced myself that no tumour could get me as long as I went to the hospital every day. While undergoing treatment, I had not felt especially dependent on the hospital personnel. Everyone had always been kind and pleasant and I had felt that I was part of the team whose common goal was to viciously attack my tumour and eliminate it completely and forever. Now that phase was behind me and suddenly I felt abandoned, as if I was standing alone in a large arena, waiting to be shot. I feared that there was an assassin out there lining me up in the viewfinder. I knew I should not stand there and make his job simple, but I had nowhere to run. Any move might reveal an unprotected flank.

It was a strange time. I had crossed the great divide between the philosophical knowledge that one day I would die and the practical understanding that my time might be very soon. This awareness was not all bad. My days now felt finite, and I was aware that each moment spent must be spent well. A note in my diary captures this sense of urgency:

My challenge is to move forward to fully claim the days which would still be mine. Without realizing it, I had begun to seek the Holy Grail. I am searching for thoughts and activities that have meaning for me now. All my former activities seem like frivolous pastimes. I must leave them all behind and focus my time and energy upon accomplishing whatever it was that I was always supposed to do with my life. I am frustrated, discouraged and depressed that I cannot discern what this might be. My body is exhausted and is begging me for time to rest and recuperate, but there is no time to waste simply recovering.

Old behaviour patterns did not help. Ever the one to orchestrate things, I had mentally planned for my physical and emotional recovery. I thought that six weeks of rest and relaxation with progressive increases in activity ought to do it. I was in deep despair at how far I was falling behind in my plan. In fact, it seemed that the harder I tried to legislate my recovery, the slower it went. I was sure that once I had achieved a certain level of activity, I ought to be able to achieve at least as much, if not more, the next day. It was not until I let go of the notion that I could legislate and ordain my recovery that I began to get better. I had to learn to listen to and respect my body. If I felt tired, I had to rest. If I was still tired, I had to take it easy for that day and perhaps the next day as well. I had a finite store of energy. When it was gone, it was gone. I could no longer run on "empty" for days at a time as I had done before the cancer.

I learned a lot about myself during those days of recovery. For one thing, I learned the importance of creating a healing environment. I had always scoffed at things like aromatherapy, but when I surrounded myself with delicious fragrances, fresh flowers and good music, I found myself healing. I gradually learned to live much less in my head and much more in my body. Even though I could not explain it medically, it helped.

The Doctor's Special Gadget: The Retrospectoscope

Ironically, it was not until I developed cancer in 1996 that I began to appreciate all I had accomplished since losing my eyesight in 1980. For more than 15 years I had laboured thinking I was slow and inefficient. I never looked at what I had accomplished; I thought of what I would be doing if I could see. I always compared myself to my sighted colleagues.

Chemotherapy made me very, very sick. I experienced a fatigue unlike any other I had ever known. This fatigue affected not only my body, but also my mind and spirit. My whole life seemed to be turned upside down by this fatigue. I had no will to do anything. It was this feeling that made me realize how remarkable my life had been before the cancer. Now that I had no energy at all, I saw how much it had taken to run my regular life. It had taken a lot of mental energy to organize my entire world. I had a computer in my brain with masses of information stored methodically, ready for instant retrieval. I did not have access to things like a notebook or telephone book. So, I memorized addresses, office numbers, phone numbers and a million other bits of information. I carried a schedule in my head of all my meetings, clinics, lectures or other obligations. I always had with me all the information I needed. I had taken this habit for granted, ignoring the fact that each step took energy and concentration. Following the diagnosis of cancer and chemotherapy, I totally lost the capacity to record, retain or recover anything in my head. I did have them recorded on my laptop computer, but it was never where I was. It seemed like too much effort to find the computer, turn it on and retrieve the information.

In order to know where things were, I had always worked hard to keep everything in its place. During treatments for cancer I did not have enough energy to stay organized. I put things down wherever I was. I did not even have the energy to remember where I had left things.

Throughout the months of treatment and for a long time afterwards, I could never find anything I wanted. It did not even help to have someone put things away for me, as they did not know exactly where things belonged. My life was misery, but I did not have the strength to remedy it. Only then did I begin to give myself credit for the extraordinary job I had done since losing my vision. I had been managing my private practice, teaching at the university, running a four-bedroom house and living a life. It amazed me that I had been able to do the medical residency. I must have had the energy of three people! Despite my current malaise, I was able to take the time to be impressed with my accomplishments of the preceding 15 years of work.

It's Hard to Kill Me

"Jane, the pathology report is dreadful. In spite of the surgery and the chemo, it is dreadful, dreadful, dreadful."

I felt as if I had been zapped with a Star Wars-type stun gun. Why was the doctor saying this to me? This could not be my pathology report he was talking about. The full horror then struck. "You will be very, very sick in three months and dead in six," he said.

I was only 44. I was starting to enjoy the fruits of earlier labours. I was in my prime and thoroughly enjoying both my professional and my personal life. I was looking forward to watching many of my projects develop. The chemo had made me extremely sick. How could the cancer still be alive in me and intent on killing me so swiftly?

When I had been diagnosed with cancer six months earlier, I was devastated at having to interrupt all my activities and put my entire life on hold. Within a two-week period, I had gone from being the chief executive officer of my life, making decisions about how and when to tackle issues, into a captive who was completely in the power of this disease. Perhaps in order to retain some sort of sense that I still had input into my life, if not control over it, I negotiated with the dark forces that had taken over. I agreed to give the disease six or nine months or however long it took to treat it and eliminate it from my life. Then, when treatment was over, I would return to my work, my life and self-determination.

Now, this felt like some kind of bad joke. If I were to believe my doctor, I would never return to my work and my precious projects. I would only have enough time to tie up some loose ends before I would become very ill and then die.

This swift and cruel death sentence, issued on October 30, 1996, had a profound impact upon my life. I have not lived in the same space since that moment. As it happens, I was with Paul Geraghty when I heard the terrible news. We turned to each other and did not know what to say. We sat in silence in the office for some time. We knew we needed to leave, but neither of us knew where to go. I held his arm very tightly as we walked through the waiting room area. I felt as if all eyes were on me. It was only mid-morning, so going for a drink was not a good option. We had already overdosed on clinic coffee. Instead, we found ourselves once more being drawn to the home of our loyal friends, Elizabeth MacCallum and John Fraser. Their reaction was very similar to my own: "How could this be happening?" We cried, ranted and raved, swore and – surprisingly – laughed together. We picked at lunch until we admitted that none of us was hungry. Eventually Paul and I returned to my home, exhausted by the emotions of the day.

I had invited a number of friends to visit me that weekend. Instead of celebrating together, we supported each other through the dreadful news. During the 72 hours of their visit, I experienced the support of my friends in a new way. For the first time in my life I felt unable to stand alone. I turned myself over to the love and affection of many people who had been integral parts of my life. We shared old experiences, recounting endless tales of adventure, misadventure and tightly interwoven lives. It was enormously satisfying to me to be able to bathe in the love of these friends. My life had been very rich and full, connected to so many others in so many ways. This affirmation remains one of the most satisfying in my entire life.

The high of those few days gradually wore off and grim thoughts and feelings took hold once again. I found it impossible to tell my family about how much time I had left. I told them the results of the treatments so far had been extremely disappointing, but no one could predict the future. I felt a sense of urgency inside me, as if a great hourglass had been turned over in the doctor's office that day and each second that passed was now extremely important. I was living with an intensity I had never known before. Twenty-four weeks sounded better than six months to me. Despite my attempts to convince myself that D-Day was still far off, I had never known time to pass so quickly.

It was hard to live a regular life in that period. I kept waiting to become ill. Where would it start? Lungs? Abdomen? Brain? Having treated many patients with this disease, I kept debating with myself which would be the preferable sites for metastatic disease. None seemed acceptable. Then I had to face the harsh reality that I had no control over the course of the disease. My body was being invaded and I was powerless to prevent the ensuing destruction. I found myself bargaining hopefully. "I hope I will be well enough to attend this or that function. After all, it will be for the last time." To my great delight, my attempt at bargaining seemed to be working. I made it to all the events I wanted, and still no sickness appeared. After I had lived through 18 of my 24 weeks, I began to reconsider the Caribbean trip I had cancelled when the countdown began. I doubted that I would become unbearably ill over the next 21 days, so Paul and I flew off to Aruba, a place we knew well, and had, under the circumstances, a very enjoyable holiday.

When I awoke on April 30, 1997, six months to the day after the initial prognosis, I wondered if I would die that day. Superstitious, I kept myself out of harm's way. I moved into a new phase of my life at this point. It was clear that the doctor's prediction was wrong: I had rushed around for six months writing my will, writing letters to my nieces and nephews and tying up loose ends, and here I was still alive. What should I do with the rest of my life?

As it turned out, the next chunk of my life was to be taken up with a different set of health concerns that no one would have expected. I had been having chest pain and shortness of breath and had now developed an abnormal cardiogram. I discussed this with my cardiologist. He thought that since I had been issued a death warrant already, there was no point investigating my cardiac status. Stunned by his approach, at first I agreed to do nothing. On the way home from that appointment, I discussed the situation with my friend Ann Dillon, who was outraged. I showed no signs of becoming ill again with cancer. I was very much alive and was only 45 years old. I began to reason with myself: I had gone through all that chemo, surgery and radiation because I wanted to live. Was I going to sit there and let myself die of heart disease? I had armed myself mentally, physically and emotionally to fight dying from cancer. Now, I had to extend that notion to include dying of any cause.

Tests revealed that I had blocked arteries. Three angioplasties (procedures that attempt to open blocked arteries using a small balloon catheter) were done over the next four months. Each was temporarily successful, but eventually the pains returned. For a time, all thoughts of cancer were gone from my head. They were replaced by terror of sudden cardiac death. I entered a period of inexplicable paradox. For months I had been dreading a slow demise with pain, shortness of breath and gradual loss of independent functioning. Now, I was afraid of dropping dead from cardiac arrhythmia.

Open-heart surgery became the only life-saving option. Less than a year after my breast surgery, I underwent an emergency bypass.

Recovery was somewhat slow as I was in a diminished physical state going into the operation. By February 1998, however, I had recovered from the heart surgery and showed no signs of succumbing to my cancer. You might think I would be elated in such circumstances. Indeed, I was very pleased to be alive and relatively well, but this pleasure was mixed with a strange sense of uncertainty. How do you live in a space and time you had thought to be impossible? My early days of living with supposedly certain and imminent death had been very surreal. Even small decisions seemed to be affected by my news. Should I buy a new winter coat? It seemed silly if this would be my last winter and I was going to be quite sick. I did not seem to need a new party dress. I could wear the old one once again. Fortunately, I reasoned that all I had to lose was some money, which I would not need after I was dead. I bought both a new coat and a new dress and felt fabulous wearing them. I kept my hair short so the agony of losing it would be less if I needed chemotherapy again.

Now my considerations took on more significance. What was the best way to spend a precious period of being alive? People asked when I would return to work. Everyone seemed to assume that this was the obvious next step for me. I suppose this thought was also comforting for them: if I slipped back into my previous patterns, people could put my cancer behind them. It had been a terrible time, but now everything was back to normal.

This assumption that I would return to work caused me great distress. It did not feel right for me. While I was pleased that physically I appeared to all as "the old Jane," I knew that I had been irretrievably altered within. I had a completely new perspective on what was important in my life. I had less energy than before the illnesses and felt the need to protect it very jealously. I wanted to spend my time and energy on activities that were deeply meaningful for me. I had missed a lot along the way pursuing a medical career. Now I wanted to read the books on my "to read" list. I wanted to listen to music and pursue other interests. I felt that life is a series of phases. Different things are important at different times. When illness struck I was in a career development phase, spending a disproportionate amount of my energy practising medicine and teaching at the university. Should I continue to pursue my professional life because I was still young and my peers were in the prime of their careers? Should I return to practice because this would satisfy so many other people? I was riddled with conflicting thoughts, but I was certain that if I knew I would be dead within the next two years, there were many things I wanted to do first. I did not have the time or inclination to waste a single second pursuing a career that would never be.

Eventually, I concluded that I was living in a very special time and space. Although the doctors maintained that my future looked short and bleak, no one can know the future. All I could know was the present. I would direct all my energy to engaging my present life most fully. I wanted to write, read, pursue my love of music and gorge myself on being with all my dear nieces and nephews. If I was to die soon, I wanted them to remember me as the auntie who went to the park and played with them, not their auntie who, although she was a doctor, was ill much of the time.

I believe that my decision contributed greatly to my survival. I have adopted an entirely new lifestyle. I am more attuned with my body. If I am tired, I sleep. I make time each day to exercise. I spend my days doing things that seem to be a good idea at the time. No longer am I driven by the clock or by a full schedule. I am more relaxed and rested than I have ever been before. I had expected to be dead in the spring of 1997; in the years that have followed, many people have told me that I have never looked better. I have not given up my academic career. I have written a number of published articles reflecting upon my experiences and this phase of my life. My energy and activity are more closely aligned and I feel as if I am working with rather than against myself.

I am grateful for this period of grace in my life. Had I never encountered cancer I would have kept pursuing my old, not so healthy lifestyle. I am not happy to have cancer, but I am proud of myself for using a terrible turn of events for something worthwhile. If this period of grace is extended much longer, I will consider activities that call on my professional training a little more. In the meantime, in an act of gleeful defiance, I am growing my hair long again.

A Creature of the Universe

My understanding of what it means to be alive deepened significantly in the spring and summer of 1998. Since becoming so ill in the spring of 1996, I had developed a secret fear of venturing any distance from my hospital in Toronto. I lived with a constant sense of impending doom. I was anxious even when visiting the cottages of friends in the Muskoka and Georgian Bay regions two hours' drive from Toronto. By the spring of 1998, I had had a six-month stretch without serious illness. I felt well enough to dare to expand my geographic surroundings. I decided that if I did not travel now, I might never get to go on several journeys I longed to make.

With some minor anxiety I set off for France with my friend Tom Fitches. We were headed for Milhars, a charming town in the southwestern part of the country, where Elizabeth MacCallum and John Fraser have a small house nestled in the hills. Tom had taken a sabbatical there the previous year and had made many friends in the area. Elizabeth was set to join us after a trip to Finland with John, who would meet up with us for four days.

Tom is an extremely talented organist. While in France the previous year, he had met some fine musicians in the Toulouse region. During our holiday, we toured the cathedrals and churches. The friends that Tom had made the year before offered us grand hospitality. We were shown many of the finest organs in France and treated to magnificent recitals as Tom and his friends played new pieces to each other. We learned the histories of these instruments, some of which were over 500 years old, and heard about musicians who had once played them. The churches themselves were incredible. I learned that some were built in a Romanesque style while others represented Gothic architecture. The buttresses were different shapes; engineering knowledge had progressed over the decades and centuries, allowing differing structure and design.

We visited churches in small villages. As we climbed the stairs, I could feel deep depressions in the steps that had been created by the streams of people who had come to worship or to drink in the beauty of this place I was visiting that day.

I was deeply moved by the concept of generations of people passing through sites of spectacular beauty. Their lives had all progressed towards an inexorable end, but still the world and life on earth remained. I identified strongly with the people who, over the centuries, had stood on this very spot.

I was particularly moved one afternoon as we visited the town of Varen and spent time in a little chapel that was built by Benedictine monks a thousand years ago. Many people were buried in tombs under the floor. Centuries of people walking upon these floors had rendered the lettering on the stone slabs difficult to interpret. We sat and prayed in the choir stalls. The energy of the souls of the persons who had prayed as I did was almost palpable. I had never felt so much one with the stream of creation as I did that afternoon. Death no longer seemed like a monster to be feared and avoided. I realized that, until this trip to France, I had been viewing my own death as a disaster specifically directed at me. My passing felt like a huge personal blow. The comfort I felt from knowing that the cycle of life had been going on for thousands and thousands of centuries was powerful and overwhelming. It gave me a great sense of peace.

The French countryside was scattered with crosses and castles marking points of historical relevance. I learned that some of these crosses were the result of Holy Wars we had studied in high school history classes. Being in the spot where these wars had been fought was an incredible experience. The spirits of those who had engaged in warfare were embodied for me. Their battles were not worthless, nor was the memory of their existence minimal.

My time in this ancient part of France was not entirely dedicated to metaphysical speculation. We also laughed and had much fun drinking local wines and eating delicious French breads and cheeses. Encountering the profound significance of being a creature of the universe allowed me to revel in an enhanced enjoyment of each moment. I no longer felt that I was an endangered species on the verge of annihilation, but one of God's creatures enjoying the riches of the present moment.

My sensibilities were heightened by my trip to France. Following my return home, I went walking in a forest park near Caledon, Ontario. One of my "sacred" places there as a child was a waterfall and gorge deep in the forest. I had found it difficult to go back to this spot since losing my eyesight. I knew intimately the beauty I would be denied seeing. But when some old friends from my Montreal days came to visit, I suggested a walk through this forest on a rainy afternoon. The parks department had created excellent walking paths through the forest, which made the going much easier. As we stood by the gorge at the cataract, one of my friends read aloud a plaque that had been placed there. It described the different rock formations that could be seen in the walls of the gorge, and the various phases this place had gone through over four million years. I was overcome by the thought of all the life that had lived and evolved here. I felt at one with a universe that had existed for much longer than I could imagine.

This experience gave me great comfort. I realized how minute one person's lifetime is in the overall schema of time. I had been in despair because it appeared that my time on earth would be shortened by 30 or 40 years. It had seemed that I was being denied half my life. Now I was beginning to understand that each person's life is merely a speck of sand in the desert. Thirty or 40 years of my life cycle was miniscule. What was important was the present moment and what I did with whatever time was to be mine. All that was certain was the past and the very present. I had used my time well. I felt comforted by thinking of all the relationships I had known, enjoyed and continued to nurture in my life so far.

Since my illness began in May 1996, I had gained an intense appreciation for each day of life. My engagement in all aspects of being alive was much more intense. Now I realized that I had gradually shifted my focus to all that I had known and currently knew rather than to all I might never know. Each person has but a very brief time on earth. Now is the time to revel in that. Now is the time to live in such a way that your presence is significant for the people who share this moment on earth with you.

When I went to England later that summer, I was deeply affected by the knowledge that Windsor Castle had first been built by William the Conqueror nearly a thousand years earlier. The kings and queens of England, although they were no longer physically present, were part of the cycle of the universe. During their time they had stood upon the land, breathed the air and drunk the water as I was doing now during my time in that place. Their bodies had died, as would mine, but the thought of death was less terrifying to me now. It was comforting to know that the universe is constantly changing and eternal. My life cycle felt like a tiny part of a much greater whole.

A House of Cards?

As I walk barefoot on the cool lawn and the sun shines warmly upon my face, I can imagine myself a part of creation and the cycle of life. This grass will wither and become cold and brown. It will be replaced in the springtime by tender green shoots, which will flourish and then die. This cycle of flourishing and then fading away is the natural order of the universe. If we believe Christian dogma, we know that the fading away is not into oblivion but rather into paradise. The book of Revelation describes well what lies ahead for us. All tears shall be dried.

Just as I think that I am firmly held in the fabric of this fantastic promise, I am thrown into the practicalities of life. I sit with a dying friend saying the Lord's Prayer and reciting beautiful psalms hinting at the wonders of paradise. Surely those who die young are the lucky ones. Why do I not find myself wishing that I could change places with my friend? Four days later at his funeral, he seems very dead and absent from us. Notions of paradise are far from my mind. Rather than being comforted by seeing his children as fresh green shoots replacing their withered father, I see sadness, despair and separation.

I struggle with the paradoxical situation of these conflicting images. At times, I am sustained by the belief that I am another tiny part of creation that is participating in the natural cycle of life and the universe. Now I am flourishing. When it is my time I too will wither and die, moving into the next phase of my journey. The smaller I can imagine myself, the more comforting this image becomes. At other times I find myself sitting in the shadow of death. It is cold and damp. Staying alive seems to be the most important thing. I rage against the thought of a stranger taking over my apartment, painting over my carefully chosen colours. Who could care for my little pet dog as I have done? I think of all the parties that will take place without me. I run as fast as I can to escape from the natural cycle of life.

Listening to the Ones Who Know

My survival has been nothing short of a miracle. When I was given a prognosis of three to six months in October 1996, I directed all my energy and attention towards getting better. I became aware of the vitality within me and focused on nurturing and strengthening this quiet but mighty feeling within my core.

I arranged for a long-term disability leave to lessen the fatigue of working and the stress of political strife in the hospital. I arranged to have massage therapy every week and surrounded myself with nice smells and soothing music. I read about many concepts to strengthen my immune system. I meditated and did imagery work and yoga. A scientist by nature and training, I found it hard to imagine how these mind–body practices could significantly influence my health, but I was superstitious enough to continue them.

At first I was busy preparing myself to die quickly. Then, having survived longer than my allotted six months, I began worrying about chest pain. I worked on regaining my health for a full nine months before achieving cardiac stability and resolving complications following the heart surgery. Then I could focus on my remaining breast.

It had always been rather fibrous and bumpy, but one area now felt different to me. Bumps usually came and went in my breasts; this one seemed to remain. Perhaps it was different because the first round of chemotherapy had wiped out my ovaries and I was no longer having cycling estrogen levels. I had had three new bumps in this breast and had had fluid aspirated from them to test for cancer. They had all been benign cysts. I had also had two ultrasound examinations. I saw the surgeon every six months, and the medical and radiation therapist regularly. I had pointed out this area to each of them. They had not been concerned about my "bump," as I called it. My gynecologist also reassured me that she felt nothing abnormal. My mammograms were negative. Still, I fussed about this breast.

In December 1998, when I visited the oncology clinic for a routine check-up, I was examined by a British breast surgeon who was spending a year with my oncologist at Princess Margaret Hospital. I showed her my "bump." She said that while it was a little prominent, it felt normal to her. I began to cry and said I felt that the area had been increasing in size for some time. She asked my surgeon to reassess the area. He told me it was still fine, but agreed to attempt an aspiration in the event that I was feeling a small cyst. But there was no cyst.

The biopsy had not been completely normal, however. I pulled up the result on the computer and found that there were some atypical cells, so I phoned the surgeon to ask how to interpret this finding. He checked that my recent mammogram had been normal (it had been) and ordered another mammogram as well as an ultrasound to be sure.

"Why are you having an ultrasound?" asked the radiologist when I arrived for my appointment. "Your mammograms are all negative. We will do it anyway, though, if you think you feel something."

His comments seemed patronizing. Several moments later, however, he had changed his tune. To his amazement he had found a worrisome area exactly where I had indicated. He was so concerned that he did a biopsy of the region right away.

"It feels gritty," he said. This, I knew, was a code word for cancer.

Three days later I began harassing my surgeon for results. He called me late Thursday afternoon. "Jane, this is not the sort of conversation I like having over the telephone. You are going to be very angry with me. There are malignant cells on that biopsy. I think that we should go ahead with another mastectomy since we cannot rely on mammograms to detect a problem. When will we learn to listen to the ones who know?"

I was reminded of the words of a radiologist at McGill. "Jane, I hope you never get breast cancer," she had said as she reviewed my films. "If you do, we will never see it on a mammogram."

I underwent a second mastectomy 10 days later. Perhaps because of the passage of time, or a different mental space, or trauma from all that I had been through since the appearance of Doris, the same coping strategies were not as effective two years later. This tumour, which I baptized Ethel, hit the waste deposit less than two weeks after her discovery, so she did not survive long enough to develop into a character I hated. I was feeling downtrodden and in despair at the thought of having to endure the whole treatment again. I offered up Ethel and the breast she had chosen to live in.

The surgery was straightforward, but afterwards fluid continued to collect in the underarm area. For eight weeks I had to attend clinic for aspiration of the area. My oncology doctor was keen that we start chemotherapy as quickly as possible. I took 10 days to recover and then began another course of chemo less than three years after the first round.

The second chemotherapy treatment was new and reportedly was much less toxic than the original medications. My bone marrow was not impressed. From the first injection, I had strong negative reactions to the therapy. My hair all fell out again and my blood cells dropped out almost to the point of extinction. I had repeated fevers and admission to the hospital for antibiotics. About halfway through the chemo I began concurrent radiation therapy. By the end of radiation, I felt as if I were dying. I begged them to stop the radiation. My doctor said that he thought it unlikely that it was the radiation making me feel so sick. I began to spike high fevers and was re-admitted to the hospital with severe pneumonia. Upon discharge I felt worse than I had ever felt in my life. Weak and battered, I returned home to begin the long road to recovery. At first, I could barely walk for half a block. Friends and helpers came every day to walk with me. Gradually I was able to walk for longer. It was a marvellous feeling to breathe freely again.

Beethoven, the Deaf Composer

One of the toxic effects of my second chemo was nerve damage. While in the hospital with pneumonia, I had complained of some subtle but worrisome numbness in my hands. A major complication of diabetes is neuropathy or nerve damage, so it was not clear how much of my current complaint was due to diabetes and how much to chemo. As the symptoms were quite mild, we elected to carry on with a reduced dose. The surgery had shown a large tumour with seven positive axillary nodes. The prognosis was very poor.

I was concerned about my nerves, especially those in my left arm. I was sent to see a neurologist who specialized in oncology. He was worried about me receiving more neurotoxic therapy, so we elected to put the chemo on hold and expected my symptoms to decrease. The numbness in my feet and right hand decreased, but to my dismay, problems developed in my left hand. Soon my entire arm became weak; within three weeks I lost all the strength in that arm. I could not feed, bathe or dress myself. My doctors unanimously diagnosed recurrence of the original tumour. Extensive examinations were done but no tumour could be seen. We sat back and awaited the tumour's physical presentation. This was devastating for me. The combination of blindness and paralysis posed a serious threat to my independence. My hands were a major source of sensory input for me and I had depended greatly upon my left arm. I had to arrange for much more assistance at home. I was not able to safely care for myself.

My options for entertainment became severely limited. My greatest source of satisfaction had been playing the piano. Following the cardiac surgery I had bought a beautiful mahogany grand piano with lovely tone. Now that I could use only one hand, the piano was silenced. I also loved writing on my computer, which I had upgraded six months earlier so that I could use the Internet and e-mail. All my addresses and phone numbers were filed there. But once again I was cut off.

The paralyzed left arm pushed me to new lows emotionally. I struggled with a response to this disaster. Part of me was praying for enough creativity to come up with solutions to the different problems, but the cogs on my overworked creativity and adaptation machinery had been worn flat by years of excessive challenge. I was angry. Surely I had been creative enough throughout my adult life. Why should I have to adapt once again? As a result of the trouble with my left arm, I had stopped writing the story of my life. There were many things yet to be recorded, but I saw the opportunity to complete the work slipping away. I knew I would not be able to die with a sense of satisfaction until this document was complete. Eventually I had to come back to the notion of creativity and adaptation. If Beethoven could adapt himself to composing music after becoming deaf, I could come up with a way of playing the piano and typing with one hand.

Slowly and painfully I learned to type with only one hand and had one of my helpers attached small buttons (the kind that you sew on clothing) to certain computer keys that I would use with my left hand. I continued to write this book using only one hand. I worked out new ways to play the piano with only one hand. As I regained some use of my left hand, I learned to play bass accompaniment with one finger.

In November 1999, I had an unusual encounter with a new doctor, a neurologist, who examined my arm and declared that the problem was not related to cancer at all. She diagnosed it as an aberrant form of Guillain-Barré Syndrome, an auto-immune syndrome in which it is presumed that the body makes antibodies against itself. I was devastated by the thought that this might represent a new disease process. The only positive aspect was that there was a possible treatment. I began taking monthly infusions of gamma globulin. This concentrated solution of antibodies caused my own immune system to slow down production of all antibodies, including those directed against my own nervous system. And so, after five months of total paralysis in my left arm, I began to see some improvement in function. By August 2000, I had good strength in the larger muscle groups but was still limited in my fine finger movements.

I feel outraged that I still struggle with so many different diseases, each calling for certain restrictions, but am slowly regaining functional independence. It worries me that no one knows what is happening in my arm, or if the problem could happen in another limb. I do not know if it is related to my cancer or if it indicates tumour activity. Neither do I know about the status of either tumour. There is no evidence of recurrent disease, but that could change suddenly. Some days I do not deal at all well with this uncertainty. On such days, each time I sneeze I think I have metastatic disease in my nose. Overall, I am in good mental health. I know that if I ponder too much the question of uncertainty or the unfairness of my position, it will make me crazy. I spend a great deal of energy maintaining myself in the present moment. I am well now and am able to cope right now. I will not upset this state of equanimity by thoughts of all that I have been through, nor dread what might lie ahead.

A New Public Persona

The experience of living with cancer was so monumental that I regularly found myself at my computer writing about it. Initially, I wrote for my own self and my own therapy. In February 1986, I met an extraordinary person in Archbishop Edward (Ted) Scott, who had retired as the primate or most senior Anglican bishop in Canada. We were very lucky at St. Clement's Church. Following the resignation of Douglas Stoute, who had been appointed dean to St. James' Cathedral, Archbishop Scott served during the interregnum while a new rector was sought. He took a great interest in my work. Quite to my surprise he suggested that I write a book about my experience as a blind physician. I told him I found that proposition overwhelming, but eventually I learned that one did not say no to Archbishop Scott! I began to share with him some of my thoughts about health, illness and spirituality. We had great talks and he offered me much support when I developed cancer and the subsequent illnesses. He encouraged me to write when I was well enough. He read my work and challenged me to continue peeling back the layers of meaning.

As I had not been expected to survive the first bout of cancer, each new day now seemed like a gift. Eventually, I was well enough to write three individual essays. The first, entitled "Dead Tired," described the physical journey I had been through and focused upon the fatigue of cancer. The second, "The Days That Will Still Be Mine," chronicled my emotional journey. I wrote the third article, "Bitter Pills to Swallow," for my medical colleagues; it talks about the profound impact of communication on healing. With Ted's encouragement I submitted my work for publication. The first two articles were published in the *Canadian Medical Association Journal*. The third appeared in the *New England Journal of Medicine*. (Note: These three articles are included at the end of this chapter.)

It seemed as if I had gone full circle – from a shy, retiring girl who could not admit any metabolic derangement to someone sending news of her health to an international audience. I think I felt freer to publish my work because I believed that I would soon be dead and would not have to live with the consequences of my decision to go public. As it turned out, my work caught the attention of many people and I have done considerable lecturing in both Canada and the United States on the subject of doctor–patient communication.

I am most grateful to Ted Scott for the changes he helped work in me and for his encouragement of my writing. When Ted developed signs of heart disease about 18 months after me, I was able to support him through his ordeal of angiography and bypass. Once more I learned that people who need help at one point in their lives may give help to others when they least expect it.

Dead Tired

Jane Poulson, MD

"Dead tired" – Reprinted from, by permission of the publisher, CMAJ 30 June 1998; 158 (13) 1748-1750 © 1998 Canadian Medical Association www.cma.ca

Before I was diagnosed with cancer I thought I knew a lot about sickness and health. In my practice as a general internist and palliative care physician I had prided myself on being a sensitive and empathetic physician, open to patients' concerns and always willing to take the time to listen. Besides, my credentials as a *patient* were impressive. I had lived with diabetes for over 30 years, and this was complicated by complete and permanent loss of eyesight when I was 27. When I was in my early forties, cardiac complications arose. I'd had 5 angiograms and 3 balloon angioplasties. I had been admitted to the cardiac intensive care unit on 3 occasions, and each time I thought it the most frightening place I had ever been.

And so, before the spring of 1996, when my long-standing fibrocystic disease transformed into an aggressive breast carcinoma, I thought I knew how it felt to be sick, tired, discouraged and scared. I thought I knew how to adapt to physical disability and limitations on energy and endurance. But I didn't know what it was like to have cancer. Quite apart from the surreal horrors of therapy, I was astonished to discover how little I had understood of what my own patients experienced.

"What did he say?"

Although for years I had taught seminars on breaking bad news and anticipating patient responses such as shock, disbelief, disorganization and difficulty understanding, I was unprepared for my own reaction to the diagnosis of cancer. At first I was simply stunned. Then the clinician in me took over, and I began to discuss the situation as if it were a third person who was in difficulty. Having sent hundreds of patients for a metastatic survey, I knew what tests had been discussed. Without my clinical experience I would have been lost.

Nonetheless, throughout treatment I had difficulty thinking clearly and rationally, and I was unable to concentrate sufficiently to read properly or follow in-depth conversations. I also had trouble retaining information and instructions from my doctors. Knowing how to access the system helped me to compensate. I could casually drop by to pick up forgotten requisitions. I could phone the radiology department to ask whether my studies had been booked and could book them myself if necessary. I knew what a CT scanner looked like and that bone scans and ultrasounds were not painful. The technology and terminology being used around me was familiar. Whenever I needed help, I knew who to ask and how to find them. Admissions were directly to the floor, bypassing long waits in the emergency room.

On the other hand, I knew the significance of what was and what was not being said to me. I knew that accounts of people in my position who lived for 10 years after diagnosis were anecdotal and by no means the norm. I carried the memory of women suffering terribly from local recurrence, breathlessness and pathologic fractures. Would I end up paralysed from spinal cord compression? I feared becoming helpless and dependent. In my practice of medicine I had tried thousands of times to sound encouraging while talking to patients and their families – while privately feeling a sense of foreboding on their behalf. And so I took little comfort from my colleagues' reassurances that all was not lost. The recollection of the misery and despair I had witnessed over the years far outweighed my memories of patients who resumed relatively normal lifestyles for prolonged periods.

Bad hair days: a whole new definition

Overnight I was catapulted from the position of one who orders and administers medications to that of a terrified and quivering recipient. The oncology clinic, which I had once thought to be so well designed for patient comfort, felt like foreign territory and was the last place I wanted to be. Five months of chemotherapy were like one enormous bout of the worst flu I could ever imagine. Although vomiting was prevented by medications, I felt queasy for 2 weeks out of every 4-week cycle. For 4 days after each injection the nausea was worst. The thought of eating was repulsive. Paradoxically, the best remedy was a small amount of "comfort food" such as pasta or bread and butter. I had several strong aversions: a veteran coffee drinker, I was sent reeling by the mere smell of coffee. I could manage tea, but only if it was weak and not too hot. Alcohol had no appeal; a white wine spritzer on ice was my best social effort. And although I always felt full after a few bites of a meal, I still managed to gain 5 pounds during chemotherapy. I thought that at the very least I should have shed a few pounds for my misery. I was grateful to the clinic nurses who reassured me that most women undergoing my treatment gained rather than lost weight. I was told to expect diarrhea. Quite the opposite was true. My whole body seemed to go on strike in response to the chemical onslaught. Everything worked slowly, if at all.

Although I was never in complete denial of the diagnosis, I had small anxiety attacks each time I went for an epirubicin injection. I wanted desperately to ask the doctors to double-check my pathology report to be absolutely certain that the injections were required.

How many times had I said to patients, "Don't worry, your hair will grow back after chemo" or "There are some really excellent wigs available. No one would ever know it's not your own hair." I had secretly found it a little strange that in the face of a potentially life-threatening disease, patients would worry about losing their hair. I had no idea how devastating it is to lose all your hair. You feel literally naked. To compound matters, the hair loss occurs when you are feeling sick, tired, nauseated and psychologically fragile. The chest has been grossly disfigured, and younger women find themselves suddenly menopausal. The combined effect is overwhelming, leaving you feeling like an extraterrestrial. Some wigs look good, but they all feel weird; you know you're bald even if the average person on the street doesn't. Wearing a hat all the time is tedious and makes you feel like you're carrying a banner proclaiming to the world that you have cancer.

Chemo was followed by surgery. Although I had explained to countless women the less aggressive nature of the current surgical approach compared with the mutilating procedures used in the past, the phrase "modified radical mastectomy" now seemed like a contradiction in terms. I took little comfort in knowing that it was merely my breast that was to be removed. Major panic arose in the operating room amphitheatre. Would I insult my surgical colleague by asking him to check the report just once more to ensure the biopsy specimens were correctly labelled and that we really had to proceed? Even at the postoperative follow-up visit, a small part of me was surprised to hear that the tissue removed was actually malignant.

My reaction to radiotherapy was another surprise. Lying on a table waiting for radiation beams to blaze at me sent chills through my core. And yet it seemed so innocuous. Every day a team of technicians shone lights on me for 15 minutes. Was this really a treatment? After the rigours of chemo and surgery, it seemed as if the radiotherapists were letting me off lightly. Yet I felt worse and worse as the therapy progressed. Was I becoming a chronic invalid?

Not just tired

The fatigue of cancer is unlike any fatigue I have ever known, not only in its severity and longevity but in its effect on my mood and spirits. In my university days I had been an avid swimmer and jogger. I knew well the exhaustion, exhilaration and then relaxation that follow profound physical exertion. Cancer fatigue is neither exhilarating nor relaxing. My muscles were soft and flabby; I felt old and decrepit. Nothing seemed to stem the tide of this deterioration. I walked as much as I could, but on some days this was not very far. During medical school and residency training, I had experienced the fatigue of being awake for sometimes 30 or 36 hours straight. This fatigue was not exhilarating or relaxing but it did respond to a hot bath and a good night's sleep. Fatigue from cancer does not. I would sleep 3 or 4 hours during the day and then wake up feeling tired and unable to climb out of bed. Sleep was never refreshing.

During chemotherapy, I felt well only for the last 3 or 4 days of each cycle. I often felt as if I had just run a marathon, despite the fact that I had been sleeping all day. I was anemic, and although erythropoietin and occasional transfusions helped slightly, the next round of chemo soon reduced me to a snail's pace. It had never taken me more than a week or 2 to bounce back from any medical problem. But the cumulative effect of repeated cycles of chemotherapy gradually wore me down. I had expected to be able to work more during chemotherapy and was discouraged to realize that I was no longer working efficiently. It took me hours to accomplish what used to take only minutes. I was accustomed to having boundless energy, and it was extremely depressing to be worn out by the slightest exertion. I was forced to plan each day carefully to make sure that I didn't overdo it.

I thought I'd be able to bounce back from surgery after 2 or 3 weeks. What I didn't factor in was that my body had just been put through a full course of gruelling chemotherapy and that I had required transfusions of both platelets and packed cells simply to allow the surgery to proceed. Nor did I arrive at my target for recuperation before radiotherapy began. It seemed extraordinary to feel more and more tired with each treatment. By the last week the technicians had to help me sit up after the session, and the walk back to the car was like a marathon.

Mind over matter?

I don't think I ever came to grips with the extent to which cancer impeded my engagement with life. I tried desperately to keep some semblance of normalcy. I took season's tickets to a chamber music series. I slept on the afternoon of the recitals but each time was desperately disappointed by my overwhelming fatigue by the second half of the performance. I used to enjoy evening concerts and plays after a full day's work. Now, even activities designed for pleasure were exhausting.

By believing that I could simply legislate myself to be better I did not make things any easier for myself. During active treatment I didn't have the energy to try to will myself better. But as soon as the treatments had finished, I set up a mental agenda for healing and recovery. One month of resting with gradually increasing activities ought to do it, I thought. It would be important to walk as much as possible to regain muscle tone. I was also anxious to resume my academic activities. It seemed an eternity since I had thought about medicine as it related to patients other than myself. During my fifth month of treatment, I had been asked to give presentations at McGill University the following February. McGill was my alma mater; many of my friends and colleagues there had been worried about me, and I thought how wonderful it would be to go back and present grand rounds. I knew that the preparation would be a lot of work, but since I had lots of time it never occurred to me to cancel or postpone. Not until it was too late. I had great difficulty focusing on my subject. The trip to Montreal, which I had never found tiring before, was exhausting. There was a major snow storm on the day of my presentation that made transportation difficult. I arrived early at the hospital to visit with friends, but by the time of the talk I could hardly stand on my feet. I was bedridden for 4 days after my folly.

I had also agreed to do some teaching at the University of Toronto. I really enjoy undergraduate teaching and thought this would be a perfect re-entry to the academic world. The course was 2 hours, 3 times each week. Because I had taught the course before, I anticipated no difficulty in preparing. But for the 2 weeks I tried to teach I spent weekends and non-teaching days in bed. I was shattered – but I had to acknowledge that this was not a good use of my energy or time. I wept on the phone asking to be replaced.

A challenge

Treatment for breast cancer takes a full year out of your life. There is no way to circumvent this fact. I tried to force my recovery with schedules and frameworks that were unattainable. Setting unrealistic goals only made me feel worse, both physically and emotionally. My healing occurred more quickly after I gave up the notion that I could legislate the return of energy and health. Letting go of that notion and giving myself over to the pursuit of rest and relaxation and to pampering myself with good music, fresh flowers and other treats was the best medicine. Telling myself that I must get back to my former activities as quickly as possible was not the right thing.

More than a year has passed since my nightmare summer of 1996. Now that I am feeling and thinking like a physician again, my mind often returns to the fatigue of cancer and its treatment. Does the chemical onslaught of chemotherapy, which attacks cells whether they are malignant or not, induce compensatory metabolic changes? Is there some sort of "sick euthyroid" state that preserves body mass and energy? Could there be some sort of uncoupling process at a muscle mitochondrion level? I am neither a biochemist nor a molecular biologist and do not have the capacity to begin addressing these issues. My contribution to the work in this field must take the form of a challenge to my colleagues in oncology and palliative medicine. Cancer-related fatigue is a definite and discrete phenomenon that significantly impairs the quality of life of cancer patients. As a profession we have taken this symptom too lightly, assuming that our patients are complaining of the kind of tiredness that everyone feels from time to time and that they could, with a few minor adjustments, soldier on. The fatigue that one feels with cancer is different; it is unique to the disease itself. Prescribing an afternoon nap or an extra hour of sleep at night is insufficient. We have made enormous strides in treating cancer pain and chemotherapy-induced vomiting. But this is only the beginning of symptom management. Fatigue is experienced by most cancer patients. We must turn our attention to delineating the cause, pathophysiology and treatment of this pervasive and depressing symptom, which perhaps does more than any other to stand in the way of the optimism of cancer patients that they will one day be well again.

The Days That Will Still Be Mine

Jane Poulson, MD

"The days that will still be mine" – Reprinted from, by permission of the publisher, CMAJ 16 June 1998; 158 (12) 1633-1636 © 1998 Canadian Medical Association www.cma.ca

I think I must have experienced the whole range of human emotions during the time I was being treated for an aggressive breast cancer that seemingly appeared from nowhere. It is an extraordinary and terrifying experience to cross the line from a philosophical grasp of the fact that no one lives forever to the realization that one has a life-threatening illness. Although I had expected and prepared myself for some of my feelings, I was frequently thrown for a loop by emotions that arose when I least expected to feel anything at all.

Shockwaves

There was anger. Even though I had exceeded recommended screening guidelines, this tumour presented out of the blue. I'd had regular radiologic and physical exams throughout the preceding 10 years. Everything had been fine, even at a routine visit 5 months earlier. Then, despite my diligence, a nasty inflammatory carcinoma suddenly appeared and dramatically put a stop to all normal activities. No one can satisfactorily answer for me the question of whether this tumour did "just appear" or whether it had been lurking for years. I tried to tell myself: "What difference does it make? You have a bad tumour now and all you can deal with is the present." It appeared at the worst possible time in my career. I had just joined the Department of Medicine at The Toronto

Hospital and the University of Toronto. This was not a good way to begin new professional relationships, but when I think about it now I ask myself, "Is there any good time to get cancer?"

There was fear. As a general internist I had cared for many patients with cancer. I was fascinated by the disease itself and really liked my patients. However, I could not imagine being able to cope with having cancer myself. Eight years of experience in palliative care only served to heighten my fears. The Toronto Hospital had hired me to establish an academic program in palliative medicine and I had set up a clinic for symptom management only 6 months before my own diagnosis. My mind was flooded not with images of people dying peacefully with good symptom management but rather of patients with intolerable pain and global distress.

None of the conditions I have lived with – not juvenile diabetes, not blindness, not heart disease – has had the emotional impact of cancer. Although other diseases have potentially life-threatening consequences, cancer carries with it a unique terror. The diagnosis of heart disease was extremely distressing but it did not make my world crumble. Angiograms looking for blocked coronary arteries are relaxing compared with MRI scans looking for cancer. The metaphors that we use in talking about cancer are distinct; words like "battling," "struggling" and "courageous fight" do not constantly arise in the context of other diseases. A diagnosis of cancer changes one's life irrevocably and carries with it a lingering foreboding. Although the physician in me knew that heart disease, rather than breast cancer, is still the leading killer of women, the statistics held no comfort for me. I was able with time to reconcile myself to my heart disease and not carry the spectre of imminent doom with me constantly. But I continue to wake in the middle of the night with gripping fear at the thought of having cancer.

There was shock and denial. I walked around for weeks feeling certain that this was happening to someone else or was not happening at all. I kept checking my office voice mail, waiting for a call from my surgical colleague to say that there had been an error in the pathology report. Life became surreal, like a nightmare. I continued with my work, but all conversations, both professional and social, left me feeling as if a thick layer of plexiglass divided me from the rest of the world. It seemed odd that people recognized me and interacted with me as they had always done. I felt that it must be written all over my face: "I have cancer." I used to be the doctor; now I was the patient.

Treatment

I was not surprised to feel fear, anger and apprehension on the days I visited the oncology clinic. What *did* surprise me was my enthusiasm to get there. I never slept well the night before an injection but always woke up early and jumped into the shower. Although I dreaded how the injections would make me feel, I never once refused to get into the car. In fact, I became rather irritable when traffic jams delayed our arrival.

Is it possible to feel positive emotions sitting in an oncology clinic? I was always comforted when I heard the familiar voices of favourite nurses or my doctor. Somehow I felt safe. Snuggling under a hand-made afghan in the treatment room made me feel comfortable and secure. "Just like a day at the spa," one nurse always quipped.

As I look back on my chemotherapy I realize that, as miserable as it was, it made me feel as if I were actively engaged in a war. I had a sense of being united with a team that was determined to kill my cancer. It was reassuring to be surrounded by knowledgeable, experienced practitioners supervising the administration of incredibly toxic drugs. Although distraught by total alopecia, including the loss of my eyelashes, I took some perverse comfort in thinking that if even the cells that made eyelashes and peach fuzz were affected by the chemo, surely the cancer could not survive. As my bone marrow flagged we started marrow growth factors. Severe anemia was reversed by transfusions of packed cells; thrombocytopenia was reversed with platelets. We seemed to have an endless arsenal of weapons to combat the cancer cells. I was in the fight of my life, with all guns blazing.

Friends and family who accompanied me remarked on my peaceful and calm countenance despite repeated setbacks. They said that I was a person of great courage and inner resources. I would like to think so. But at least part of my calm during those months came from satisfaction at what we were doing to my tumour. *I* could always be shored up with transfusions and antibiotics, but the tumour had no recourse.

Having had such a rough ride with chemotherapy, I wasn't prepared for my emotional reaction to the sudden discontinuation of therapy. The original plan had been to do chemo first and then operate. Surgery was to be followed by more chemotherapy. However, the pathology reports after surgery were so discouraging that it was felt we should move directly to radiotherapy. Instead of being thrilled at avoiding more chemo, I pleaded for more of the dreaded poisons. When I was told firmly but kindly that chemotherapy was not working against the tumour I had a whole-body reaction. I went hot and cold; I had goose bumps and felt weak at the knees. I shook all over and was not at all certain that I could stand up and walk with dignity through the waiting room to the car. Although I understood that one could not go on treating cancer endlessly with chemotherapy, losing this avenue of treatment precipitated the most violent emotional response I had ever experienced.

I had to wait several weeks for the surgical site to heal before starting radiation. During that time I was relentlessly tormented by images of tumour cells flooding through my veins, each choosing a cozy spot in my liver or lungs to nest and raise a family. At last, we moved into the radiotherapy phase: 30 treatments administered daily, 5 days a week. I was more terrified of the radiation than I had been of the chemotherapy. Soon, however, I settled into the routine of daily treatments and weekly consultations. Once again, I developed a sense of certainty that radiotherapy would be successful in blasting this invader out of my body.

Anticlimax

During treatments, I kept myself going with thoughts of how wonderful it would be when my life was no longer determined by doctors' appointments and hospital visits. I looked forward to feeling well again and resuming my regular activities. I expected some acknowledgement of the fact that I had graduated from therapy: a diploma of some sort, or anything concrete to let people know what I had been through. Instead I simply walked out of the hospital with an appointment card telling me to return in 3 months. A journal entry from that time captures my dismay and confusion.

> I have just finished my 30th and last radiotherapy. For 8 months I have been sequentially poisoned, nauseated, anorexic, anemic, neutropenic, thrombocytopenic, febrile, infected, constipated and fatigued.... I do not have another doctor's appointment for 3 months: that is 90 days. Surely, this is the day I have been waiting for.

During chemotherapy, days were no longer called Monday, Tuesday or Wednesday, but day 1, 2, 8 or 12. Each day had its own significance. Days 1 and 8: injections. Days 4 and 11: stop ondansetron. Day 14: stop cyclophosphamide. Days 15 through 22: take filgrastim and watch for infections. Day 28: start over again with day 1. Surgery followed on the heels of chemotherapy. My days were now called post-op

day 1, 2 or 10. Post-op day 8 brought the discouraging pathology report…. On post-op day 12, I began radiotherapy; before long my days
were called radiation day 1, day 2, and so on. Christmas and New Year's
had an additional significance, as no treatments were given on those days.

At the beginning, I felt as if radiation day 30 would never dawn.
Now it has come and gone, and I am bemused by my strange lack of
enthusiasm. I have kept myself going with positive images of waking up
on the first day when there was no treatment to be given: day 1 of my
life. Tonight I struggle with a more stark and frightening reality. My life
has been irretrievably altered. I do not think or feel the same. What
once seemed so important to me now seems irrelevant. I am beset with
strange and unfamiliar feelings. I do not know myself or my life. My
challenge now is to reclaim day 1 for my own and to move forward to
claim all the days that will still be mine.

I was not prepared for the loneliness and sense of abandonment
I experienced. After months of frequenting the hospital and dealing with
experts in the field, it seemed inconceivable to spend 3 months without
seeing any of the staff I had come to rely on to kill this tumour. The
pathology reports suggested that we had failed to eradicate my tumour
successfully. At any moment it could surface again somewhere else. I
have had to let go of my image of full-scale battle. Now I think in terms
of guerrilla warfare. Initially I felt protected by the big guns; now I feel
as if I am standing alone in the middle of an arena – defenceless, and
waiting to be shot. It all feels like a grotesque game of hide and seek. We
have used our biggest guns and failed in our attack. Should the cancer
reappear, the arsenal available for battle will be less impressive.

I had been looking forward to redirecting all the energy I had
funnelled into health concerns toward normal activities and enjoying
my friends. Instead, I found it difficult to attach myself to the world as I
knew it. None of my former interests seemed particularly relevant. I was
consumed by the need to search for something precious and significant.
Another journal entry captures my virtual panic:

Without realizing it, I have begun to seek the Holy Grail.
I am searching for thoughts and activities that have meaning for
me now. All my former activities seem like frivolous pastimes. I
must leave them behind and focus my time and energy upon
accomplishing whatever it is that I was always supposed to do
with my life. I am frustrated, discouraged and depressed that I
cannot discern what this task is. My body is exhausted and is

begging me for time to rest and recuperate. I know now, however, that my time is finite; I don't wish to waste a single, precious moment simply recovering.

Strangely, everyone and everything else appears to be
as it always was. It is only my interior world that has been
smashed, irretrievably rearranged and then given back to me.
How am I to fit a shattered and unrecognizable self into my old
world? Connecting with old things and old people is complicated by the fact that my dramatic and radical transformation is
not apparent to anyone else. I am still "the old Jane" to them.
They have been waiting for 8 months for me to return to my
teaching, my career and all the other signposts that the cancer
was a self-contained nightmare and is now finished.... But I know
that I can never return to my former space. The challenge before me is to acknowledge this fact, to meet and know this new
person that I have become and to live differently in the world.

In the first 6 months after therapy, things I had always taken for
granted caught me by surprise. Everyone appeared to live in and for the
future. They spoke of holidays they were going to take the next year.
My desk was covered with notices of meetings scheduled 2 years hence.
I received a new credit card and realized with a chill that I could easily
expire before this piece of plastic did. I had no dread of the future but,
rather, a sense of a deep void as I regarded the horizon of my life.

There were practical concerns. Did it make any sense to buy a
new winter coat if this were to be my last season? Why buy a party
dress? Surely I could wear my old dress one more time.

My emotions were not all negative. The enormous support and
positive reinforcement I received from loved ones sustained me from
the moment of first diagnosis and carried me at times when I could not
stand alone. My family and friends laughed with me and wept with me.
Throughout the whole experience I felt loved. This gave me the ability
to hope for the best and to go on living in a fully engaged manner despite the nightmarish circumstances.

A different lens

Now I am more than a year past treatment. In a paradoxical way,
I think I can say that I feel more alive now than ever before in my life.
Another journal entry:

I see all that I do now through a different lens.... When you presume to have infinity before you the value of each person, each relationship, all knowledge you possess is diluted. My life is now concentrating before me. This the most painful yet most enriching experience of my life. I have found my Holy Grail: it is surrounding myself with my dear friends and family and enjoying sharing my fragile and precious time with them as I have never done before. I wonder wistfully why it took a disaster of such proportions before I could see so clearly what was truly important and uniquely mine.

I am now awaiting my fourth 3-month follow-up visit. The pathology reports notwithstanding, the disease has not behaved as predicted. I long to move forward, but feel restrained by the sword of Damocles hanging over my head. It is difficult to strike a balance between reasonable watchfulness for symptoms of return and excessive vigilance. I had never noticed before the dry cough brought on by low humidity in my home. I must actively remind myself that cancer patients can have coughs or minor aches and pains just as they did before the diagnosis. This departure from the expected course of the disease has also given me a period in which I have felt relatively well, and thus the chance to do things that I thought I would never be able to. My emotions are generally more muted than before; neither fear nor anger are quite so acute. My denial has been slightly reinforced. I continue to live largely in the present, although I am now beginning to plan some trips several months from now. I cannot think much beyond this point. I am delighted by my involvement with life, and I am living with a passion unlike any I have ever known. I know that I cannot ultimately sustain such intensity but, for the moment, I enjoy nature, friends, family, music, art, sleep and relaxation as I have never done. I have a new dog who is a delight. Should this period of grace continue, no doubt my emotions will continue to mute gradually as I take up more of the activities that once formed a framework for my life.

Cancer continues to permeate my consciousness when I least expect it, but it no longer dominates my existence. I cannot say that cancer has been a positive experience, but my enhanced appreciation of being alive has been a gift. I only wish that I had been able to connect with this passion within me in some different way. What I would like to say is this: Live fully every moment of your life. Do not wait for everything to be threatened before you realize the value of all you have.

Bitter Pills to Swallow

Jane Poulson, MD

The New England Journal of Medicine, *June 18, 1998*
© *1998, Massachusetts Medical Society. All rights reserved.*

I learned more about comprehensive cancer care when I became a patient in 1996 than I had during a residency in medicine or in practice as an internist and palliative care physician in a teaching hospital. When I was given a diagnosis of aggressive inflammatory carcinoma, I found myself transformed from one who orders and administers medication to a terrified recipient. Until then, I had felt that I was a particularly empathetic doctor who listened to and, I thought, heard the stories of my patients. It was a shock, then, to undergo the foreign and surreal experience of becoming a patient.

I had given countless seminars on the topic of "breaking bad news." The second half of each seminar was about "patient responses and how to be most helpful." I knew patients often reacted to their diagnosis with shock, horror, denial, and disbelief, but I was unprepared for the emotional roller-coaster ride precipitated by my discussions with the hospital staff after the diagnosis. I soon realized the number of bitter pills I had unwittingly delivered to patients during my 15 years of practice. Statements are made routinely by doctors who are oblivious to their catastrophic effect on patients. I became aware of this fact only when it was my turn to be on the receiving end of such statements as the following.

"Our newer technologies are so much better"

Perhaps telling patients that medical technology had improved in recent years simply made the discussion easier for me as the doctor bearing bad tidings. I had thought that it would be helpful to patients to learn that we had made tremendous advances in technology and supportive care. I tried to explain to patients requiring a colostomy that the new appliances and adhesives were far superior to the older ones. I had noted that few patients seemed encouraged by this fact, but I felt better having some good things to say about the procedure.

In a similar vein, I often told women about the history of breast surgery. The original Halsted procedures were far more mutilating than the much simpler approach used these days. Now that it was my turn, the term "modified radical mastectomy" seemed a contradiction in terms. I found little comfort in the knowledge that it was merely my breast that was to be removed, and not the pectoral muscles as well.

It was not helpful – and it actually augmented my distress – to be told how quickly the surgery was done. It seemed that since I would have to stay in the hospital for only two or three nights, my despair should be correspondingly less intense. Patients who have received bad news and are dealing with the prospect of upcoming surgery are frightened and angry. Trying to minimize the seriousness of the procedure they are fearing serves only to heighten their anxiety. Patients should be encouraged to express their fears and emotions. Once they have done so, it may then be helpful to speak about the positive and more hopeful aspects of the illness. Warning: Don't be surprised if the patient is still upset during future meetings, or if you have to explain it all again.

"Don't worry – your hair will grow back"

How many times had I reassured patients about to undergo chemotherapy that their hair would grow back? Probably hundreds. In the meantime, fabulous wigs were available. "No one will ever know you're wearing a wig." Occasionally, I would secretly wonder why they were so inconsolable about losing renewable hair when they could potentially lose their lives.

I had absolutely no comprehension of how devastating the physical changes associated with even early-stage cancer can be. There I was, engaged in a battle for my life, and weeping on day 21 of the first cycle of chemotherapy because my hair – which would grow back – was slithering away down the drain. Losing my hair was more upsetting than any of the other physical consequences of cancer therapy.

A bald head always made me feel naked. Yes, there were some very cute cotton hats or scarves. Yes, my wig was a dead ringer for my natural hair. But both hats and wigs felt suffocating. Regular people do not wear hats indoors. Wearing hats inside was almost as humiliating as walking around bald. Out of doors, the first puff of wind struck terror to my heart. I had to choose between walking along with my hand on my head or chasing after a truant wig.

Alopecia comes just at the time when the patient is feeling physically ill, tired, and demoralized. The body in which you are living feels quite foreign. These symptoms combine to cause great anguish. We cannot prevent anticancer drugs from causing alopecia. We can, however, be more attuned to the ways in which our patients express the nightmares they are living. Patients' despair about physical signs like alopecia or skin color often provides an entrée into the more global despair they are feeling. It is therefore not sufficient simply to tell patients that their hair, eyebrows, and lashes will grow back or that their normal skin texture and color will return. Even if patients are not expressing concern about these changes, as practitioners we must recognize that although the primary target of our chemical assault is neoplastic tissue, self-esteem and the quality of life are innocent victims. Recommendations about support groups or counseling are just as important as prescriptions for prochlorperazine in helping our patients live through the experience of cancer.

"Your procedure is canceled today"

Cancellations or postponements are sometimes unavoidable. Discharges are postponed, or treatments may be delayed. This is frustrating for physicians trying to provide good and efficient care. Most of us, however, have little appreciation of the effect that delays have on our patients.

We know that ultrasound examinations, radiology, and computed tomography are painless and relatively simple procedures. Many patients do not know this. All patients awaiting even simple tests are anxious about what the results may show. Considerable mental energy and emotion are required to prepare oneself for these investigations. As a result, the news that there will be a delay is a bombshell for the waiting patient.

I was terrified of radiation treatments. As a medial professional, I was ashamed of my fear and knew it to be irrational. Only with great mental effort was I able to get myself to the clinic for the first two treatments. At the end of the second treatment, the technician told me that the machine would be down the following day for routine maintenance. I was shattered. The following day was Friday. That meant three days without therapy. My fear of radiation changed to terror at the possibility that my tumor would spread in the interim. Yes, I understood why machines needed servicing. The technician was rather detached as he prepared the room for the next patient. He seemed surprised by my reaction, and he obviously had no understanding of how hard it had been to make myself come for the treatments.

We cannot avoid delays in procedures or therapy, but if we had a better understanding of how patients feel while waiting for tests, we could be more empathetic and diminish the impact of delays. The shorter the time that remains before a procedure, the more devastating it is when the procedure is canceled. All health care practitioners must have a better understanding of the psychology of being ill. We are too often nonchalant about procedures or treatments and do not stop to think how it feels to be in the patient's shoes.

"I have a really great case"

As a teacher of medicine, I have been in pursuit of "great cases" for two decades. A non-medical friend used to take exception to my use of the term. I always thought that he was being rather stuffy until I found myself "a great case."

The various treatments for my cancer complicated the management of several concurrent medical conditions. One day, discouraged, I sat in an examining room waiting for the return of my physician. I heard him talking to a resident about "a great case" he had. It was a good example of how one thing can seem to make everything else go wrong – the classic domino effect. I began to weep when I realized that I was the great case.

We will always require good illustrative cases for educational purposes. We must, however, refine the methods used in clinical teaching in the corridor and at the bedside. Physicians must remember that although patients may be invisible because of curtains or thin clinic walls, they are not out of earshot. The attitudes revealed and the manner in which cases are discussed can be devastating to the listening patient. Worse still is raucous laughter while doctors are discussing your problem. Patients know that the worse their dilemma, the more interesting they are to the doctors who are talking about them.

Before any discussions about a patient take place, the participants must ensure that their words cannot be overheard by anyone, especially the patient. In addition, we must broaden both our approach to and our understanding of our patients. If we fail to acknowledge that they are first and foremost people struggling with an illness, this attitude will be evident to all concerned. Teaching physicians must remember that they are transferring more than knowledge during clinical interactions. Physicians who are callous and insensitive toward their patients will encourage the same characteristics in those whom they teach. As I have learned by bitter experience, anyone can become the next great case overnight.

"You are not eligible for this study"

As an academic physician, I was raised on clinical trials. I believe very strongly in evidence-based medical practice. Studies need to be vigorously designed if the results are to be useful. An important premise, of course, is that the groups of patients receiving different treatments are all similar at the outset. Particularly during my residency, we searched diligently for patients to enroll in clinical trials. Often as the interview with a new prospect proceeded, it became apparent that the patient was not suitable for the study after all. "You are not eligible for this trial" was the explanation we always used. This was not so disturbing to patients considering a trial of new antihypertensive medications. Life would carry on with the old medication. That statement could be shattering, however, when the stakes were much higher and the patient believed that an experimental treatment might make the difference between life and death.

My pathology report indicated that my tumor was relatively drug-resistant. The outlook was grim. Panic-stricken, I immediately thought about bone marrow transplantation. When I learned that I was "not eligible" for ongoing studies involving transplantation, I was distraught. Was I supposed to die quietly because no researcher had thought to try transplantation at this point in the disease trajectory? At that moment, it felt as if the only life-saving option for me was being denied for arbitrary reasons.

Detailed discussion on a subsequent visit made me realize why transplantation was not a good option at the time. I was considerably comforted by this discussion. I know that my family and I would have felt resentful and bitter had I been denied this treatment only because of the design of the trial.

I am in no way proposing the discontinuation of clinical trials. I do, however, feel that the language of the clinical-trial world should not be used with desperate patients who are considering various treatment protocols. The term "eligible" is commonly used in everyday speech in different contexts. In an emotionally charged medical situation, it carries the connotation that the patient is being denied something desirable. If a patient is found to be ineligible for a clinical trial, this information must not be transmitted in a manner that implies that useful treatment is being withheld.

Conclusions

It is virtually impossible for one person to know exactly how another is feeling unless he or she has been through a similar situation. It is neither practical nor desirable that physicians experience a serious illness as part of their education. This does not mean that we cannot teach physicians to be more sensitive in their interactions with patients and to communicate better. I do not believe that most physicians intend to be callous or insensitive. I, myself, used all the classic phrases I have quoted here while in practice. I thought that I was being a sensitive physician and had no idea of the effect my words were having on my listeners. I learned to say these things from teachers who worked with me during my formative years. No doubt there are doctors who learned the same phrases from me.

Several suggestions may help. We must increase the time students spend learning the psychology of illness while they are doing clinical work. Many medical colleges now offer courses on this topic during the first years of training. Such courses are much less effective, however, when they are taught in a non-clinical setting. Several minutes could be reserved during bedside and clinical-teaching rounds for patients to describe how they are feeling. This approach would not only expose trainees to patients' emotions, but it would also present patients as real people rather than simply objects of interest for budding physicians. Too often, clinical teachers speak about patients but rarely speak to them as people. Role-playing is an effective method of allowing students some sense of how it feels to receive bad news from a doctor. With the opportunity to play out the scenarios in many different ways, students can experience the difference between good and poor communication.

Finally, our profession ought to be working on effective methods for practitioners to deal with the stress of work. Many physicians prefer to keep a detached attitude toward patients, because it is too difficult emotionally and too time-consuming to encounter the suffering that accompanies human illness. This approach is not advantageous for either patients or doctors. There have been some strides toward improving doctor-patient relationships, but there is still much more work to be done. Perhaps increased attention to this aspect of patient care and the more interdisciplinary approach practiced these days will help doctors to do a better job of communicating with their patients.

And behold, the LORD passed by, and a great and strong wind rent the mountains, and broke in pieces the rocks before the LORD; but the LORD was not in the wind; and after the wind an earthquake; but the LORD was not in the earthquake;

And after the earthquake a fire, but the LORD was not in the fire: and after the fire a still small voice.

And it was so, when Elijah heard it, that he wrapped his face in his mantle, and went out, and stood in the entering in of the cave. And behold, there came a voice unto him....

I Kings 19:11-13

Chapter 12: Something
of an Educational Interlude

Jane's School for Helpers Who Really Want to Help

No, We Are Not in the Same Boat
She: "Do you have a problem with your eyesight?"
I: "Yes, I am completely blind."
She: "Oh, gee, I know exactly how you feel. I have worn glasses since Grade 4."
Another: "I know exactly how you feel. I am blind without my glasses."
Another: "I know exactly how you feel. I can't drive at night without my glasses."
I: "No, you do not know how I feel. You make me feel angry when you try to pretend we are in the same position. Please simply say that you are sorry that I must carry such a burden."

No, I Am Not Lucky
She: "Do you have a problem with your eyesight?"
I: "Yes, I am blind."
She: "Oh, gee, you are lucky you do not have cancer. My neighbour's sister was diagnosed with breast cancer last week."

Everyone who does not have cancer is lucky, including the person who is trying to point out that my situation could be worse. Please simply say that you are sorry that I am plagued with such a problem.

No, There Are No Advantages to Being Blind

She: "Do you have a problem with your eyesight?"

I: "Yes, I am blind."

She: "You must have amazing hearing. I think that I might be losing some of my hearing."

Another: "Oh, well, you will have so much more vision than those of us who can see."

Another: "You are lucky that you do not have to see all the terrible things going on in the world."

There is nothing good about being disabled. Do not let your discomfort allow you to make the mistake of pointing out to me the many advantages of my circumstances.

Spare Me the Platitudes

She: "Do you have a problem with your eyesight?"

I: "Yes, I am blind."

She: "Oh, well, God never sends us more than we can handle."

Another: "You blind people are so brave. I really admire you."

Neither your concepts of God's mercy nor your admiration for the disabled is helpful. Simply say that you are sorry. If you wish to express admiration, please direct it specifically to me or speak about the activities of another disabled person. The circumstances for someone who is blind are quite different than for someone who is deaf or physically handicapped. Speaking of 'the disabled' as if they were a homogenous group is annoying to an individual person dealing with a specific problem. It is extraordinary to me how often people run off to find me a wheelchair upon learning that I am blind.

As a society, we are uncomfortable communicating with anyone who is "different." We tend to speak in a louder voice and more slowly. We use diminutives such as "dear." I do not believe that people are consciously being insensitive. Most people are unaware of how they address a disabled person. They are also unaware of the impact of their well-intentioned but thoughtless words. Listen to yourself the next time you talk to someone who has a disability. Remember that disabled people are, first and foremost, people, just like you.

Many, many people ask what seems to me a very silly question: "Would you rather have lost your sight in adulthood or have been born blind?"

Both situations are dreadful. I think that people who ask this question are awkwardly trying to get at a deeper issue: How does someone who once could see adapt to the world with no vision, not even light perception? Reflecting on this matter has revealed some interesting paradoxes to me. I consider myself a very visually oriented person. When I am trying to orient myself I imagine myself standing at the centre of a circle. From there I determine where is north, south, east and west. Rather than groping about in my apartment when I feel lost, I identify a piece of furniture and then make a picture in my mind of the room in which this furniture is located. From this mental picture I know how to move in the desired direction.

When I first lost my eyesight, I drove people to distraction with questions about minute details of a person's appearance. Most of the time, they answered that they had not noted whether the person was wearing glasses, and could not remember what type of clothing the person was wearing. Initially, this information was critical to me, but over the 20 years of my blindness, I have lost that need to be factually correct about the appearance of persons or objects.

Travelling Mercies

In 1984, I travelled to Southern California with a group of medical colleagues to attend a conference. We took several extra days to see California. In San Francisco, I could not see the sharp inclines as we rode the streetcars. I could not see the sights and lights that surrounded us the night we had dinner in Chinatown. But the worst experience was the next day, when we travelled south to visit a Redwood National Park. It was an extraordinary place. We travelled to the top of an enormous rock face to look down on the coast below. Hundreds of barking seals were sunning themselves, and huge waves crashed against the rock. My colleagues eloquently described the breathtaking view. Some of the trees were 2000 years old. One trunk was so huge, a hole that had been made in the trunk was so big you could drive a car through it. My colleagues had me walk around several trees to get an idea of their circumference. I was unable to control my rage – I could not see these things. I was so angry with God, I could not enjoy any of my sensory experiences. How could God create such natural beauty and allow it to be impossible for another creature (me, for example) to see it? I could not wait to leave the park.

This experience is in sharp contrast to my visit to southern France 15 years later with my friends Tom Fitches and Elizabeth MacCallum, when my senses were fully satisfied. It was springtime. The air was rich and full of the fragrance of lilacs. At one point we walked past a cemetery marker of someone who had fallen hundreds of years ago during the religious wars. As my arms traced the shape of a cross carved centuries ago by the Cathars, I could feel wisteria entwined within the intricate cross. It rained a lot and the small streams that had sprung up all over the place raced and rippled down the mountainside. The air was fresh and cool and blew through the trees, which were just coming into bloom. I could tell from the sound that these trees were extraordinarily tall; the dappled sunlight that warmed my face told me that their growth was dense. My knees and legs reminded me how mountainous this area was. We walked past fields of flax, which I identified by its distinctive smell. My hair had grown just long enough after the chemotherapy to catch gusts of wind and flutter, if only a little. As we walked, I turned towards the breeze to enjoy this gentle tousling of my hair. After a long, cold, difficult winter in Toronto I basked in the luxury of this warmth and freshness with great delight.

The smells of southern France lingered in the food and the wines we consumed. The fragrance of the bakery first thing in the morning when we went to buy fresh bread was intoxicating. In fact, here I was able to make my orientation maps much more by smell than by visualization. A lush rosemary hedge grew along one side of the garden; a large patch of lavender grew near the door. The distant sound of a train told me how vast was this open space around us.

I enjoyed Tom's and Elizabeth's descriptions of what they were seeing, but even if they had never said a word, I had vivid visions of this beautiful region of the world. Human language alone is insufficient to describe such majesty. I wished I could see these glorious surroundings, yet I was able to relish their beauty without the benefit of sight. It was a decidedly spiritual experience, one that enabled me to marvel at God's creation. I also made an important discovery on this trip. My overwhelming anger during previous travels had been transformed into a certain sadness which, while it was still painful, was no longer debilitating.

Mindfulness

When in December 1998 I sensed that I was finally living on borrowed time and that at any moment my original tumour could recur and kill me within a matter of months, I consulted with a psychiatrist whose specialty was psychological support of persons with medical disease. She worked extensively with transplant patients, who also lived with the knowledge that their immediate futures were uncertain. She and I focused on the idea of trying to take life in very small stages, dealing only with real rather than anticipated problems. She recommended that I do a new program at the hospital called "Mindfulness-Based Stress Reduction." The program, which was developed at the University of Massachusetts, was designed to help people with chronic pain. (It has now been extended to involve persons with a variety of medical conditions that are unlikely to be permanently cured by standard therapy.)

I enrolled with some trepidation: it was a group program, and this would be my first time in a group setting. It had been all I could manage to admit privately to a psychiatrist that I was feeling overwhelmed by all the challenges I was facing. It was little comfort to me that the uniform response was, "I would be much more concerned about you if you said you were coping well!"

In my social and professional interactions I always seemed calm. Now, for the first time ever, I would have to admit to a group of strangers that I was feeling stressed. I would have preferred to present myself as a physician observing this new methodology at work rather than as another neurotic patient.

The leaders must have read my feelings. Their opening statement was that this was not group therapy. People would have an opportunity to speak if they wanted to, but there was no obligation to participate. In fact, they had quite a tight agenda and there was not a lot of general discussion. The leaders were very skilled. Persons attending an intensive program for relief of stress generally are quite anxious to talk about their issues. At times the leaders had to be quite directive in preventing the whole thing from degenerating into a muddle of sad stories.

There were three basic arms to the program. The first was meditation. After learning certain fundamentals of meditation practice, we were instructed in how to observe our physical, mental and psychological state. When we noticed something, we were to concentrate intensely upon it. For example, if we felt an itch, we were not allowed to touch it but rather were to focus upon it intently, describing its characteristics and our responses to it. To my very great surprise, this intensive focus upon a symptom transformed the experience. The logic behind it is that when you have a condition that cannot be taken away, you have to learn to adapt to it and not fight it. An itch is a small symptom, but is used as an analogy for pain. We were to apply the same techniques to pain as we did to unscratched itches. This approach of focusing intently upon a symptom had incredible results for patients with physical complaints such as pain.

The second thrust was yoga. We started off gently; we were invited to do each movement only as much as we comfortably could. Some people started moving limbs only inches each time. By pushing ourselves to a certain point each day, our tolerance and flexibility improved progressively.

The final thrust was to be mindful of everything around us. We learned this skill by minute analyzing of the smallest events. In time, we were given exercises each day that required us to write about individual events. This was an amazing process. I chose my morning shower. I had always thought of showering as something I did each morning to keep clean. I would be in and out of the shower in several minutes; while I was in there I usually thought about what I would wear that day. By showering mindfully, I felt the hot water hitting my skin, the massage of the stream of water on my back. I began bathing with soaps that smelled good and brought me sensual pleasure. I felt the drops of water running down my back and the rough touch of the towel. I felt the soft plush rug upon my bare feet. By being mindful, I transformed a routine activity into a positive experience. Similarly, we learned to enjoy the smell of our coffee, the warmth of the mug in our hands and the rich flavour. We would follow the sense of the coffee descending our esophagus.

Mindfulness training taught us to be fully in the moment. There is nothing we can do about past events. We have no idea what lies ahead. The only thing we can know or control is the present moment. The program encouraged us to bring an open mind to each new event or interaction during the day. Thus, we would attempt to leave behind the emotions engendered in a previous interaction and approach the next with a fresh slate. We tried to observe our "knee jerk" reactions to certain situations and to develop a method of actively responding rather than reacting in the usual pattern.

I have been amazed by the impact this course continues to have on my situation. I did not learn anything new from the program, but the way it was integrated and presented rekindled in me many important things I had learned over the years. I was delighted to get back to my meditation practice. The form of meditation taught in this course was quite different from the mantra-based format I had learned to practise at the Benedictine Priory in Montreal, but I was encouraged to make the practice my own and eventually ended up with a mixture of centring prayer, Christian meditation and a more Eastern meditation format. I found it extremely calming and helpful to meditate on five statements, which I would repeat over and over again.

1. This is my moment. May I live in it well.

Of all the ideas and concepts presented or reframed during my mindfulness training, perhaps none was more powerful than that of being fully present in the moment. This concept has been most helpful for me in several different ways.

One of the occupational risks of being a palliative care physician is that I have been present at hundreds of deaths. As my specialty was cancer pain management, I have known and tried to help many people who were experiencing severe pain from their disease. Most I was able to help somewhat, but many persons died in considerable discomfort. Almost more difficult than seeing someone in pain is attending the bedside of someone struggling to breathe. As I am now entering the more advanced stages of a malignant illness, I sometimes worry that I will not be able to manage the symptoms of advanced disease. I have arranged for two of my colleagues to care for me, but in the back of my mind dreadful images lurk. I find myself transposing the symptoms of different patients onto myself, imagining myself not only with intractable pain but with shortness of breath and paralysis as well.

My meditation upon the present moment has helped me move past these frightening images. Whenever my panicked mind begins this irrational journey, I keep returning myself to the present moment where my symptoms are manageable and I am doing well. I do not tell myself that things will get worse. The critical point is that I am in the present moment and I am well.

Perhaps a more profound interpretation of living well in the present moment is having a constant awareness of being alive and of all the pleasures this can entail. I use this meditation a lot when I am happy or content. At the lake, I sense the warm sunshine on my back, the breeze on my face, the water lapping at the dock and the cold beer going down my throat. Mindfulness has taught me that each moment can be and deserves to be celebrated. While I can still feel sad at the prospect of not seeing my nieces and nephews grow up, or missing out on many years of drinking beer on the dock on Georgian Bay, being present to the joys of each moment enhances the everyday experiences of my life.

Mindful observation of the world around me has also brought me into constant awareness of God in my life and of my existence as part of the universe. While I am out walking, I feel the sun, hear the leaves rustling in the trees and smell the flowers from a beautiful garden. The sun, the trees, the garden and I are all co-creations of God. Seeing life in this way has always been important to me, but I find it particularly comforting in this autumn of my life cycle. Mindful observation of each moment has given me a language for exploring and enhancing my spirituality.

2. *In the calm and the storm, may I hear the still, small voice of God.*

This meditation reminds me that I can find the sacred in the secular with the smallest effort. I am awed by the power of creation in fierce thunder and lightning storms and in gale force winds that nearly blow me off the rocks in Georgian Bay, or in the still calm of dawn breaking over Lake Muskoka. When I tire of the petty politics of organized religion and the autocratic and self-serving positions the Church sometimes adopts, I need only spend some time quietly observing the wonder around me to find reassurance that God created the earth and we, His creatures, have created organized religion.

3. *May the darkness be overcome by the power of your light.*

Many things constitute darkness. Light represents all that is positive, is peaceful and leads to grace.

In its most literal form, the darkness is the world I live in, where I do not recognize light or shadow. Most visually impaired persons have distorted, reduced or impaired refraction of light that makes vision very difficult. I have no sensation of light at all. I can look directly into the sun; if it weren't for the sensation of warmth and daytime sounds, I would not know whether I was gazing at the sun or the moon. In addition to being a major disability, this makes me feel cut off from the rest of the world. When I meditate upon the power of light, I am connecting to the peace within me, which can overcome the sense of loneliness I often feel. I am connecting to the energy that reaches out and links me to the world around me even though I can't see it. I am connecting to that part of my mind that thinks in brilliant colours.

Darkness is also the chronic depression I have battled since I was 13 years old. For many years I treated this as an unwelcome personality trait. I tried to bar its presence, suppress it or destroy it. Over the past decade, my enlightenment has led me to realize that this shadow person is as authentic as the bright, outgoing entertainer and the kind and gentle caregiver who live in me. Proceeding towards the light has helped me to integrate these persons into one real, albeit complicated, person.

The darkness also represents the darkness of this world. Light is God's forgiveness of us all.

4. I am the lamb of God; may I live with grace.

Of all the fruits of the Spirit, I value grace most highly. I have always striven for grace and composure in dealing with the twists and turns of life whether or not the outcome is favourable for me. I believe that it is this gift of grace that has allowed me to let go of so many things I thought I needed and to turn myself to the mystery of adaptation and venturing forth through uncharted waters. There is always a great temptation to dig in my heels and say that something is unacceptable. This sort of energy makes me angry and bitter. Instead, grace creates openness to searching for other ways to do something or to receiving pleasure from unexpected sources. Grace is not saying that everything is the way I want it. It is the strength to carry on in the face of adversity. When I am meditating, I must sit very quietly to tap into this profound but gentle force.

5. The Lord is my shepherd; I am safe.

This meditation connects me to the concept of a transcendent God. When I am worried about what will happen to me, especially not being able to cope with the symptoms of advanced disease, I find great comfort in the image of God the Shepherd caring for me, one of the sheep in his flock. I love the pastoral nature of this meditation. I have read many works that visualize what heaven is like. I have read about our bodies, or the energy that is our body, becoming part of the energy of the cosmos. Somehow, I find that notion rather lonely. Although it may sound narrow and very earthbound, I love to think of God holding me as one of his lambs. Of all my meditations, this one leaves me with the greatest feeling of peace.

In addition to these meditations, I have found breathing exercises to deal with my emotions or feelings to be very helpful. For example, I focus on breathing in peace, courage or vitality; or I breathe in an unwanted emotion, such as despair or fear, and breathe out these same emotions transformed into peace or courage. I like the feeling of control I have when I can transform negative feelings into something good.

I must say that the scientist, the rational "Westerner" in me, found all these ideas absolutely preposterous at first. How could two health professionals sit there telling us about transforming emotions by breathing with them? How could I, a doctor, sit there and listen? They often introduced their exercises by recounting some Buddhist or Eastern tales or fables. The one that I found most ridiculous has turned out to be a long-lasting and important friend.

A man is being chased by a tiger. He is running quickly but suddenly comes upon a cliff. He is about to be eaten by the tiger when he sees a small vine hanging over the edge of the cliff. He grabs onto the vine and leaps over. He is feeling smug, looking up at the hungry tiger, when he hears growling from below. Another tiger appears at the base of the cliff. He realizes that he has to hold tight to the vine until the tigers give up their quest. Then a tiny mouse appears and begins to nibble on the vine. He panics and looks around him for help. All he sees is a bush with a big red strawberry on it. He reaches out and picks the berry and pops it into his mouth. It is perfectly ripe. He feels his teeth sink into the flesh of the berry. The sweet juice trickles down his throat. It is the best strawberry he has ever eaten. The moral of the story is that there is nothing more he can do to protect himself from impending disaster. Still, he stops and thoroughly enjoys the experience of eating the strawberry without thinking about the tigers or the mouse.

To my surprise, I listened intently to this silly little story. Some weeks later, one of my teachers called me at home to see how I was. Since I had started the course, I had been diagnosed with a malignant tumour, had had surgery and was beginning chemotherapy. My hair had fallen out. When he asked me how I was, I said that my wound had not healed, the chemo was stronger than I had thought, and my hair was all out. To my horror he asked me what the strawberries had been that day. He was serious. This completely changed the focus of my thinking; I had to recall things such as a relaxing hot shower, a mug of hot coffee and many other good things. He was not promoting "Pollyanna" behaviour. He was reminding me that although there were many harsh realities in my life, I did not have to let myself be overpowered by them.

I began once again to restrict myself to the minute and things did not seem so overwhelming.

I did not realize the power of this line of thinking until December 2000. My brother, David, was going through an extremely difficult time with his business. Many companies had gone bankrupt and he was suffering terribly at the thought of losing all he had worked towards and being unable to support his family of six. He had imagined himself in debtors' court; I was trying to find a way to support him. I kept pointing out that none of the things he feared and was losing sleep over had happened. I told him that his challenge was to restrict himself to coping with his current reality. Each night he would call to tell me all that had gone wrong that day. In desperation I told him the strawberry story. He was quiet for a moment, no doubt thinking his sane, rational sister had lost it. Then we began to talk about it. He had been reduced to tears that morning when his youngest child drew him a special picture and wanted a cuddle. His immediate reaction was to feel sad and guilty because life would be so hard for her if he had to declare bankruptcy. I told him he had missed the whole point. The significance of that event was not the possibility of future sadness but the comfort of a daughter's love and innocence.

In the days that followed, he would tell me about the "strawberries" he had received that day. This did not relieve him of the stress of the difficult events, but it did give him a slightly different window on his world. When this painful time was finally over and his financial worries were resolved, we discussed these months of strain and all the things I had written to him: not to worry about things that had not happened, and to deal only with the present realities. It was a useful exercise for both of us to go back over the letters we had sent each other. I wouldn't say I changed my brother's approach to life, but I did become aware of how much the mindfulness program has helped me stay firmly rooted in the present moment, to enjoy what is good and to wait until tomorrow to worry about what the future might bring.

Not Just Tired

Jane Poulson, MD

© 2001 *Lippincott Williams & Wilkins.* Journal of Clinical Oncology, *Vol. 19, No 21 (November 1), 2001, pp. 4180-4181. Reprinted with permission.*

Here's the case: A 46-year-old palliative care physician attends a follow-up visit with her surgeon 2 months after multimodality therapy for inflammatory breast cancer. During the examination, the surgeon asked her how she was getting along. She replied that she was feeling somewhat better than at the previous visit but was plagued by fatigue and lack of energy: "I am feeling as if I can hardly put one foot in front of the other at times." "I sure know how you feel," he said reassuringly. "I was on call last week and I have never seen the service as busy. I didn't stop all week. I still haven't caught up yet. A day or two off would be so nice right about now, wouldn't it?" As I was that patient, I wanted to shake my doctor by the collar of his lab coat and scream. "No, that's wrong! You have no idea how I feel!" But I did not have the energy. I could not seem to find the words or language which would make the doctors, nurses, and other health care professionals understand just how tired I was."

My health care providers were keenly interested in my level of pain and shortness of breath. These symptoms seemed very important to them. It did not seem to register with anyone, however, when I said that the most overwhelming symptom for me was fatigue. My anger and dismay with the many health care providers who "just didn't get it" were tempered by the recollection of countless conversations I had had with my own patients who were complaining of fatigue. With some discomfort, I recalled making "supportive" suggestions, such as "Try to get an extra hour's rest at night" or "Be sure to have a little nap in the afternoon." Other helpful discussions included commentaries bout North American lifestyles and what a fastmoving world we were now inhabiting. Everyone was overworked and exhausted. It was becoming the norm of the 1990s. I would also cheerfully remind the patients that their bodies had recently been through a lot. Despite the fact that the majority of my clinical practice was spent with oncology patients, I had not realized the enormity of the problem about which my patients complained.

A problem of semantics

The problem for patients, as I see it now, is that patients and professionals are using the same terminology, "tired" or "fatigue." Because they are using the same words, they mistakenly presume that they are speaking about the same phenomenon. This is the root of the problem. The deadening fatigue which invades the very bones of cancer patients is totally unlike even the most profound fatigue of an otherwise well person, even a busy doctor. When I was healthy, I remember feeling different types of fatigue. After a good run, the physical exhaustion felt wonderful. My muscles would feel soft and supple. Many people become addicted to running because of the phenomenon of "catching their second wind." There is no "endorphin rush" with cancer fatigue. Fatigue after a busy night on call did not feel wonderful, but it did respond to a hot shower and a good night's sleep. When healthy, I did not realize the energy required for activities of daily living, such as bathing, dressing, or sitting upright in a chair.

During cancer therapy I always felt the exhaustion of prolonged exercise but without any positive attributes. My muscles felt soft and flabby. I imagined tensile myofibrils being replaced with a putty-like substance. My limbs felt heavy. The quality of my sleep was changed. The mere act of sleeping itself seemed like work sometimes. Sleep was not restful and refreshing. I never awoke in the morning feeling energetic and anxious to greet the day.

Prolonged symptoms

During my therapy, I kept myself going with the understanding that chemotherapy and radiation were a necessary evil and that fatigue went along with the package. I and many others were disappointed when, at the end of treatment, I did not revert to my old energetic self. Cancer fatigue is not limited to the physical realm. My brain felt tired and so did my spirits. I seemed to have lost my zest for life. Even though I continued to participate in activities, I lacked my usual enthusiasm and sometimes felt I would rather be sitting on the sidelines. The fatigue continued with almost no change for months. For sure, there was a gradual improvement in my energy, but the incremental improvement was small and very slow.

Anemia is frequently promoted as a major cause of fatigue. Transfusions certainly helped when my hemoglobin level was very low, but the beneficial effects subsided after it reached a level of about 105 to 110 g/L. Depression, no doubt, contributes to the fatigue; however, in the 6 weeks leading up to my diagnosis, I was feeling distinctly unlike myself and wondered why. I was doing a lot of teaching at the time. Before each tutorial, I sat at my desk thinking that it was such a long walk to the amphitheater. I usually enjoyed the medical students, but that spring I had to fight the urge to dismiss them at the break. This mental fatigue and inability to focus my thinking persisted for a long time after the acute phase of the illness and its treatment. For many months, I found myself quite content to simply sit doing nothing. I had neither the physical energy to move nor the mental energy to read or to contemplate.

Because I did not understand cancer fatigue, I did not help myself in the recovery period. I started from the premise that at the end of treatment my body had returned to its former energy metabolism. I presumed that patterns of exercise and activity which had previously worked would be reasonable. I set up a recuperation plan for myself. I began walking and assumed that the pace and duration of my walks would increase each week. I allowed myself to continue with afternoon naps initially but was dismayed when these did not shorten nor become unnecessary. In short, I made what I thought would be a reasonable recovery routine, but I feel drastically short of the mark. My body was not responding in a recognizable fashion. What had been reasonable expectations formerly were now far too ambitious.

Helpful interventions

How can we help our exhausted cancer patients and families for whom prolonged symptomatology is difficult to comprehend? Health care professionals must recognize that cancer-related fatigue is different from fatigue experienced by otherwise healthy persons. Caregivers and family must also be so educated. While exercising or a nap may be helpful suggestions to normally fatigued persons, these may not be the solutions for cancer fatigue.

It must be recognized that each patient is unique. The extent to which cancer fatigue disrupts normal activities will vary widely. In an effort to be encouraging, many colleagues reassured me that many women with breast cancer continue with all their family responsibilities as well as work full time. Rather than helping me, this made me feel somewhat inadequate or lazy because I was so tired. It also led me to fear that my fatigue was all in my head and that if I could only get a grip on my emotion I would be more productive.

Patients must be reassured that recovery eventually does occur but may be prolonged and incomplete. Rehabilitation may not follow a predicted course. The healing trajectory is unlikely to be straight. Patients should be encouraged to pursue light to moderate exercise as much as possible to preserve conditioning. Exercises such as yoga are helpful as the exercise can be tailored to each day's energy level. Patients should be encouraged to create a healthy and pleasing environment. Many modalities should be suggested, eg, healthy diet, regular sleeping habits, and creation of a restorative environment with fragrance, sound, and visual effects.

Physicians and patients must understand that recovery may not be complete. Four years later, my total physical capacity is less. It seems to be harder to replenish my energy and every activity seems to take more energy than it once did. My physical and, I believe, mental abilities have much sharper boundaries than before. By this I mean that when I can no longer carry on with an activity, this margin is very clear. Attempts to finish a task or pursue a project are unsuccessful. Empty is empty. I do not seem to have a safety margin where, although the needle is on E, there is still energy so spare. Before my illness, I never considered whether I would have enough energy to embark upon a project or activity. Now, this is a serious consideration. Patients should be encouraged to prioritize activities to ensure limited energy is optimally utilized.

Fatigue is a devastating symptom that deserves the same attention as pain, nausea, dyspnea, and other well-recognized complications of a malignant illness. Oncologists must recognize its common presence and ask the right questions to elucidate its dimensions.

Surely, fatigue is a problem deserving of a priority for research on its etiology and treatment. We now recognize that many tumor symptoms flow from an aberrant inflammatory response in concert with chemical stimuli that may be produced directly by the rumor. There is no doubt that general counseling and psychologic guidance are helpful to patients and families facing the problems associated with overwhelming fatigue. It is to be hoped that in the near future these approaches will be complemented by therapies soundly based on our understanding of the pathophysiology of fatigue with proven successful interventions.

Then they cried to the LORD in their trouble,
and he saved them from their distress;
he sent out his word and healed them,
and delivered them from destruction.
Let them thank the LORD for his steadfast love,
for his wonderful works to humankind.
And let them offer thanksgiving sacrifices,
and tell of his deeds with songs of joy.

Some went down to the sea in ships,
doing business on the mighty waters;
they saw the deeds of the LORD,
his wondrous works in the deep.
For he commanded and raised the stormy wind,
which lifted up the waves of the sea.
They mounted up to heaven,
they went down to the depths;
their courage melted away in their calamity;
they reeled and staggered like drunkards,
and were at their wits' end.
They cried to the LORD in their trouble
and he brought them out from their distress;
he made the storm be still,
and the waves of the sea were hushed.
They were glad because they had quiet,
and he brought them to their desired haven.

Psalm 107:19-30

Chapter 13: Running out of Borrowed Time

Despite the fact that the entire world was buzzing about the advent of Y2K, I felt detached and outside the hype. It never occurred to me that I would live long enough to see the new millennium arrive. I made no attempt to update my computer equipment or prepare for unknown calamity. As we moved into December 1999, I realized that, barring an accident, I too would live to experience this momentous event. I spent the evening alone, as I prefer to do on New Year's Eve. I tuned into the New Year celebrations around the world on television and went to bed confident that if tiny African countries could safely make the transition into the new millennium, surely North America would manage it too.

January 1, 2000, was a symbolic milestone for me. The fact that I had made it that far was a tangible example of how little we know about the future. All we can know is the present moment. This event spurred me to be very proactive in extracting every drop out of this unexpected gift of life. I threw fiscal conservatism to the wind and began pursuing things I had only dreamed of before.

I have a passion for music, and love listening to live broadcasts of the Metropolitan Opera from New York. I asked my Benedictine friend Paul Geraghty in Montreal if he would meet me in New York and attend a live performance; he was more than happy to oblige. He called his friend Timothy Meyer, whom he had met at the Benedictine monastery. We arranged to stay with Tim, who lives in New York, and take him with us to the performance.

We chose my favourite opera, *La Traviata*. What a thrilling night! I had reserved excellent seats so that we would miss nothing of the event. My friends described the Chagall paintings in the lobby, the shimmering golden stage curtain, the rich red velvet-covered seats, and beautiful crystal chandeliers everywhere. They helped me create a vivid picture of this scene in my mind. I believe that this was possible because I could see for the first three decades of my life and I still have a technicolour vision of the world, although the accuracy of my mental image is not as important to me as it once was. They described what they saw; from there I could build my scene without asking for minute details. That particular night was especially glamorous; it was the night of the Millennial Ball for the members of the Metropolitan Opera Foundation, who attended in all their finery.

Scattered throughout the audience were these wealthy patrons of the opera, all competing with each other for the title of "Best Dressed." My friends told me of dresses with no backs, or tantalizing and suggestive lack of fronts. There were slim, slick black dresses as well as fluffy, flouncy gowns that made their owners look as if they were about to take off into orbit. There were many different kinds of hairdos that defied gravity. I shuddered to think of how awful the hair must feel to the touch! During each intermission, these patrons were served champagne in fluted glasses by white-gloved waiters in a circular lobby with giant portraits of famous opera singers on the wall. The whole scene was reminiscent of the ball in Cinderella. And we, the visitors from Canada, felt like the Ugly Stepsisters looking on enviously.

But of course this was not just an opportunity to observe the rich and famous of New York, it was also an opportunity to hear sublime music about a beautiful woman who dies too young. The moving performance eclipsed all of my expectations. I shall never forget it.

Muskoka

I am not sure when my appreciation for natural beauty was transformed into awe and a sense of being in the presence of God. I certainly have strong recollections from childhood of being in places that made me wish to be silent and where I was filled with a special feeling. One of these was the "Big Rock" at the cottage at Lake of Bays in Muskoka. Not far from our cottage was a sheer rock face rising several hundred feet straight up from the water. In its shadow the water was green and always cool. Kids liked to go there because the fishing was good. I fished there, but I never did catch anything. I liked to take my canoe there and sit by the edge of the rock. I felt a sense of mystery, almost fear, knowing that this place was different from other places around the lake. From Sunday School I knew that God had made the mountains long, long ago, but I did not understand at that time that the presence of God was stirring the sense of awe and mystery within my soul.

I used to unknowingly commune with God in the very early morning by the lake. On many Muskoka mornings, the day began without a breath of air. The lake was like a sheet of glass. I would waken early and go down to sit on the dock. It was so beautiful that my sister and I would automatically speak quietly, if at all. There was a sunken wharf just off our dock that attracted many fish. While the water was so still, the sunlight reflecting off the sunfish sent dazzling reflections of emerald, sapphire and ruby. We dropped our fishing lines into the water and watched the fish inspecting our worms. The fish were so beautiful we never kept anything we caught. I worried about throwing them back in with a sore mouth, but we could not bear to kill them. As an adult, I still commune with God as I sit at the edge of a lake at the beginning or end of the day. It is marvellous for my soul to be still and listen to the water gently lapping against the shore.

These formative years at Muskoka have had a long-lasting influence on my sense of spirituality and nature. I have very vivid dreams in fabulous bright colour of the panoramic view from our dock. Since I have been blind for over 20 years, most of my dreams take place in strange, shadowy images, but not the dreams that take place at our cottage.

Many people believe that science is gradually replacing our need for the concept of God, the Creator of the universe. I have found the opposite to be true: the more we know about science and biology the more I am in awe of God and the natural world. One of my most amazing moments in medical school was seeing, for the very first time, a baby being born. I suppose I must have seen something similar on television or instructional videos, but to witness the start of a new life was a phenomenal moment for me. The attending physician was asking me questions about the delivery, but my mind was stuck on the miracle of that little head appearing from the body of the labouring mother. I remember wanting to touch the perfect little ears and count the tiny toes and fingers. I knew that I had witnessed a miracle that humans could never achieve on their own. To this day, when people ask me why I believe in God, I reply that anyone who has witnessed the birth of a child could only believe in God the Creator. The miracle is enhanced by our knowledge of the minute reactions that have taken place during embryonic development and response to breathing air.

I have made nine trips to the Caribbean since becoming blind. It is incredibly therapeutic for me to walk along a shoreline feeling the sun on my face and the breeze on my body and in my hair. It was not until my later trips, after facing my mortality through cancer, that sitting on the shoreline of the Caribbean took on a new and deeper significance. I find I can sit on the shoreline for hours and marvel at the constancy of the wind and the waves. I feel very strongly the presence of those trade winds and am transported by the awareness that these winds have been blowing the waves ashore in this place for thousands of years. I am greatly comforted by the image of these same winds blowing waves against the same shore long after my death. It makes me feel alive and one with the universe.

The sands, wind and waves symbolize for me the changelessness of eternity. My mortal frame will change when I die, but sitting beside the seashore fills me with positive feelings that transcend the mortal pleasures of the warmth of the sun and the smell of the sea air.

When, after a number of months, no objective signs of advanced disease appeared, I became rather blasé about my mortality. This changed later in 2000, when I experienced my first recurrence of disease. It was shocking in some ways to learn that I did indeed have living cancer cells proliferating within me. I sat pondering this new reality in the late afternoon on the day I learned this news. Everything felt completely different. As if to mirror my mood, the skies darkened and there came upon the earth the type of strange stillness that can only precede a storm. Before long, the heavens opened and rain and hail bucketed down. There followed the most fierce thunderstorm I have ever experienced. Lightning flashed and thunder crashed simultaneously.

Following a violent crack of lightning and thunder, my front door burst open and in ran my friend Douglas Stoute. It was a dramatic entrance and could not have been done any better had it been scripted. He had heard my bad news and had come to be with me, a custom he had followed for a number of years. I had some great talks with Douglas on these occasions because he is able to talk about the current issue without apology and without avoiding the difficult stuff. Many people were shy or too polite or reluctant to talk about the subject of my potential death, but with Douglas I could be very candid. We spoke about why I was so certain that there was a God.

That day I was speaking about God and natural science. During a pause in our conversation, a huge lighting bolt ripped through the sky. We both laughed as we spoke about this, but I felt the presence of God very much in that bolt of lightning. The message to me was that of an eternal and mighty God in control of the universe. There was so much more to the cosmos than my limited exposure in my life so far on earth; it would take faith to give myself over to that energy but I felt a strong and comforting invitation to do so. I felt God telling me to have courage to live my life fully even as it appears to be closing in on me, and to have faith to live knowing that I will be transformed into an eternal creation. All the energy of that lightning would be available to me for protection.

Nobody Can Fix Everything

As I reread these pages I notice that I have shied away from writing very much about my mother. Where do I begin to write about my complicated relationship with my mother, Barbara, known affectionately as Bobbie to her friends and family or as Mrs. P to most of my friends? Where does any daughter begin to describe such an intricate, complex and multi-layered relationship, which becomes increasingly more nuanced and dense as the years pass?

In part, it is the fluidity of the mother–daughter relationship that makes it so complex. During the course of a lifetime, the relationship develops from one where the child is entirely dependent upon the mother, through developing independence, to where the mother is dependent upon her child. I observe the agony of friends as they face the trauma of dementia in their aging mothers. Even when the mother no longer recognizes her own offspring, still the daughter visits and cares for her mother as lovingly as she does for her own precious children. The roles of "mother" and "child" rotate back and forth over the decades. When this rotation takes place smoothly all is well. When this rotation is less gradual or more apparent or less satisfactory to both sides, stresses occur in the relationship.

When I was little, my mother and I were very close. I was seven years old when my brother, David, was born. Mom was in the hospital for seven days and my sister and I spent this time at my grandmother's house. I was devastated at being separated from my mother. I called the hospital frequently to speak to her. A very mean old nurse took the phone one day and told me that I was not allowed to phone Mom for three days. Those three days were torture to me. Nothing could console me. I could not wait for her to come home.

Mom was always home when we got in from school. There would be some fresh baking and a nice after-school snack waiting for us. My favourite day of the week was Friday, when our cleaning lady, Anna, came. We did not have to make our beds that day as our sheets would get changed. When we got home from school the house would smell fantastic. The smell of the waxed and polished kitchen floor combined with ginger or cinnamon or oatmeal cookies is one of the most comforting memories of my childhood.

No matter what disaster befell us, Mom seemed able to fix everything. Then came my diabetes. For the first time in my life, something had happened to me that my mother could not fix. No one in my family had died that I could remember; this was the first experience for me of an irreparable and permanent event. Initially, I had a hard time with my mother's embracing of the medical plan. I felt betrayed by her when she offered me diet ginger ale rather than juice or milk. For a long time I felt that Mom was part of the enemy team making my life miserable. This feeling was significant until the point when I took responsibility for managing the diabetes myself.

When does a daughter become an adult in her own right? Perhaps when she leaves home for the first time. I left my parents' home in 1970 to attend Queen's University. I called home every Sunday night to speak to my family; despite the distance, I felt closer to them than ever. Mom worried about me. While I lived at home, Mom had been in control of my diet and adhered to it quite strictly. She also knew when I had doctors' appointments and was aware of any changes to routine care. My move to Queen's and more independence gave me the responsibility for my own health. This was a good growing experience for me, but it was hard for Mom to know how things were going. She wanted to ask about my health but I loathed talking about it. Diabetes was my own private hell. My custom of depending mainly upon myself during tough times began here.

Many mothers and daughters draw closer when the daughter marries and becomes the manager of her own household. The experience of becoming a mother creates a shared bond that only mothers can understand. Mom and I will never share these experiences. It was very clear to my mother right from the start that my marriage was neither supportive nor happy. She visited me as often as she could because of her heartfelt concern for me.

When my marriage ended, Mom was accepting of my divorce. I felt like a failure, but I never detected a moment of disapproval from my family. For this I was grateful. They were sad to see me so disappointed, but I never felt that they were feeling shame about the situation.

In 1985, when I bought a house of my own in Lower Westmount, Mom loved to visit, but she was not involved in the daily running of my house and my life. When I moved back to Toronto in 1992, I had my own apartment, but Mom became much more involved in the daily management of my world. This new pattern developed innocently enough. It is not easy for anyone to move to a new city, but the situation was much more complicated because I was blind. It was natural for Mom and everyone else to pitch in and help me with the move. I had not organized where I would do my food shopping, dry cleaning, banking or pharmacy errands, so at first I was very grateful to Mom for picking up different items for me and for smoothing the transition. Slowly, I found myself slipping back into some of the maladaptive patterns I had known in Montreal. Just as I had relied upon willing friends to help me with errands, I started to let Mom meet many of my everyday needs. While there is nothing wrong with this situation on the surface, the relationship between a volunteer helper and the person receiving help is very different from that of a helper being paid to help someone. When someone is helping you out of the goodness of their heart, it is hard to say that the time they are suggesting does not suit you. It is hard to ask them to return something because it is not exactly what you wanted. If you are paying someone by the hour, it is not as difficult to ask them to wait for you while you are doing something else.

A major loss related to blindness is the loss of privacy. You are no longer free to run off and do something silly, self-indulgent or even sinful. I have not found my way around this loss. It was somehow mitigated by hiring someone to accompany me on outings, but you cannot "hire" your family. It is difficult to ask a mother or sister to accompany you to buy an extravagant outfit and then refuse to say why you are making such a purchase. If you do say why you need such an outfit, the door has been opened for questions and follow-up about the event, and this can be an invasion of privacy. I cannot even satisfy a major craving for Oreo cookie ice cream without invoking the help of someone else. The less closely I am related to that helper, the greater the sense of privacy for me.

Moving back to Toronto had a major impact on how I viewed myself. In Montreal, I called a taxi and went where I wanted to go. Mom, in her generosity, was always ready to drive me anywhere. In fact, she and her sisters found it somewhat insulting when I said I preferred to travel to most places by cab rather than in a private car. Living independently, organizing my own transport and making decisions by myself were all important features of how I saw myself. With a plethora of willing helpers, I found my boundaries becoming blurred, but I found it hard to speak of my need for privacy and personal boundaries when my helpers were offering boundless love, energy and generosity of spirit.

Most people have not known the feeling of profound physical dependence upon others and the mindset that creates. Most people who are helpers are doing their good works out of generosity or love. You hope that you have made life a little easier for the person you have helped and that they appreciate your efforts. As someone who has required a lot of help over the past two decades, I can only say that it is not easy to require help and that it is much easier to give help than to receive it. I have found myself feeling quite conflicted sometimes. I am truly grateful to whoever has helped me, but at the same time I feel angry and that makes me feel guilty. The helper/recipient relationship is complex. Mom and I have struggled with it, trying to keep the dialogue open so we can tell each other when our feelings are being hurt. Sometimes we succeed; sometimes we fail.

One night Mom was at my home, having delivered some groceries. She had been so helpful, I did not want to tell her that I did not feel like visiting with her and that I had several phone calls I needed to make. While she was there, one of the people I wanted to speak to phoned me. I took the call; it went on longer than I had expected and I did not feel comfortable cutting it short. Mom got up and went into the kitchen, where she opened the fridge, took out some meat and proceeded to cook it. When I got off the phone, she was feeling very efficient and helpful for having prepared a tasty meal for me. She expected me to be grateful for her help and impressed by her efficiency.

I was very upset that she had opened my fridge, made a decision and then proceeded with her plan. She was hurt by my reaction. I tried to explain that I felt my territory had been invaded and that it was important for me to be in control of my own house, even down to such seemingly trivial things as what to do with the items in my refrigerator. But she could not understand my point of view. It seemed clear to her that I have difficulty cooking and that she had saved me a lot of trouble by preparing a meal that would last for several nights.

I am not sure that we will ever completely resolve these differences in perspective. Nevertheless, it is both important to me, and a credit to her, that we are prepared to discuss this issue whenever it arises.

How Strange, How Strange

I live a paradox. While I would definitely change certain things about my life if I could, I would also say that I am happy. This paradox has allowed me to reflect on happiness and how to maximize it. While health and physical well-being have a significant impact upon our happiness, there is more to it than that. For much of my life I have experienced considerable physical distress. Diabetes caused the emotional commotion of my adolescence as well as blindness and heart disease. It is a constant all day, every day. If I choose to disregard my blood sugar, in the short run I am thirsty and lethargic; in the long run, I damage my nerves and kidneys. Yet even though I carry the burden of diabetes with me at every waking moment, I am still happy.

I think of all the patients I have known over my years of practice. Their apparent level of happiness has rarely been correlated to physical well-being. Many people with serious chronic pain and disability such as rheumatoid arthritis appear to be less cranky and more satisfied with their lives than many patients with intermittent or short-term ailments.

It is becoming more and more clear to me that whatever this thing called happiness is, it is often a result of reflecting upon and appreciating the positive aspects of being alive. Three concepts fuel my constant consumption and love of life.

The first of these is the pleasure I find in personal relationships. I love deeply the people in my life and am endlessly nourished and sustained by the scores of relatives and friends who populate my world. I have retained meaningful contact with friends going as far back as my days as a Brownie when we gathered around a *papier mâché* toadstool at St. Clement's Church. Several of those Brownies formed into a secret group known as "The Lonely Hearts" Club during the rigours of the early dating years. The members of the LH Club were bridesmaids for each other and have all been in attendance at the funerals of our respective parents. I continue to laugh with the friends I have made dating back to John Ross Robertson School.

These relationships have meant different things to me at different stages. In high school, friends provided company at a dance. The following night they consoled you and pointed out that you were not the only one who was not asked to dance. At other times they were accomplices in schemes too zany to describe.

My desire to see my nieces and nephews grow up induced me to leave Montreal for Toronto, a drastic and potentially disastrous professional move. Battling progressively more serious diseases in my later years has shown me how much I depend upon these relationships for my very life.

I am certain that attitude and determination play a major role in survival. During difficult moments in treatments or slow recovery, I sometimes wonder why I bother to pursue any more interventions. Surely there is a moment when it is appropriate to give up. Then I start to think about all the parties and events I would miss and I decide to offer up my beleaguered body for more. Most significantly, I have learned to allow myself to be loved for everything I am, including blind eyes, deranged metabolism and cancerous breasts. When I reached a new low point and could no longer sustain myself physically or emotionally on my own, my friends and family were there to see me through.

What might have been utterly unendurable has been transformed into an affirming experience. Some psychologists might say that I am nothing more than a Type A, driven personality. I prefer to think of myself as being full of passion and enthusiasm. When this is activated, I find extraordinary and seemingly limitless drive to accomplish amazing things. My passion for practising clinical medicine was so great that I had to try it. I believe that my passion is tempered by wisdom. I did not want to be a bad doctor, nor did I want to do medicine to the exclusion of all else. I needed to give it my best shot and see for myself what I could do. This burning desire has kept me going during many difficult times.

Another of my passions is music. After losing my eyesight, I threw away all my piano music in a fit of pique. I missed my music so much that I eventually bought a piano and took lessons, trying to learn from audio cassette instructions read by my teacher. (There is Braille music available, but I chose not to learn Braille.) While in Kingston I had sung with the Kingston Choral Society. I missed choral music, so I asked the director of music at the Montreal Cathedral if I could sing with them at specific concerts. I could not sight-sing, which is essential for a regular chorister, so members of this choir would make recordings of the soprano lines and I would memorize the notes and words. Whenever this seemed to be too much work, thinking of how I felt when in performance with choir and orchestra kept me soldiering on.

My Body Is Suffering, but My Spirit Is Calm

While I would like to think of my energy and passion as merely personal attributes, I am aware that this is not so. My aggressive pursuit of happiness and meaning from a life few would lust after is fuelled by a force greater than I possess. My infinite energy is the result of my deep and abiding faith in God, my creator. I believe that I entered into a covenant with God at the time of my birth. God gave me my life; my part of the covenant is to live as fully as I can. My covenant does not require that I be thankful for or rejoice in the travails. I hate having diabetes and being blind. I rail against my body, which is constantly failing me and severely limiting my activities. I long deeply for the imagined joys of an intimate relationship with a beloved mate. I wish I had had a child. My covenant has required that I repeatedly let go of my images and desires, and that I acknowledge that they are not realities in my current journey. In letting go I have learned about the richness of being alive.

I hate being so dependent, physically and emotionally, upon others in my community. Letting go of the notion that "normal" or "real," "complete" or "valuable" people do not need help allowed me to see the complex interactions needed to permit function in our world. Living this truth has made me realize my own worth and see the contribution my encumbered body makes in the wider world. Although I dream of jumping into a car and doing errands independently, I am open to the wonders of relationship and community. Would it not be worse to believe that you were completely independent and needed nothing from those around you? There is much comfort in seeing yourself as part of a mutual and interdependent community.

Trying to embrace a whole different paradigm has taken years of reflection, prayer and meditation. It is very easy to fall into the trap of getting my priorities wrong. I must remind myself that physical ability and beauty are evanescent features that ultimately dwindle for all of us. The only realm that has continued to grow and flourish for me is that of being fully alive every moment of my life. I can only access the energy, patience and strength to do so from my connection to God. My most valuable personal asset is my willingness and ability to be still and know my creator.

Happiness is a state of mind, an approach to life, a way of relating to the world around you. We each hold the possibility of our own happiness within us. No person or object can make us happy. We have very little control over the events and circumstances of our lives.

We rarely are able to choose our destiny. The only choice we have is how we respond to what happens to us. We may choose to deny reality and strive to eliminate unwanted challenges, or we may engage the events of our lives and pursue the journey down a different road. Pursuing alternate ways of thinking or being does not have to be enthusiastic or joyful. It is probably more authentic if it is somewhat tentative. Our creation covenant with God only asks us to be willing to take the road that stretches before us. It is only in going down this road that I have encountered my soul. It has only been in encountering my soul that I have been able to fully enter the mystery and marvels of being alive.

Dr. Jane Poulson died in the Grace Hospital, Toronto, on Tuesday, August 28, 2001. She was 49 years old. Her ashes are buried beside her father's in the courtyard of St. Clement's Church, Toronto.

I come to the end – I am still with you.

Psalm 139:18

Appendix: Poems

Imagine...

...waking up in the morning knowing that your blood sugar is neither too high nor too low
...knowing this to be so without stabbing your finger
...thinking about food as it tastes and smells rather than as grams of carbohydrate, or fat
...eating a meal without "shooting-up" first
...doing as much exercise as you want without worrying about hypoglycemia
...feeling anxious just before a presentation and knowing your blood sugar is not plummeting
...going through a day without thinking about your health
...leaving a doctor's office feeling that you are not a failure
...eating a triple chocolate fondant with a honey centre and nuts without guilt
...eating another

Frustration (What They Cannot Teach in Rehabilitation)

I cannot see the luminous clock face.
I cannot distinguish my pills.
I cannot retrieve dropped pills before my dog does.
I cannot find the fallen bar of soap in the shower.

I cannot see the runs in my panty hose.
I cannot check that my socks match.
I cannot find my suit jacket.

I cannot put on my makup.
I cannot pour boiling water into the small teapot.

I cannot use a knife and fork properly.
I cannot see the food spilled on my suit.
I cannot see the lipstick on my teeth.
I cannot check that my glass eye is right side up.
I cannot hail a cab.
I cannot use the rotating door alone.
I cannot find the button for the handicapped door.
I cannot use the banking machine.
I cannot use the alternate route.

I cannot use notes for my presentation.
I cannot see their graphs or slides.

I cannot see how much money I gave him.
I cannot see how much change he gave me.

I cannot play racquet sports.
I cannot play golf.

I cannot play curling.
I cannot play Scrabble.
I cannot play cards.
I cannot play computer games.
I cannot read the newspaper.
I cannot find the CD I want to hear.
I cannot find the correct book on tape
    from this pile of cassettes.
I cannot leaf through a magazine.
I cannot "people watch."
I cannot paint.
I cannot sight-sing.
I cannot play new piano music.

I cannot use Windows.
I cannot surf the web.
I cannot use most home pages.
I cannot click here for anything.

I cannot see the sun or moon or stars.
I cannot see the beauty of springtime.
I cannot see the glorious bouquet of flowers.

I cannot see the wasp about to sting me.

I cannot see the beautiful babies.
I cannot watch then grow.
I cannot see them play hockey.
I cannot admire Halloween costumes.
I cannot read their favourite books.

I cannot make them understand that I cannot see them.

I cannot see the smiles and welcomes.
I cannot avoid speaking to certain people.
I cannot see the expressions of the audiences I am
    addressing.
I cannot see the faces of my friends and dear ones.

I cannot look into the eyes of the one I love.

I cannot tell you how many things I cannot do.

I cannot tell you how angry I am.

Dreams

I dream…

of waking up with the sunshine flooding through the
window into my eyes

of lying on the dock gazing at the twinkling sky and
shooting stars

of driving my car through the mountains of Vermont

of walking through a garden in the spring with magnolia
trees and apple and cherry blossoms

of curling up with a good book

of reading the Saturday papers with a pot of coffee

of watching the world go by

of my beloved's face smiling at me

of life after death

About the painting on the back cover flap

I created this painting for the *Canadian Medical Association Journal*, to accompany one of two articles written by Dr. Jane Poulson about her experience of living with cancer.

Dr. Poulson was both a doctor and a patient. I asked myself, how can I represent a person being both at the same time? I settled on the playing card motif, since this graphically tied the two together: when viewed from one position, she was Dr. Jane Poulson, scientist and doctor; her diagnosis of cancer turned her upside down, making her into a patient.

There was also a slightly fatalistic element in the choice of the card motif. Dr. Poulson's story was an especially profound one for me, as I had just buried my mother, who died after losing her battle with cancer in 1991. Much of Dr. Poulson's evocation of what it is like to be a patient with cancer brought back painful memories for me. This sadness infused the image I created; I could not help but think of Tarot cards and of someone being dealt an ominous future. Sadly, for Dr. Jane Poulson, this turned out to be the case.

Frederick Sebastian
Ottawa